Love, Language, Place, and Identity in Popular Culture

Communication Perspectives in Popular Culture

Series Editors:

Andrew F. Herrmann, East Tennessee State University and Art Herbig, Purdue University, Fort Wayne

Communication Perspectives in Popular Culture examines the integral role that popular culture plays in scholarship and teaching. We use it to critique culture and to exemplify theory. We use it to understand public discourse as well as help us to explain the role that those discourses play in our daily lives. The way popular culture helps construct, define, and impact everyday reality must be taken seriously, specifically because popular culture is, simply, popular. Rather than assuming that popular culture is an unimportant place of fantastical make-believe with no impact beyond the screen, this series studies popular culture and what it can tell us about identity, gender, organizations, power, relationships, and numerous other subjects. The goal of this series is to provide a glimpse into the differing relationships between academic research and a number of popular culture artifacts from a variety of perspectives to create a space for larger discussions.

Recent titles in the series:

Love, Language, Place, and Identity in Popular Culture

Romancing the Other

Edited by
María T. Ramos-García
and Laura Vivanco

LEXINGTON BOOKS
Lanham • Boulder • New York • London

The cover image is provided under the Creative Commons License (https://creativecommons.org/licenses/by/2.0/) and can be found at https://www.flickr.com/photos/izzonme/32658008657/.

Published by Lexington Books
An imprint of The Rowman & Littlefield Publishing Group, Inc.
4501 Forbes Boulevard, Suite 200, Lanham, Maryland 20706
www.rowman.com

6 Tinworth Street, London SE11 5AL

British Library Cataloguing in Publication Information Available

Library of Congress Control Number: 2019920460

ISBN: 978-1-4985-8938-3 (cloth)
ISBN: 978-1-4985-8940-6 (pbk)
ISBN: 978-1-4985-8939-0 (electronic)

Contents

Preface

This volume comprises a selection of the papers presented at the *First International Seminar on Languages and Cultures in Contact in the Romance Novel*, held at the University of Las Palmas de Gran Canaria (Canary Islands, Spain) in June 2017. The seminar was organized within the framework of Research Project FFI2014-53962-P, funded by the Spanish government, through MINECO (Ministry of Economy and Competitiveness), and developed between 2015 and 2018. This project, titled *Discursos, género e identidad en un corpus de novela rosa inglesa ambientada en Canarias y otras islas atlánticas* (Discourses, Gender and Identity in a Corpus of Popular Romance Fiction Novels Set in the Canaries and Other Atlantic Islands), has already inspired a number of publications exploring the various aspects suggested in its name, including Otherness, which is the focus of attention in this work. The chapters in the current edited volume provide theoretical, empirical, and practical bases for an understanding of the crucial relation between factors such as love, language, place, and identity and the perception of the Other within Popular Culture, and particularly in Popular Romance Fiction.

As the leader of the research project organizing the seminar this volume emerges from, I would like to express my gratitude to the contributors who have made it possible. My warm thanks of course go to the editors, Dr. María Ramos-García and Dr. Laura Vivanco, for their enthusiastic engagement, careful review, and invaluable suggestions to enrich the original papers. I'm also very grateful for the support of the publishers, particularly Nicolette Amstutz, senior acquisitions editor for Lexington Books, in charge of both *Media, Film, Communication, and Rhetorical Studies* as well as *Latin American Studies*. Her patience, continued assistance, and tireless cooperation in preparing this volume for publication proved to be most encouraging.

María Isabel González-Cruz
ULPGC Professor in English Studies

Introduction

María T. Ramos-García and Laura Vivanco

"Entre las varias actividades de amor sólo hay una que pueda yo pretender contagiar a los demás: el afán de comprensión. [. . .] Llámase en un diálogo platónico a este afán de comprensión [. . .] "locura de amor." Pero aunque no fuera la forma originaria, la génesis y culminación de todo amor un ímpetu de comprender las cosas, creo que es su síntoma forzoso. Yo desconfío del amor de un hombre a su amigo o a su bandera cuando no le veo esforzarse en comprender al enemigo o a la bandera hostil." (Ortega y Gasset 1914, 20–21)[1]

Did you understand this epigraph? If José Ortega y Gasset's words are in your native tongue do they reassure you that, although the language of this volume is English, you are not among strangers? If the quotation is unintelligible to you, or difficult to understand, is the language in which it is written an intimation to you that you may be traveling with us into the unknown? Is that an intriguing thought or a worrying one?[2] Fredric Jameson has suggested that,

> from the earliest times, the stranger from another tribe, the "barbarian" who speaks an incomprehensible language and follows "outlandish" customs [. . . is one] of the archetypal figures of the Other, about whom the essential point to be made is not so much that he is feared because he is evil; rather he is evil *because* he is Other, alien, different, strange, unclean, and unfamiliar. (1981, 115)

The criteria used for Othering the outsider are varied, and change across time, cultures, and contexts but the Other tends to come into existence via discursive processes by which powerful groups, who may or may not make up a numerical majority, define subordinate groups into existence in a reductionist way which ascribe[s] problematic and/or inferior characteristics to these subordinate groups. Such discursive processes affirm the legitimacy and superiority of the powerful and condition identity formation among the subordinate. (Jensen 2011, 65)

Otherness as such has been studied in many disciplines, from philosophy (where it has its origins in the nineteenth century with Hegel) to sociology, and in the 1980s "the questions of the other and otherness took the geographical world by storm" (Staszak 2009, 2).

In literary studies, approaches to Otherness have their origins in Antonio Gramsci's studies on hegemony, as well as in Lacan, Levi-Strauss, and Levinas, and later in Michel Foucault's work on power. The term Othering was coined by the cultural theorist and literary critic Edward Said in his book *Orientalism* (1978), and the concept of the Other is key in different theoretical frameworks both in literary and cultural studies. Simone de Beauvoir stated in *The Second Sex* (1949) that even though "there are other *Others* than the woman, she is still always defined as Other" (2011, 167) and in 1979 feminist scholars Sandra Gilbert and Susan Gubar noted that

a woman is denied the autonomy—the subjectivity—that the pen represents, she is not only excluded from culture (whose emblem might well be the pen) but she also becomes herself an embodiment of just those extremes of mysterious and intransigent Otherness which culture confronts with worship or fear, love or loathing. (Gilbert and Gubar 2000, 19)

Women authors have, however, found a welcoming home in popular romance fiction. Perhaps because of its association with women, the romance genre is, without doubt, the most Othered or marginalized of all popular genres of literature. Romance novels have received far less academic attention than crime or science fiction, and when second wave feminist critics did examine it in the 1980s they concluded that romance novels were a patriarchal tool to keep women satisfied in their subordinated role. Although scholarship became more varied in the 1990s, the field of popular romance studies can really only be said to have emerged very recently, with the publication of Pamela Regis's *A Natural History of the Romance Novel* (2003). Since then, the scholarly attention to the genre has grown exponentially.[3]

Not surprisingly given this history, in the critical work on the genre gender has tended to take precedence over other forms of Otherness. However, critics have also addressed other types of difference, especially with respect to the pervasive whiteness of the genre. Jayashree Kamblé, for example, has devoted an entire chapter in her *Making Meaning in Popular Romance Fiction: An Epistemology* (2014) to this topic. Regarding the Other as an object of desire, the sheikh subgenre has received significant attention, in part because of the fame of E. M. Hull's *The Sheik* (1919). Hsu-Ming Teo's *Desert Passions: Orientalism and Romance Novels* (2012), for example, traces the history of the subgenre, while Amira Jarmakani's *An Imperialist Love Story: Desert Romances and the War on Terror* (2015), as the title implies, concentrates on the sheikh novel after 9/11.

This volume aims to contribute to the body of work on Otherness in romance with a focus on the geographical Other in less studied spaces, such as the Canary Islands, Madeira, the Antilles, Mexico, and Native American reservations in the United States, the social and ethnic Other in historical romances set in Britain, as well as the fantastic Other in paranormal romance and steampunk, which often offer a sobering commentary about contemporary society. This project, which originated in a symposium in the Canary Islands in 2017, does not pretend to be exhaustive in its exploration of Otherness, but a contribution to the ongoing research in the genre and hopefully a first step into new areas of inquiry. One of its most unusual features is the inclusion of two sociolinguistic studies of languages in contact in novels written in English but set in Portuguese and Spanish-speaking islands. This is an important area to explore given that language can be used in a tokenistic way to create a sense of the exotic, while more clearly demarcating the distinction between the Us and the Other.

The volume is divided into two parts.

PART I. PLACE, TRAVEL, HISTORY, AND LANGUAGE

The chapters in this section illuminate the extent to which, in the second half of the twentieth century, notions about Otherness and representations of the Other in popular romance and related popular narratives still retained much of the ideology of Anglo ethnic and racial superiority of a previous era. While postcolonial critics have studied these attitudes when referring to the faraway Other (the East vs. the West), most of our texts in this section deal with Spanish and Portuguese locations (i.e., settings supposedly not so different culturally to those of their English-speaking authors). However, these novels' approach, ideologically and linguistically, is eerily similar to that of Orientalism, as María del Mar Pérez-Gil illustrates in "Britannia's Daughters: Popular Romance Fiction and the Ideology of National Superiority (1950s-1970s)" and María Jesús Vera-Cazorla in "'And they Drive on the Wrong Side of the Road': The Anglo-centric Vision of the Canary Islands in Mills & Boon Romance Novels (1955–1987)." In romances written in the aftermath of the Second World War and the Suez Crisis, a time when the UK was in decline as an imperial power, Pérez-Gil identifies an underlying "belief in Britain's superiority, and the occasional imperialist residue underlying this belief." In these novels the British heroine embodies the nation's superiority, and the "freedom and independence enjoyed by British women are measured against the submissiveness that often defines southern European women." However, as Vera-Cazorla's chapter demonstrates, such British views of foreigners depend upon mistaken or outdated understandings of their culture and politics. While General Franco's family policies were admittedly pro-natalist and anti-feminist, even before his death Spain was seeing "transformations in the Spanish family in the opposite direction to the political, legal and religious guidelines of the regime." British romances set in Spain persisted in hewing to stereotypes about Spain and the Spaniards and thus while those published in the closing years of his regime seem outdated, those written after his death can appear "shockingly anachronistic."

Romance novels are not alone in clinging to outdated stereotypes. Maureen Mulligan's "Cross-Cultural Romance and the Shadow of the Sheikh" shows how old fictional tropes about the Other, specifically the captivity narrative and mixture of attraction and repulsion found in E. M. Hull's *The Sheik* (1919), had made their way into successful non-fictional travel narratives written by women in the 1980s: *An Indian Attachment* (1984) by Sarah Lloyd and *Nothing to Declare* (1988) by Mary Morris. Casting herself in the role of romantic heroine, each author feels an "immediate need to succumb to the charms of the powerful, inarticulate, brooding, dark, handsome lover whose main attraction seems to be that he comes from another culture and therefore represents the Other." However, since reality differs significantly from the patterns established in popular fiction, both authors become dissatisfied with the relationships and abandon their Otherly lovers.

María Isabel González-Cruz and Aline Bazenga take a sociolinguistic approach to inter-cultural relations, analyzing the representation of languages in contact in island novels: the former examines the uses of Spanish in novels set in the Canary Islands, and the latter the uses of Portuguese in novels set in Madeira. Both authors observe significant parallels in the type of strategies the authors employ to indicate their linguistic awareness, although some minor differences can be noted in the uses of the secondary language in the texts they analyze. Thus, after describing the close relationship between language and identity, González-Cruz justifies the linguistic analysis of literature and then studies the role Spanish plays in the construction of Otherness in six romances set in the Canaries. She illustrates the sociolinguistic strategies employed in the texts to represent characters' identities, namely the use of metalanguage and the insertion of Spanish words (borrowing), and phrases and sentences (codeswitching). These mechanisms, which prove the authors' awareness of the other culture and language, work as identity markers that emphasize socio-cultural closeness and create affective bonds with the Other. Besides, the study also reveals that a considerable number of Hispanicisms have been consolidated into the English lexical repertoire. Following the same line of inquiry, Bazenga offers a quantitative and qualitative analysis of similar strategies for the representation of language contact in four romances set in the Portuguese-speaking island of Madeira. She shows the authors' language awareness through the strategies they employ to recreate the bilingual environment of the novels' settings and to characterize and portray the different characters according to their language competence. However, her findings also confirm the writers' poor knowledge of Portuguese address terms, which constitute a highly coded and complex system. In fact, their general knowledge of the Other tends to be superficial and often inaccurate, as proved by the lack of diversity of Portuguese words used, including some confusion between Portuguese and Spanish.

All the foregoing chapters examine texts written by native speakers of English, about native speakers of English, who travel abroad and thus come into contact with the Other. Ramón Soto-Crespo, by contrast, examines texts in which there is no clear binary of Self and Other, written by authors native to the places about which they write. These authors are themselves in the geographical and ethnic margins in the field of English literature: he analyzes a number of works of Caribbean romantic historical fiction and finds that they complicate Whiteness, challenging the reader to rethink how we read racialized class differences, developing his concepts of "white trash" and "trash fictions." In the texts examined by Soto-Crespo, the proliferation of "trash" forms of otherness often brings conflict and death in its wake and can make "it impossible for the protagonists to find love."

Though they examine a range of forms of Otherness, what all the chapters in this section have in common is a sense that Otherness is an unresolved issue. The Other may attract, but the discourses of Otherness are still strongly moored in colonialist attitudes. Some privileged Others may be assimilated into the in-group, but by and large, the Other remains a feared, often despised, unknown.

PART II. TENSIONS AND TRANSFORMATIONS

The chapters in this section examine how specific authors have responded to Othering from the 1990s to the present. While the strong preponderance of white authors and white characters is still the norm in English-language popular romance, in spite of the current debates and challenges to the status quo, there is without doubt an increased level of awareness and diversity in the genre. This change is, however, incremental, and fraught with tensions and contradictions.

Johanna Hoorenman notes how romance novels with Native American protagonists have mostly been written by white authors for a white audience. Those novels tend to be set in an idyllic, ahistorical past which avoids periods and events that would force their authors to address the violence against, and oppression of, Native Americans throughout the U.S.'s past. Hoorenman focuses on Kathleen Eagle who, though not a Native American herself, has close ties to, and experience of living among, the Lakota Sioux. By depicting contemporary Native Americans while showing their ties to their history, Eagle's *Fire and Rain* (1994), she suggests, avoids "the stereotypical depiction of Native people in historical settings" which have served to deny the continued existence of Native American people and their cultures into the present.

As the twentieth century drew to a close and the twenty-first arrived, the romance reading and writing community began to show greater awareness of Othering and its consequences. Laura Vivanco offers the steampunk romance *Riveted* (2012) by Meljean Brook as an example of a romance which explicitly addresses Othering in a variety of forms. This includes an exploration of gendered Otherness. In general in romance novels the patriarchal positioning of women as the Other is reversed: the dominant tendency with regard to gender would seem to be towards emphasizing the appeal of the male Other, who has often been depicted as the binary opposite of a female protagonist, on the assumption that "The more strongly emphasized the contrasts between hero and heroine are, the more the confrontations between the two take on a sense of the heroic" (Barlow and Krentz 1992, 17).[4] Nonetheless, Susan Ostrov Weisser has suggested that

> Modern romance ideology takes two opposing sides on likeness, namely that a) opposites attract, and b) we love others because we have so much in common with them. Oddly, no one seems bothered by this conceptual paradox. Furthermore, lovers who are too different may be threatening to social harmony (such as interracial couples until fairly recently), but lovers who are too much alike (for example, of the same sex) can be equally threatening. (2013, 80)

Brook's novel challenges readers to question negative attitudes towards those who have been considered too "threatening," and therefore been Othered, because of their sexual orientation, disability, race or ethnicity.

Challenging stereotypes of the Other is difficult, not least because it has tended to be harder for those who are Othered to have their stories reach a wide audience. *Riveted* acknowledges its author's debt to those who have highlighted forms of prejudice and exclusion in popular romance and seems to call for more of their stories to be told. However, attempts to diversify popular romance and challenge Othering have met with varying degrees of success and even resistance, and it would be a mistake to assume that those who have been Othered will themselves automatically and invariably produce texts which are unproblematic and celebrate diversity.

María T. Ramos-García draws attention to the dual and often contradictory dimensions of racial and ethnic diversity in paranormal romance: the "real" one based on the race of the characters, and the metaphorical one based on the supernatural species represented and their dynamics. In this context, she analyzes J. R. Ward's *Black Dagger Brotherhood* series and concludes that Ward's texts offer a disturbing social and racial subtext of separation and prejudice, while Nalini Singh's *Psy-Changeling* series appears to offer a utopian near-future alternative-reality world in which physical differences in skin color, facial features and origin have lost all meaning, however this happens at the expense of cultural diversity. Furthermore, drawing on Amira Jarmakani's observations on the sheikh novel after 9/11, Ramos-García demonstrates how in Singh's work humanistic liberalism is conflated with neoliberal economic values.

In Lisa Kleypas's fiction Inmaculada Pérez-Casal discerns an ongoing attempt to depict greater diversity in a sub-genre of romance (Regency and Victorian romance) which tends to "focus almost exclusively on the lives and loves of upper-class, (white) British characters": Kleypas includes heroes who are Other due to their social class, ethnicity, or both. However, as Pérez-Casal observes, Kleypas's heroes have to choose between a total erasure of their difference or being permanently relegated to the margins of the society they marry into.

As stated in the epigraph to this introduction, Ortega y Gasset claimed that the desire to understand is an unavoidable symptom of love and he mistrusted any man who claimed to love but who made no effort to understand the Other (1914, 20–21). Knowledge and understanding come in a variety of forms, however. As Edward Said has cautioned, there is

> a difference between knowledge of other peoples and other times that is the result of understanding, compassion, careful study and analysis for their own sakes, and on the other hand knowledge that is part of an overall campaign of self-affirmation. There is, after all, a profound difference between the will to understand for purposes of co-existence and enlargement of horizons, and the will to dominate for the purposes of control. (2003)

The texts examined in this collection bear witness to that dichotomy. Our omissions, given that the protagonists of the texts we examined are predominantly young, neurotypical, cisgendered, and allosexual, hint at the existence of many additional Others who have hitherto largely been judged undesirable and unlovable.

NOTES

1. "Among the several activities of love there is only one with which I can try to infect others: the eagerness to comprehend. [. . .] In a Platonic dialogue this urge to understand is

called [. . .] 'the madness of love.' But even if the urge to understand things were not the original form, the genesis and culmination of all love, I believe that it is its indispensable symptom. I mistrust the love of a man for his friend or his flag when I do not see him make an effort to understand his enemy or the flag of his enemy" (translated by Evelyn Rugg and Diego Marín 1963, 34–35).

2. Dr Eileen Cheng-yin Chow has tried a similar experiment to the one we have engaged in here with our epigraph. In front of lecture halls full of U.S. students she began by addressing them in Chinese and found that the experience encouraged her audience "to think about how language informs but also discomfits, how we always have differentiated access—and how reluctant we are to challenge existing power structures [. . .] And how we assume people who don't speak our language must be . . . lesser than. Or are worthy of suspicion, derision, in need of 'guidance' [. . .]. Unless they have power over you." (2019)

3. For a more detailed description of the evolution of popular romance studies see Eric Murphy Selinger and Sarah S. G. Frantz's introduction in the collective volume *New Approaches to Popular Romance Fiction* (2012).

4. Not all romance novels reverse this position: there are, of course, a substantial proportion of romances with heterosexual protagonists which emphasise similarity and familiarity. Former Mills & Boon editor jay Dixon, for example, has noted the existence of "the boy hero of the 1920s and 1930s, [. . .] the boy-next-door of the 1950s" (1999, 63). For obvious reasons, a binary and gender-based opposition between a hero and heroine will also not be found in romances featuring same-gender couples, non-binary protagonists, or a central relationship involving more than two protagonists.

REFERENCES

Barlow, Linda and Jayne Ann Krentz. 1992. "Beneath the Surface: The Hidden Codes of Romance." In *Dangerous Men and Adventurous Women: Romance Writers on the Appeal of the Romance,* edited by Jayne Ann Krentz, 15–29. Pennsylvania: University of Philadelphia Press.

Chow, Eileen Cheng-yin. 2019. Tweets of 29 January 2019. https://twitter.com/chowleen/status/1090100070001901568 .

de Beauvoir, Simone. 2011. *The Second Sex,* translated by Constance Borde and Sheila Malovany-Chevallier. London: Vintage.

Dixon, jay. 1999. *The Romance Fiction of Mills & Boon, 1909–1990s.* London: UCL Press.

Gilbert, Sandra M. and Susan Gubar. 2000. *The Madwoman in the Attic: The Woman Writer and the Nineteenth-Century Literary Imagination.* Second Edition. New Haven: Yale UP.

Hull, E. M. 1919. *The Sheik.* London: Eveleigh Nash Co.

Jameson, Fredric. 1981. *The Political Unconscious: Narrative as a Socially Symbolic Act.* London: Methuen.

Jarmakani, Amira. 2015. *An Imperialist Love Story: Desert Romances and the War on Terror.* New York: New York University Press.

Jensen, Sune Qvotrup. 2011. "Othering, Identity Formation and Agency." *Qualitative Studies,* 2.2: 63–78.

Kamblé, Jayashree. 2014. *Making Meaning in Popular Romance Fiction: An Epistemology.* New York: Palgrave Macmillan.

Ortega y Gasset, José. 1914. *Meditaciones del Quijote.* Madrid: Publicaciones de la residencia de estudiantes. http://bibliotecadigital.jcyl.es/es/catalogo_imagenes/grupo.cmd?path=10124294 .

Ortega y Gasset, José. 1963. *Meditations on Quixote,* translated by Evelyn Rugg and Diego Marín. New York: W. W. Norton & Company.

Ostrov Weisser, Susan. 2013. *The Glass Slipper: Women and Love Stories.* New Brunswick, NJ: Rutgers University Press.

Regis, Pamela. 2003. *A Natural History of the Romance Novel.* Philadelphia: University of Pennsylvania Press.

Said, Edward. 2003. "Orientalism." *CounterPunch*, 5 August 2003. https://www.counterpunch.org/2003/08/05/orientalism/

Selinger, Eric Murphy and Sarah S. G. Frantz. 2012. "Introduction: New Approaches to Popular Romance Fiction." In *New Approaches to Popular Romance Fiction: Critical Essays*, edited by Sarah S. G. Frantz and Eric Murphy Selinger, 1–19. Jefferson, NC: McFarland.

Staszak, Jean-François. 2009. "Other/Otherness." *International Encyclopedia of Human Geography*. Oxford: Elsevier Science.

Teo, Hsu-Ming. 2012. *Desert Passions: Orientalism and Romance Novels*. Austin, TX: University of Texas Press.

1

Place, Travel, History, and Language

Chapter One

Britannia's Daughters

*Popular Romance Fiction and the Ideology of National
Superiority (1950s–1970s)*

María del Mar Pérez-Gil

In an essay published in 2003, Hsu-Ming Teo argued that almost all previous work on romance fiction had focused on questions of class, gender, and sexuality, neglecting issues such as colonialism, race, and ethnicity (2003, 279) which are as relevant as the former in understanding the structures of power underlying these texts. In her study of desert romances, Amira Jarmakani agrees that these novels "speak directly about the construction of race, gender, sexuality, religion, nation, and civilization" (2015, 120). Admittedly, the romance hero and heroine have traditionally embodied certain stereotypical constructions of masculinity and femininity, which explains why gender has occupied a central position in scholarly studies of romance fiction. Nonetheless, as Patricia Hill Collins has observed, "race, class, gender, sexuality, ethnicity, [and] nation . . . operate not as unitary, mutually exclusive entities, but as reciprocally constructing phenomena" (2015, 2). Broadening our critical perspectives so that they examine more than one facet of the protagonists' identities is, therefore, a necessary task if we wish to fully understand the cultural and political ideologies that subtend these narratives.

One of the elements of romance novels that still remains underexplored is their involvement with discourses of nation-building, particularly in twentieth-century Britain. According to Gabriele Linke (1997), the popular romance genre has contributed to bolstering the national image of Britain and the United States through the transmission of their values, history, and collective memory. In the case of Britain, Linke uses a number of novels set in African and Arab countries in the late 1970s and the 1980s to illustrate the persistence of a colonial mentality that emphasizes British superiority. Other scholars, like Teo (2003, 2016a) and Deborah Philips (2011), have worked along similar lines, examining the presence of racial hierarchies in early and mid-twentieth century romance texts set in the former colonies.

This chapter looks at how the belief in Britain's superiority, and the occasional imperialist residue underlying this belief, also find a way to substantiate themselves in romance novels located in southern Europe. In these narratives British values are presented as superior in contrast to the primitive nature attributed to southern Europeans. The novels analyzed cover the time span from the 1950s to the 1970s, a period in the history of Britain when the Empire was moving inexorably to its end, although part of the population still clung to belief in Britain's political and moral supremacy.

ENGLISHNESS AND NATIONAL SUPERIORITY

Britain's decline as an imperial power began after the Second World War and reached a critical point during the Suez crisis of 1956, when the country suffered an "international humiliation" (Mandler 2006, 215). The gradual loss of the colonies caused contradictory feelings in the British people. Some felt nostalgia for past glories while others saw the end of the Empire with a "sense of relief" (Ward 2001, 91). In the 1960s and 1970s, the political, intellectual, and cultural scene was dominated by the Left, for whom nationalism and patriotism were outdated concepts (Richards 1997, xi). National identity came to be associated with the ideas of "racial superiority," "imperialism," and a "hierarchical status quo" (Richards 2001, 366), which were felt to be inappropriate and no longer tenable.

Although emotional distance from the notion of patriotism was the rule among the intelligentsia and the political Left, the belief that Britain was still a dominant power did not completely wane. In fact, Margaret Thatcher's call to revive the country's lost greatness partly explains her rise to leader of the Conservative party in 1975 and Prime Minister in 1979. As Stuart Hall affirms, Thatcherism sought to bring people together under the defense of national identity and Englishness (1998, 29).[1] The Conservative party aligned itself with the ideology of cultural racism and upheld a concept of Englishness that racially and ethnically marginalized groups perceived as a source of exclusion (Hall 1996, 235). According to political scientist Stephen Haseler (1996), this belief in the racial superiority of white Britons continued well into the last decades of the twentieth century, as seen in the racism against the multicultural Others living, or coming to live, in Britain during those years.

Approaching romance fiction from a politically aware stance shows how these narratives have been complicit in promoting a discourse of Englishness and the ideology of imperialism. Linke argues that in many Mills & Boon romances the "distinction between the national self and the other" is more visible when the heroine travels overseas and her own culture is compared with that of African and Arab countries. She observes that Mills & Boon romances located in the former colonies keep alive the memory of the Empire and its association with a "glorious, prosperous Britain" (1997, 207). Although there are feelings of "admiration" and "adoration for the exotic other" (1997, 208, 207), the sense of British superiority is deeply rooted, as well as the "mission of bringing British civilization to the less advanced peoples and cultures" (1997, 207). These novels portray the Other as primitive, while constructing some of the British characters as role models (1997, 208).

In the same vein, Philips has shown how 1950s romance novels set in Africa and Asia are imbued with the imperial ideology. The white hero and heroine, says Philips, embody the concepts of Englishness and progress. For example, in Kathryn Blair's *The House at Tegwani* (1950), one of the novels she analyzes, South Africa is presented as a picturesque, exotic, and idealized country where racial conflict is absent. The black South Africans are cast in the role of loyal servants and primitive people whom the heroine "civilizes" and domesticates by teaching them manners and proper behavior and by making them abide by British customs in the domestic sphere of the house (2011, 119, 128). In other novels, the hospital is the space where the white hero and heroine evince their "superior knowledge" (2011, 129) and professionalism. The hospital is the "paradigm for an Africa in need of education and technological enlightenment, and it is British expertise which is shown to provide it" (2011, 124). The general view conveyed by these narratives is that Africans and Arabs "need to be managed" and supervised by the British (2011, 127). However trained and educated the fictional Other may be, their wild and instinctual nature may sooner or later erupt (2011, 125).

The ideology of British supremacy, as I contend, also runs through some of the novels set in southern Europe (Spain, Portugal, Italy, and Greece). These 'exotic' locations, as they were still regarded in the 1970s, are portrayed as inferior in terms of gender roles and social conventions. Their traditionalism is emphasized and contrasted with the modernity of England. In Violet Winspear's *Dearest Demon* (1975) the heroine, who travels to southern Spain to nurse a young invalid, feels "as if time had turned backwards and she found herself in the nineteenth century" (146). We are also told that southern Spaniards are a "feudal people who cling to the old traditions" (161). In *The Child of Judas* (1976), Winspear describes the Greek village women as "people deep-rooted in the traditions of their past" (154–55) and adds that "England seemed many miles away with its modern way of life" (155). In *A Nurse at Barbazon* (1964), Kathryn Blair refers to Portugal as a country with "ancient things and traditions" (100). This atmosphere of old-time customs and rules foregrounds the cultural distance between England and southern Europe.

The pastoral descriptions of the landscape are sometimes linked with the social and economic underdevelopment of the people, who nevertheless seem to live content with their lot. Art historian Alicia Fuentes Vega claims that the idealization of primitive locales into "rural arcadia[s]" (2013, 226) offers a limited perspective of reality that tends to overlook the political situation in the country and the economic hardships of the people. Moreover, such an idealization conceals the hidden, neocolonial desire for everything to remain in its current underdeveloped state, as the "rural paradise" that tourists have discovered will vanish when economic progress makes its appearance (Fuentes Vega 2013, 232) and changes forever both the landscape and the people. A romanticized view of the poor is explicit in some romance novels. In *A Nurse at Barbazon*, the village fishermen are said to be "simple, happy people" who "relax so utterly" (105) because nothing bothers their minds. In Kay Thorpe's *Olive Island* (1972), protagonist Nicky Brent travels to Perata on the island of Corfu to work in a hotel. Perata is described as a "pretty but primitive" village where many of the houses have neither electricity nor running water. Even so, the people are the "gayest and happiest" (35) Nicky has ever known.

In this novel, the character of the English and that of the Greeks function as opposites. Almost from the start, Corfu is pictured as a languorous place where time moves at a different pace. The hard-working, restless nature of the English contrasts with the indolence of Corfiotes. On arriving on the island, Nicky observes that the strong bodies of the men who work in the terminal building do not match the amount of energy they put into their work:

> [Nicky] looked out on the scene of activity, admired the symmetry of the Greek physique and reflected that the potential suggested by rippling muscle and strong hard back had seemingly little bearing on the amount of effort employed. Siesta was half an hour or more away, yet the languorous movements of the men out there already embraced its threshold. Life had a pace and inevitability all of its own in this corner of the world. (6)

The novel makes clear from the beginning the differences between the Greeks and the English. Gerry Copeland is the chief representative of the company for which Nicky works in Corfu. He is always "at the gallop" and unable to "run himself down" (8) because so much work needs to be done in the hotels. In contrast, the Greeks appear lazy and indolent. Words like "lethargic" (17) and "idle" (18) are connected with the islanders, whose sluggishness clashes with the English sense of duty. For instance, the road to Perata is bad and perilous so a new road is being built, but things are not given the importance and urgency they deserve. Nicky sees a "bright yellow digger standing idle"; of "the men who must have been working on the site there was no sign" (18), as it seems to be the siesta hour.

In her analysis of romance novels set in Greece, Laura Vivanco has pointed out the connections between climate, character, and geography. She states that the "association between hot blood, an ardent nature and a hot climate" may explain why Greek heroes have been more attractive to romance authors and readers than foreign northerly heroes (2017, 90). I think the relation between climate and character is also manifest in the stereotypical attribution of some specific negative traits (for example, laziness) to the peoples inhabiting the cultural and imaginary geography of the hot south, a spatial construct of national and ethnic prejudices. The languorous atmosphere that Thorpe associates with Greece in *Olive Island* is likewise present in Jean S. MacLeod's *The Valley of Palms* (1950), a novel set in the Canary Islands, Spain. The "vagueness of island life, that attitude of 'sufficient unto the day'" is regarded as something "typical of all tropical countries," where the sun unmercifully "saps" the "energy" of men (36), but, curiously enough, does not seem to affect the British characters. In this novel, the Spanish siesta serves to emphasize the hard-working nature of the British as opposed to the laziness of Spaniards. Although Edward Barnard, the heroine's uncle, regards the siesta as quite necessary, he has not conceded to the "Spanish custom" and keeps on working in his room in the "hour of rest," having "no time for coffee" (46). The hero, Michael Rayner, also works all day in the fields and the heroine, Elizabeth Barnard, does not "want to rest, even in the heat of the day," as there is "too much to see, too much to learn" (46). Edward Barnard's illegitimate son, born to a Canarian mother, is a "Spaniard through and through" in looks and character (92). He takes after his father only in his hard-working nature, which explains why he does not sleep during siesta.

These texts celebrate the superior moral qualities of the British, their courage, their unfailing struggle to do what is right, and their sense of duty. In *The Valley of Palms*, Michael Rayner embodies the British man who never surrenders. He does not accept defeat and is not easily beaten by adverse circumstances. His stubbornness is said to be a "typical British characteristic" (74). Despite having lived for many years in Spain, Edward Barnard feels British to the core and has "never really given up his British nationality" (162). For him, the tenant farmers in Spain are less hard-working than the English and they "haven't the guts of the yeoman breed." Spaniards are "[l]azy as sin, most of them! *Mañana!* Leave till tomorrow all you should have done today!" (44). Barnard calls the men working his lands "rascals" (61) and thinks it essential to be harsh with them. Although in this novel and in others like *The Valley of Desire* (1955), which was published under the pseudonym Catherine Airlie, MacLeod describes the inhabitants of the Canary Islands as "industrious" people who work hard to make the earth produce all kinds of fruits (Airlie 1955, 47), she nonetheless resorts to the stereotype of Spanish indolence to exalt the moral standards of her own nation.

The Valley of Desire was published during Winston Churchill's second mandate as Prime Minister (1951–1955). Churchill possessed an imperialist and "decidedly racist side" (Haseler 1996, 39). For him, the idea of Empire was "integral to the greatness" or "racial superiority" of Britain (Brendon 2011, 30). References to the English *race* are found in the romance fiction of this and later decades. Whiteness defines the English, in contrast to the darkness that exoticizes southern Europeans and essentializes them as visually, ethnically, and culturally different.

Some of MacLeod's novels from the 1950s and early 1960s set in the Canaries racialize ethnic groups with the aim of highlighting the cultural and physical differences that separate the British from their Others. Sociologists Stephen Cornell and Douglas Hartmann argue that the racialization of ethnic groups occurs when one of them regards the other as inferior, either physically, biologically, or morally. The Other is categorized as everything the white subject is not:

> in defining others, we implicitly define ourselves, if only through unspoken contrast. If "they" are evil, "we" must be good; if "they" are notable for their laziness or dim-wittedness or violence, it goes without saying that "we" are notable for the opposites. At the heart of racial identification lie the claims we wish to make about "them" and about how different "they" are from "us." (2007, 30)

In *The Valley of Desire*, MacLeod articulates an esthetic hierarchy that includes the racialization of the lower-class local characters. The Spanish woman who cooks for the hero is "short" and "broad-featured" (59). His housekeeper is a "stout" woman (49), and the local doctor is a "small" man (60). Although the aborigines of the Canary Islands (the Guanches) seemingly had clear eyes and fair hair, MacLeod depicts their descendants as swarthy. For instance, Ramón Machadas, one of the local characters, is said to be a "small, thick-set young man" (74) of dark eyes whose "breadth of shoulder and swarthiness" (75) suggest that he descends from the Guanches. Airlie attributes him a wild, primitive nature only restrained by "the veneer of civilization" (75). In *The Valley of Palms*, Edward Barnard's illegitimate son takes after his Canarian mother in looks: he has "dark, unruly hair," "heavy brows and rather low forehead" (47) which MacLeod, prey to physiognomic conjectures, associates with scant intelligence. Later in the narrative, she will employ the expression "high, intelligent forehead" to describe another character (63). Barnard's illegitimate son is a passionate, domineering man who must learn to control his unruly nature. He is contrasted with the hero—Michael Rayner—an upright, honest man who typifies the British ideal of manhood.

WOMAN AS NATION

As noted by jay Dixon (1999), the portrayal of romance heroines has changed over time, as has that of heroes. Romance fiction reflects the gradual shifts concerning women's sexuality, independence, and economic status. In the period between the 1950s and the 1980s, the archetypal heroine is an ordinary girl with a job. She is "working class or middle class with at least a high-school education and increasingly some form of higher education" (Jensen 1984, 88). Although not a "raving beauty," the heroine has some personality traits that make her particularly attractive (Jensen 1984, 88). Her sensibility, intelligence, and noble-mindedness contribute to her idealization.

This female type should not only be seen as a didactic role model (in an Austenian manner) but also, I argue, as a symbol of Britain. In romance novels set overseas, the heroine represents an ethical ideal in terms of nation and gender. According to sociologist Barbara Einhorn, "nationalisms construct and functionalize women through discourses of appropriate *femininity*" (2006, 199). The narrative of woman-as-nation is "translated into a moral imperative requiring women both to 'represent' the nation through moral virtue and social norms, and to reproduce the national/ethnic group in biological as well as cultural terms" (2006, 202). The romance heroine functions in ways similar to those mentioned by Einhorn: as a representation of the moral values of England and of the values that should define the feminine. She is honest, hard-working, responsible, and committed to high moral principles.

The heroine of *Dearest Demon*, nurse Destine Chard, complies with this ideal. In line with Mills & Boon's traditional politics of gender, Winspear rejects the increasing sexual license of women in 1970s Britain. Destine is unlike the "brash and over-eager females crowding out the nice girls and making them feel freakish because they don't indulge in every form of licence" (137). The heroine makes it clear that she is not like other English or European women of "easy virtue" (53) who go on holiday to Spain to flirt with Spaniards. Destine is wholly devoted to her work after her husband's tragic death when they were heading for their honeymoon. Her (English) efficiency surpasses that of Latin nurses, who have been unable to treat adequately the young Spanish invalid who is now under Destine's care. Winspear articulates a patriotic discourse through the figure of the heroine. Destine feels proud of belonging to a nation that is still "the most glorious of all" (164). The history of England, she states, is made of "selfless" and "sacrificial" people who will always fight to make their country great. Much like their brave ancestors who fought against cruel, stronger enemies and defeated them, the English nowadays are "a people who could still be rallied to fiercely defend" their country (164). The 1970s, when the novel was published, was a period of economic and (post-imperial) identity crisis in Britain (Gifford 2008, 49). In this fragment, which verges more on a speech, Destine seemingly becomes a mouthpiece for Winspear, who appeals to the readers' sense of pride in being English and the deeply romantic view that they have of their own nation, even though the "worm of reality" (163) may be slowly destroying that view. Destine's thoughts reaffirm the continuity between past and present. The patriotism of the English, so the heroine believes, may still be aroused if the country needs it.

In 1970s romance novels, the message that Britain still stands as an example for other countries to follow is most visible in terms of gender. Gender creates a hierarchical gap between Britain and southern Europe, whose alleged backwardness is reflected in the submissiveness of the women and the primitive masculinity of the men (Pérez-Gil 2019). Although the presence of a feminist discourse in British romance novels from this decade should be studied in relation to the Women's Liberation Movement and its widespread impact on society, this discourse can also be related to what historian Antoinette M. Burton calls "imperial feminism" (1990, 295). According to Burton, the "national and racial superiority" that Britons proclaimed during imperial rule was evident in the condescending way in which British feminists treated Indian women. In the Victorian period, British feminists did not regard Indian women "as equals, but as unfortunates in need of saving" (1990, 295). British women felt under the moral obligation to help their Others, and the Empire was the place to carry out this civilizing mission. Moreover, the colonized woman "served as a foil against which British feminists could gauge their own progress" (1990, 295) and demand greater equality if Britain was to appear to the world as a civilized nation. The emancipation of British women should come first and, then, that of colonized women, whom British feminists would help in their fight. As Burton argues, by comparing their situation to that of Indian and Turkish women, British feminists could show their greater achievements and the higher degree of civilization Britain had reached.

This imperial feminism also runs through the romance novel in the post-imperial age. In some contemporary sheikh romances, the white woman's burden still remains to help other women out of patriarchal oppression. As Jarmakani has shown, some sheikh romances are built on the imperialist fantasy that the heroine will bring liberation and change to the patriarchally oppressed Arab women. This act of liberation is, however, another form of "imperialist power" that seeks to emphasize the capacity of the white woman to help and teach the sheikh in the process of modernizing and civilizing his country (2015, 107), thus improving the condition of Arab women. In the narrative, these women act as a foil to the heroine and serve to highlight her superior qualities (2015, 112–13). In her analysis of contemporary sheikh romances, Teo observes that American authors depict modern, independent heroines who travel to Arab countries and refuse to adapt to the patriarchal norms. Like Jarmakani before her, Teo asserts that the heroine serves as a role model for Muslim women, who generally "stand cowed, passive, silenced, and submissive" (2016b, 191). These novels position "American women as the authoritative educators and liberators of women from other races, cultures, or nations" (2016b, 194) and situate the United States as a modern, democratic nation, in contrast to the lack of freedom and the authoritarian political rule in Arab countries.

I think a similar position with respect to gender underlies many novels from the 1970s set in southern Europe. The freedom and independence enjoyed by British women are measured against the submissiveness that often defines southern European women. In Katrina Britt's *The Spanish Grandee* (1975), one of the female characters explains that Spanish men are "very scornful" about the feminist movement and that women are "all on the men's side" (92), to which the heroine replies that, in a few years' time, Spanish women "will have no alternative other than to accept the changes progress will inevitably bring into [their] lives" (92). The Women's Liberation Movement has brought dignity to British women and it will bring it to Spanish women when they wake up and reclaim their independence: "Women's Lib doesn't mean that the women want to rule the home. Far from it. The idea of the whole thing is that they should not be treated as chattels, unpaid housekeepers, by their husbands and to receive the same payment for any career they choose on equal merit" (92). References to arranged marriages, the patriarchal division of roles that confines women to the home, or their silent obedience to the men in the family, who take the decisions on what is best for women, constitute the Other as inferior with regard to gender issues.

The second feminist wave influenced British romance authors to introduce a critical discourse against patriarchy that served to enlighten many women readers about their rights. This discourse is tainted with some ethnocentrism in the novels portraying the regressive gender system in other countries, as compared to the more evolved condition of women in Britain. In *Dearest Demon*, Destine protests that "women aren't slaves" and that they are "entitled to share in all the rights and privileges that men have enjoyed" (96), which includes the ability to have a career and to "express [themselves] beyond the confines of the home" (106). Englishwomen possess these rights; in contrast, Latin women are more prone to "appreciate male arrogance" (107) and to accept men's decrees as part of the natural order.

Progress is symbolized by the heroine. In *A Nurse at Barbazon* the Portuguese hero dislikes the fact that the heroine plays tennis in shorts and is surprised that, in England, she goes alone to the cinema, a freedom that would not be permitted to Portuguese girls. Unlike southern European women, English heroines do not submit to the tyranny of men. With a few exceptions represented by authoritarian matriarchs and emancipated local women, usually cast in the role of the heroine's rival or the "evil" woman, southern European females are less free than their English counterparts. In Blair's novel, we read that Portuguese women have no freedom to choose their husbands because marriages are arranged, something that the heroine describes as "inhuman" (165). Anne Mather provides a similar view of Portugal in *Rachel Trevellyan* (1974). In this country, women do not argue with men; they are "mild and agreeable, totally feminine in every way" (20). The English heroine strikes the hero as being the opposite. Her insistence on wearing trousers shows the modernity and emancipation of Englishwomen and becomes the symbol of her rebellion against Portuguese customs.

CONCLUSION

Popular romance novels are narratives through which national hierarchies have been reaffirmed. As cultural historian Jeffrey Richards states, literature, cinema, and television intended for the masses "have functioned as propagators of the national image, both in reflecting widely held views and constructing, extending, interrogating and perpetuating dominant cultural myths" (1997, 25–26). Approaching romance fiction through the ideology of cultural and national supremacy helps to deepen our understanding of many of these texts and to see their enmeshment in political debates.

These novels usually rely on stereotypes that construct the Other through a hierarchized vision of national and gender difference. The idealized geography of the exotic and the experience of traveling overseas are a means to provide readers with the necessary escapism associated with this genre. However, these narratives also become a medium through which authors can proclaim that Britain is still a glorious nation, a beacon of progress and civilization.

NOTE

1. I will use interchangeably the terms "British" and "English." Although the great majority of the novels analyzed use the term "English," there are others in which "British" is preferred.

The research for this chapter is funded by the Spanish Ministry of Economy and Competitiveness under grant FFI2014-53962-P, which is here gratefully acknowleged.

REFERENCES

Airlie, Catherine. 1955. *The Valley of Desire*. London: Mills & Boon.
Blair, Kathryn. 1950. *The House at Tegwani*. London: Mills & Boon.

Blair, Kathryn. [1964] 1980. *A Nurse at Barbazon*. London: Mills & Boon.

Brendon, Piers. 2011. "Churchill and Empire." In *Churchill and the Lion City: Shaping Modern Singapore*, edited by Brian P. Farrell, 10–35. Singapore: NUS Press.

Britt, Katrina. [1975] 1981. *The Spanish Grandee*. New York: The Romance Treasury Association.

Burton, Antoinette M. 1990. "The White Woman's Burden. British Feminists and the Indian Woman, 1865–1915." *Women's Studies International Forum* 13, no. 4: 295–308.

Collins, Patricia Hill. 2015. "Intersectionality's Definitional Dilemmas." *Annual Review of Sociology* 41: 1–20.

Cornell, Stephen, and Douglas Hartmann. 2007. *Ethnicity and Race: Making Identities in a Changing World* (2nd ed). Thousand Oaks: Pine Forge Press.

Dixon, jay. 1999. *The Romance Fiction of Mills & Boon, 1909–1990*. London: UCL Press.

Einhorn, Barbara. 2006. "Insiders and Outsiders: Within and Beyond the Gendered Nation." In *Handbook of Gender and Women's Studies*, edited by Kathy Davis, Mary Evans, and Judith Lorber, 196–213. London: Sage.

Fuentes Vega, Alicia. 2013. "Greetings from the Rural Paradise. Touristic Images of the Spanish Countryside during the 1950s and 60s." *The European Conference on Arts & Humanities 2013. Official Conference Proceedings*, 225–38. Nagoya: The International Academic Forum.

Gifford, Chris. 2008. *The Making of Eurosceptic Britain: Identity and Economy in a Post-Imperial State*. Aldershot: Ashgate.

Hall, Stuart. 1996. "The Meaning of New Times." In *Stuart Hall: Critical Dialogues in Cultural Studies*, edited by David Morley, and Kuan-Hsing Chen, 222–36. London: Routledge.

Hall, Stuart. 1998. "Brave New World." *Marxism Today* (October): 24–29.

Haseler, Stephen. 1996. *The English Tribe: Identity, Nation and Europe*. Basingstoke: Macmillan.

Jarmakani, Amira. 2015. *An Imperialist Love Story: Desert Romances and the War on Terror*. New York: New York University Press.

Jensen, Margaret Ann. 1984. *Love's $weet Return: The Harlequin Story*. Bowling Green: Bowling Green State University Popular Press.

Linke, Gabriele. 1997. "Contemporary Mass Market Romances as National and International Culture: A Comparative Study of Mills & Boon and Harlequin Romances." *Paradoxa* 3, no. 1–2: 195–213.

MacLeod, Jean S. [1950] 1977. *The Valley of Palms*. London: Mills & Boon.

Mandler, Peter. 2006. *The English National Character: The History of an Idea from Edmund Burke to Tony Blair*. New Haven: Yale University Press.

Mather, Anne. [1974] 1983. *Rachel Trevellyan*. Toronto: Harlequin.

Pérez-Gil, María del Mar. 2019. "Representations of Nation and Spanish Masculinity in Popular Romance Novels: The Alpha Male as 'Other.'" *The Journal of Men's Studies* 27, no. 2: 169–82.

Philips, Deborah. 2011. "The Empire of Romance: Love in a Postcolonial Climate." In *End of Empire and the English Novel Since 1945*, edited by Rachael Gilmour, and Bill Schwarz, 114–33. Manchester: Manchester University Press.

Richards, Jeffrey. 1997. *Films and British National Identity: From Dickens to Dad's Army*. Manchester: Manchester University Press.

Richards, Jeffrey. 2001. *Imperialism and Music: Britain 1876–1953*. Manchester: Manchester University Press.

Teo, Hsu-Ming. 2003. "The Romance of White Nations: Imperialism, Popular Culture, and National Histories." In *After the Imperial Turn: Thinking with and through the Nation*, edited by Antoinette Burton, 279–92. Durham: Duke University Press.

Teo, Hsu-Ming. 2016a. "Imperial Affairs: The British Empire and the Romantic Novel, 1890–1939." In *New Directions in Popular Fiction: Genre, Distribution, Reproduction*, edited by Ken Gelder, 87–110. London: Palgrave Macmillan.

Teo, Hsu-Ming. 2016b. "Orientalism, Freedom, and Feminism in Popular Romance Culture." In *Romance Fiction and American Culture: Love as the Practice of Freedom?*, edited by William A. Gleason and Eric Murphy Selinger, 181–203. New York: Routledge.

Thorpe, Kay. [1972] 1973. *Olive Island*. Toronto: Harlequin.

Vivanco, Laura. 2017. "A Place 'We All Dream About': Greece in Mills & Boon Romances." In *Greece in British Women's Literary Imagination, 1913–2013*, edited by Eleni Papargyriou, Semele Assinder, and David Holton, 81–98. New York: Peter Lang.

Ward, Stuart. 2001. "'No Nation Could Be Broker': The Satire Boom and the Demise of Britain's World Role." In *British Culture and the End of Empire*, edited by Stuart Ward, 91–110. Manchester: Manchester University Press.

Winspear, Violet. 1975. *Dearest Demon*. London: Mills & Boon.

Winspear, Violet. 1976. *The Child of Judas*. London: Mills & Boon.

Chapter Two

"And They Drive on the Wrong Side of the Road"

*The Anglo-centric Vision of the Canary Islands in Mills
& Boon Romance Novels (1955–1987)*

María Jesús Vera-Cazorla

Romantic novels located outside the United Kingdom offer British readers the possibility of enjoying a predictable but also unexpected plot, as the Otherness of one of the protagonists changes the expected behavioral patterns of the romantic relationship. Although popular romantic fiction has been criticized for being highly formulaic, novelty in the locations allows for an infinity of new situations, colorful foreigners, and cultural misunderstandings. Thus, many writers place the action in another country, with characters from other cultures. Exotic locations have appeared in Mills & Boon novels since at least the 1920s. One of those exotic settings for British authors and readers is the Canary Islands, a place that has been associated with paradise and the exotic since Classical antiquity. In the romantic novels set in the Canary Islands, an English female protagonist comes to the islands, usually to work or visit a relative.

This chapter offers a discussion of nine romance novels set in the Canary Islands, focusing on how the Spanish fictional Other is created through discourse. These romance novels, aimed at a heterogeneous group of readers, were published by Mills & Boon and Harlequin between 1955 and 1987. The novels I will be analyzing in this chapter are Catherine Airlie's *The Valley of Desire* (1955), Jane Arbor's *Golden Apple Island* (1967), Kay Thorpe's *An Apple in Eden* (1973), Iris Danbury's *The Silver Stallion* (1973), Pippa Lane's *Nurse in Tenerife* (1978), Sally Wentworth's *Dark Awakening* (1984), Elizabeth Oldfield's *Beware of Married Men* (1986), Claudia Jameson's *An Engagement is Announced* (1987), and Jenny Ashe's *The Surgeon from San Agustin* (1987).

Mainland Spain "had traditionally remained off the beaten track for the Grand Tour, which focused on France, Switzerland and Italy" (Mulligan 2017, 17). However, foreigners have always been present in the Canary Islands: first as pirates, explorers, and slaves, and later as cane-growers, traders, scientists, and Victorian travelers who came to the islands either to improve their health and benefit from the islands' weather, or because they were on their way to America or Africa. In the nineteenth century, the figure of the individual visitor gave way to that of the tourist, a traveler who joins "a package tour in search of recreation, fun and health" (Morales Lezcano 1986, 124). The British community that resided in the islands between the late nineteenth and early twentieth centuries played an important role in the development of the Canarian economy and the beginning of tourism. Regarding the timeline of the novels, five of them appeared towards the end of the Franco dictatorship and the beginning of democracy, when the first tourist boom occurred in the islands and the British were starting to have more detailed information about Canarian life and customs. In fact, although the British airline Aquila Airways began the first regular weekly flights between the UK and the Canary Islands in 1949 (Alzola 2017), it was not until the 1960s that tourism became an essential factor in the local economy.

According to Ruth Wodak et al. (2009),

> If a nation is an imagined community and at the same time a mental construct, an imaginary complex of ideas containing at least the defining elements of collective unity and equality, of boundaries and autonomy, then this image is real to the extent that one is convinced of it, believes in it and identifies with it emotionally. The question of how this imaginary community reaches the minds of those who are convinced of it is easy to answer: it is constructed and conveyed in discourse, predominantly in narratives of national culture. National identity is thus the product of discourse. (2009, 22)

The imagined communities we called nations are created through discourse. This discourse of national identity manifests itself especially in each nation's customs, traditions and differences from other nations. The Other is unfamiliar, sometimes fascinating but, above all, different from us. In the novels published in the 1950s, the Canary Islands appear as an exotic and romantic place near the African coast. In some novels, the existence of Canarian aborigines is mentioned in order to underline the difference from mainland Spain and emphasize the image of the islands as a paradise. That exoticism tends to disappear in later romances when one might think that the knowledge about the islands was greater. Most of the books I analyze in this chapter were written when tourism was no longer reserved for the few; even so, the lack of information about the islands is noticeable. These British writers place special emphasis on difference, on Otherness, and they do this through an Anglo-centric discourse.

In this work, I discuss the way the authors of these nine romance novels express their Othering of the foreign country. From her position of privilege, since she is a self-sufficient independent woman who comes from a rich country, the English female protagonist faces the challenge of understanding unfamiliar customs in her search for love. When describing the encounter between the protagonist and those new customs, these writers reveal their Anglo-centric view of the islands. As Maureen Mulligan states about travel writing,

> What we may perceive naïvely as an unmediated, objective description of a place is always and inevitably filtered through many levels of social, cultural and linguistic discourses of which the author may be unaware but which condition the image created in the text. (2017, 8)

ROMANCE NOVELS AND STEREOTYPES

Although to a person who is not used to reading them genre romance novels may seem very similar, many readers and devotees of the genre recognize the unmistakable characteristics of a particular author or the different plot possibilities, as An Goris points out:

> Contrary to the widespread stereotypical image of the romance novel as repetitive and formulaic—and hence literarily worthless—the handbooks [on how to write romance] define and locate the genre's success precisely in its ability to integrate familiarity with innovation, thus offering its readers experiences of both comfort and surprise. The romance author must give the reader what she wants and expects, but differently. (2012, 76)

Within their predictability, these novels tend to offer an unexpected plot twist and sometimes an original or exotic location far away from the reader's routine. Setting the story in Spain, or more specifically in the Canary Islands, provides the reader with an unusual destination where a love story could become real, always within the genre conventions. According to Deborah Philips, "The fantasy of true love has always involved a measure of international travel, and Mills & Boon heroines have found their heroes across the world" (2011, 114). In many of the romances set in the Canary Islands, while both the male protagonist and Canarian traditions contribute to the required exoticism, many stereotypes related to Spain, Spaniards, and the paradisiacal image of the islands give the reader a sense of familiarity.

According to Isobel Lindsay, "The importance of national stereotypes lies not in whether they reflect a reality, past or present, but whether they are part of our consciousness and, as such, may influence behaviour" (2015, 133).

The long history of British-Spanish relationships has impacted the emergence of different stereotypes and there are references to some British stereotypes about Spaniards, such as their chauvinism, religiosity, passion, and the
importance of the family, in many of these novels.

OTHERING THE FOREIGN COUNTRY

In a socio-historical and cultural approach to the discourses of Spanish national identity, José Igor Prieto Arranz (2012) examines the image of Spain
from the British perspective from the sixteenth century. For centuries, this
image has been linked to Catholicism and religious fanaticism, especially
since the reign of Mary I of England. During the reign of Elizabeth I, support
for the English government and the Church of England became synonymous
with patriotism. Prieto Arranz affirms that the Anglo-centric discourse of
British identity, prolific in the eighteenth century, is based on the concept of
freedom and was clearly constructed in opposition to the tyranny of both
France and Spain. During the reign of Elizabeth I, the discourses of national
and religious identity merged in England, especially in the years following
the unexpected defeat of the Spanish Armada. This national-religious discourse remained in force during the second half of the nineteenth century and
the first half of the twentieth.

It would be natural to believe that this English image of Spain has
changed with the arrival in Spain of English tourists and residents from the
1960s onwards:

> During the 1980s, increasing numbers of British people began migrating to
> Spain's coastal areas. Attracted by the warmth, the cost of living and the
> potential for a leisured lifestyle, and aided by portable pensions and capital
> gained during the property boom of the 1970s, they were the outcome of a
> phenomenon which began in 1960s with cheap air travel and mass package
> tourism. (O'Reilly 2002, 179)

However, the image of Spain held by those expatriates has not changed that
much. Sociologist Karen O'Reilly has studied the attitudes of the English
living in the south of Spain on a permanent basis. According to these mi-
grants, Spain is a country of "bullfights and passion, quaintness and backwardness, blood and revolution, peasants and traditions" (2002, 182). The
British residents find in Spain the values of community, caring, sharing, and
responsibility that they used to associate with a historical bygone Britain, so
for them Spain offers an escape to the past (183). According to María del
Mar Pérez-Gil, "the othering of the foreign implicitly reveals how the self
builds up his/her own national identity [. . .] in this process the self's own
prejudiced views incidentally come to light" (2018, 943). Therefore, the

authors of the romance novels subconsciously write about their concept of Britishness and of Spanishness.

THE ANGLO-CENTRIC DISCOURSE OF OTHERNESS IN ROMANCE NOVELS

In Elizabeth Oldfield's *Beware of Married Men*, the English hero complains to the female protagonist that he must remember how to drive "on the wrong side of the road" (1986, 64) when they are in Lanzarote. Not on the other side of the road, but on the "wrong" side of the road, even though the countries in which motorists drive on the left are in the minority. The sentiment is echoed in Claudia Jameson's *An Engagement Is Announced* (1987): the female protagonist acknowledges that she has no experience of driving on the wrong side of the road. This kind of discourse characterizes British customs as normal and correct and is evident in other aspects of the novels. In *The Valley of Desire* it is the narrator who Others Spaniards by saying of one of the Spanish characters that, "Like most of her race, Sisa attached very little importance to time and distance" (Airlie 1955, 121). This type of discourse of national identity permeates all these novels to a greater or lesser degree. This Anglo-centric discourse and the potential of stereotypic image construction shapes British cultural consciousness of the Spanish by offering readers patterns of expected behavior.

In most of these exotic romance novels, a young British woman comes to the islands and meets the male protagonist, usually a Spaniard or an Englishman who has lived on the islands for many years. Many of the Spanish male protagonists are chauvinists. Thus, in *Nurse in Tenerife* (1978), Trudy Forrester is reluctant to leave Midthorpe General Hospital and go to the island of Tenerife to take care of her stepmother for a year as she is in love with handsome Dr. Derek Larridine, who works at the hospital. In Tenerife, she meets Dr. Martina ("Mr. Tenerife"), the island's richest man and a famous surgeon, who falls in love with her. However, Trudy loves Derek even though he is far away in the United Kingdom. When Trudy has only recently arrived on the island, an English woman points to Dr. Martina and tells her he is as "Chauvinist as any Spanish male" (Lane 1978, 17). This idea of the machismo of the Spanish man is present in many of the novels. However, the most chauvinistic male protagonist is undoubtedly Dr. Riviero from *The Surgeon from San Agustin* (Ashe, 1987). Dr. Hannah Day runs a little hospital beside San Agustin beach, but she needs an assistant to take on some of the workload. Dr. Ramon Riviero, a chauvinist Spanish doctor from the region who has been working in India, needs a job while he recovers from a severe illness. Although he resents working for a woman and is in the midst of many family problems, Hannah falls in love with him. Ramon uses the word *mujer* (woman) as if it were an insult and expresses himself in the following ways:

> "You think you can command me, *mujer*?" (Ashe 1987, 13)

> "Anyway, a woman alone is a sad sight." He shrugged. "For your sake I hope it is a man."
> "That's . . ." Hannah controlled her sudden outburst and said in quieter tones, "That's both patronizing and sexist."
> "Probably," he shrugged. (26)

> "Typical—let the woman get the juice! You could easily have done it while I was getting ready."
> "Don't nag." And she was already obeying him, with a smile on her lips. (61)

> "You ought to have known I wouldn't trust my precious car to a mere woman!," he grinned. (66)

Machismo is reflected in several Spanish characters throughout the novels, male dominance in sexual encounters being one of these forms. Particularly during the 60s and 70s, there is an increasing correlation between the rising demand for gender equality and machismo in romance novels (Kamblé 2014, 87). This is portrayed in the books, in which an English woman protagonist is independent and empowered although attracted to a chauvinist Spanish male. Though the heroine is not always involved in a non-consensual sexual encounter, the Spanish male figure nonetheless exhibits a threatening alpha-male personality. According to María Teresa González Mínguez, the macho hero of the 1970s Mills & Boon romance "is commanding, dominant, cruel, sexually aggressive but also tender and supplicating" (2010, 185). For this author, the appearance of this type of male protagonist was due to the eroticization of the Latin and Arab hero; "the books link sex with violence and rape" (2010, 190). However, Jayashree Kamblé abstains from applying the term rape, as "the level of rape is avoided by documenting the heroine's feelings of sexual arousal" (Kamblé 2014, 103).

Even though *The Valley of Desire* was published long before, in 1955, the male protagonist behaves like the typical Latin macho hero of the 70s. Rape used to be understood almost as a cultural expression of the excessive love felt by the exotic protagonist. Jayashree Kamblé argues that "The racially foreign character—with his potentially reactionary beliefs about women—is invoked because he is assumed to be synonymous with heterosexual identity" (2014, 100). Thus, in *The Valley of Desire*, Charles, the half-English half-Spanish cousin of the protagonist's brother-in-law, admits to her that "I wanted you more than anything in the world" (Airlie 1955, 188). He says that he was very much in love with her, and that he wrongly believed that she loved Nicolás, her brother-in-law at the time. Although he does not commit rape, he apologizes to Barbara for having thought about it, excusing himself with the following words:

> "I thought I had a right to take you." He laughed abruptly. "Remember that I am not wholly English!" (Airlie 1955, 188)

Despite his *machismo* and conceit, the female protagonist is attracted by his strong masculinity and confidence.

In contrast, many of the young Spanish females that appear in these novels are portrayed as women who are subordinated to their roles as wives and mothers. Franco's regime meant a break with the family law of the Second Spanish Republic. Thus, equality between legitimate and illegitimate children was annulled, contraceptives, adultery, and cohabitation were penalized, women's work outside the home was hindered—especially if married—coeducation was forbidden, large families were encouraged, religious marriage ceremonies were compulsory for the baptized, and the Church was given the power to determine grounds for matrimonial separation and invalidation of marriage (Iglesias de Ussel 1990, 242). Celia Valiente Fernández characterizes Franco's family policy as pro-natalist and anti-feminist. Since population growth was one of its main objectives, his policy tried to remove married women from the workplace, confining them to the domestic sphere. Motherhood was defined as the main obligation of women to the family, the state, and society and it was considered a function incompatible with work outside the home. During the first two decades of the regime there were clauses in a large number of work regulations affecting public and private companies which made it mandatory for female workers to retire upon marriage, as well as the requirement that married women receive their husband's authorization to sign a work contract or to trade (Valiente Fernández 1996, 151–54).

The social dynamics of these laws are reflected in the novels' portrayals of Spanish characters. Some novels describe how women do not participate in conversations when they are with British visitors or merely repeat opinions they have learned from their fathers or husbands. In *An Apple in Eden*, Eve's young sister announces her engagement to an unknown Spaniard in the Canary Islands, so Eve decides to go to Tenerife to meet her sister's fiancé, Juan Perestrello. There, she learns that Juan has a twin brother, Ramon. Soon after her arrival, her sister admits that she no longer loves Juan, but that she has fallen in love with Ramon. However, Ramon himself seems very interested in Eve. In this novel there are many references to the differences between English and Spanish women, their expected behavior and way of

life. In the following quotation, Ramon tells Eve about family values in
Spain:

> ". . . Perhaps while you're here we can do something to alter your opinion of
> the Latin male. You are looking for a husband yourself?"
> "No."
> "Then you should be. In Spain you would already be the mother of three at
> your age. Our girls marry young and stay married." White teeth flashed in a
> smile. "The little ones keep them out of mischief."
> "What a wonderful reason to have children," she said with sarcasm, and
> succeeded only in widening the smile into a grin. (Thorpe 1973, 11)

In many of the early novels the authors mention that arranged marriages are
very common in the islands: girls' parents choose husbands for them from
among the families they know. In *An Apple in Eden*, Ramon and Juan's
grandmother does not support this tradition and, as their mother complains to
Eve,

> "Were it not for her both of my sons would already be husbands and fathers,
> with wives chosen from among the families of our acquaintance." (1973, 31)

However, these remarks are not accurate, as they do not reflect the real
marriage customs of the islands. A reference to arranged marriages also
appears in *Golden Apple Island*. In this novel Fran Page and her mother fly to
the nonexistent island of Canaria following the recommendation of Mrs.
Page's doctor. On the estate of Fran's supposed grandfather, Don Diego de
Matteor, Fran reconnects with her cousin Gil, with whom she has always
been a little in love. However, he is in a relationship with Elena Merced, a
beautiful singer of flamenco and fado. Fran is afraid to confess to her domineering grandfather that she is not really his blood granddaughter, but the
daughter of her adoptive father's brother. In this book, reference is made to
an imaginary tradition called the Marriage Fair that, according to Fran's
grandfather,

> dates from the time when a father could ask a price, in cash or in kind, for his
> daughter's hand in marriage. He would invite all the eligible bachelors he
> could muster, wine them and dine them well, and the "wares" would go to the
> highest bidder. (Arbor 1967, 60)

The role of Spanish women as mothers, associated with the idea of large
families, is frequently mentioned in these novels, including those that were
published long after the end of Franco's dictatorship. The Civil War had
killed a large percentage of young men, so a policy was established with the
purpose of replenishing the population. In 1943, large families were defined
as those that included four or more children. The pro-family measures con-

sisted mainly of giving them a higher amount of family subsidy, and preferential treatment with respect to taxes, public transport, loans, public housing, rates in educational centers, and stays in residences, hostels, camps, spas, and public hospitals. Family policy was not a set of covert or little-publicized measures, but a recurring theme in the rhetoric of the regime. The demographic concerns were emphatically outlined in official speeches and writings. As another example of the visibility of these policies, the granting of prizes to the most prolific families in the country represented one of the best-known rituals of the time, as the mass media covered these events widely, offering the public photographs of the winning families, extensive information about them and interviews with their members (Valiente Fernández 1996, 153–54).

Some authors writing in the 1980s and 1990s continued to assume that Spanish families would be large, since the Catholic Church, a very public ally of the Franco regime, upheld the strict prohibition of Pope Paul VI against artificial contraception defended in his encyclical *Humanae Vitae* (1968). Although religion is not explicitly mentioned in the novels, there is an implicit association between Catholicism and large Spanish families, especially compared to the smaller-sized British family:

> "So there is something to be said for our own instincts in favouring the large family," commented the other. "In Spain one would never be left entirely alone as you and your sister were." (Thorpe 1973, 31–32)

Closely related to the subject of religion and the prudishness that gained strength after the Spanish Civil War, there are several references to the fact that a man and a woman, if not married, need to be chaperoned. In some cases, this rule is not very strictly adhered to, especially if the woman is not Spanish. In the following case, Rosanna del Rey takes advantage of this custom to try to get Lucie away from Joel and Hallam's house:

> "I'm afraid that we—that is Hallam and I—have offended the local conventions of propriety. Señora del Rey and Rosanna have pointed out to us the iniquity of allowing a young woman—and one of our own country-women at that—to remain under our roof." (Danbury 1973, 52)

However, the economic development of the sixties encouraged social change. Urban growth, the increase in the number of women working outside their homes, the rise in the school enrolment rates of both sexes, the spread of a degree of economic well-being, among other factors, favored important transformations in the Spanish family in the opposite direction to the political, legal and religious guidelines of the regime. Even before the death of Franco, people were living with attitudes that did not match the structural surface that his regime represented. Without that reality, democratic change would not have been possible (Iglesias de Ussel 1990, 243–46). These novels do not reflect those changes, but show viewpoints and attitudes that were already beginning to disappear.

Thus, although *Dark Awakening* was published in 1984, when the socialist government led by Felipe González, elected in 1982, was planning modernizing legislation on issues such as the decriminalization of abortion and equality for women, it contains a shockingly anachronistic scene. Minta marries Dane Fenton, a half-English half-Spanish businessman, against her father's wishes and comes to Gran Canaria. She is happy on the island until she meets Delia Nelson, her husband's ex-lover, who warns her that Dane has married her to get financial security from her father. The protagonist, who is pregnant, has an accident and her husband calls a doctor. The two men argue in Spanish and finally the doctor assures them that everything is well and wishes them many more children, making him, in the words of Dane, "A man after my own heart!" (Wentworth 1984, 155). However, Minta wonders if her husband is talking about her and her baby as if they were his possessions:

> She could hear them talking outside on the landing, and felt a burning resentment that the doctor could discuss her with Dane as if she had no rights over her own body. But maybe they still regarded a wife as just another of the man's possessions in the Canary Islands. (155)

The difference in women's rights in Spain and Great Britain was a theme that romance authors kept very much in mind and, although Spanish legislation had changed, these writers suggest that the mentality of the general population had not, in spite of all the evidence to the contrary. However, not all Spanish women who appear in these books reflect Franco's ideal woman. There are two clear exceptions, Elena Merced from Arbor's *The Golden Apple Island* (1967) and Rosanna del Rey from Danbury's *The Silver Stallion* (1973). These two women, antagonists of the British female protagonist, are portrayed in a very different way from the rest of the Spanish women. Both are very beautiful and sensual women, and economically independent, either because they work or because of the wealth of their family. Their way of dressing and behaving does not match the appropriate female behavior of the time. The singer Elena Merced is an independent woman who works and travels on her own. As for Rosanna del Rey, she belongs to a rich Canarian family and is used to behaving as she pleases. Nevertheless, when she realizes that artists Joel and Hallam seem very interested in Lucie Durant, she quickly reminds them of social conventions and that a single woman is not allowed to live with two single men under the same roof. However, at the end of both novels the male protagonist finally chooses the innocent and poor British protagonist against a bold demeanor and explicit sexuality of the kind one might associate with Carmen, the heroine of Georges Bizet's famous opera.

In addition to gendered stereotyped traits, a characteristic feature of Spanish people is, according to the English, their pride, a trait cited in many novels, especially when describing the male protagonist. In the next quotation, however, pride is mentioned as a national quality:

> "Do you think we should offend the family if we gave them presents?" Lucie asked Joel.
> "No. I think they'd be most grateful, but not anything obviously expensive, for they have a fierce pride, like all Spanish people." (139–40)

There are numerous references to Spanish indolence and their habit of leaving everything to *mañana*, as the following examples illustrate:

> By the time he had finished listing tasks for the following day, Lorenzo's chirpiness had faded into shell-shock. Jorja doubted whether he had absorbed all the instructions. If by a miracle he had, she was convinced at least half had been put on "hold," to be attended to at some vague date in the future. Hard work did not appear to have a high rating on the Spaniard's list of priorities. (Oldfield 1986, 62)

> Hannah smiled. "Mine is only a small clinic. I only bought it as a way to stay in the sun and do as little work as possible. I'm not ambitious, Señor Riviero. I believe in taking life as it comes."
> The fat man laughed. "You do not have to explain that attitude to me. All Spanish people believe in *mañana*, you know. It comes naturally to them." (Ashe 1987, 76)

> "Oh, you'll not see her [señora Perestrello] before five," was the indifferent reply. "She takes her siesta very seriously." (Thorpe 1973, 20)

The novels also suggest that many of the great advances in local industry are due to the English; in some cases, this notion could be justified, but in others this Anglo-centrism seems exaggerated. As an example, an English resident in Gran Canaria asserts that "Spaniards blew their brains out all over the place at the time of the Cochineal Disaster, and it took a handful of Englishmen to show them the way back to prosperity through fruit and vegetables" (Airlie 1955, 69). The implication is that when the natural dye cochineal was supplanted by artificial colorants, Spaniards could only respond in a dramatically emotional manner, while Englishmen pragmatically thought of turning to other crops.

When there is an antagonist in the novels, whether male or female, they are characterized more like a national stereotype than a real person. As we have seen, if the antagonist is a Spanish woman who competes with the protagonist for the love of the hero, she is usually dark, attractive, exotic, and arrogant. Either an alluring folk singer or a rich girl from high society on the islands, she represents everything that the shy English rose is not.

On the other hand, when the antagonist is male, he is usually a British man who is romantically interested in the protagonist and represents the virtues of Britain against the backwardness of the islands. A clear example of this male antagonist is Rendle Jervis in *Golden Apple Island*. Rendle is hardworking, reliable, and calm; however, he cannot avoid showing his prejudice against Canarians. On the island for work purposes, he makes fun of many of the local customs and yearns for his mother country:

> When she [Fran] felt ensnared by the web in which she was involved at the Quinta, his [Rendle Jervis's] very prejudice was refreshing. With him she could relax and, listening to him talk "England" to the disparagement of any-where else, she could almost persuade herself she would be glad to go back. In Rendle's view the civilized world only began at the cliffs of Dover or London Airport, and since it was to be her world again from now on, there had to be comfort in supposing he was right. (Arbor 1967, 147)

While Rendle shows Fran the work he has been doing for her grandfather, he takes the opportunity to show his resentment against Canarian workers:

> They left the car and walked. "It's fabulous," Fran marvelled, "what you've achieved in the time!"
>
> "Round-the-clock shifts, siesta cut to half an hour and the sky the limit for the wage-bill, and we could hardly achieve less." Rendle added with his custo-mary jaundice, "Not that the building comes anywhere near English standards. Jerry, a lot of it, but what can you expect?" (148)

However, rather than feeling anger at his prejudice, for Fran her compatriot represents the mundaneness and the routine of home in the face of the new sensations she experiences on the islands. At the end of the novel, Fran recognizes that she is not in love with Rendle, but with Gil, and admits that the Englishman represents the tranquility and stability of their country of origin. She says "I think because by contrast Rendle looked sane and English and balanced, against something that was shaming and fantastic and cruel. Alien and hateful" (177). Gil and Rendle become representatives of the idio-syncrasies and distinctive features of their respective countries and, to all appearances, Rendle offers a more suitable partner for the female protago-nist. This is a clear example of a protagonist letting her passions and emo-tions guide her instead of what she believes would be the logical best fit for her.

At the beginning of this chapter, I stated that national identity is a product of discourse. A final example of such discourse can be found in the following scene from *The Silver Stallion*. Lucie Durant goes to a villa far away from the city of Las Palmas de Gran Canaria in search of Joel Barron. She goes by taxi but upon arrival she dismisses it, even though the driver offered to wait for her. Once the visit is over, she finds she has no way to go back to Las Palmas and the housemaid calls a delivery boy who was going towards the city, and he agrees to take her back as a favor:

> She handed him the equivalent of the taxi fare she had paid and he examined the peseta notes.
> "Too much!" he muttered.
> "No, keep it. Good luck."
> He shrugged, pocketed the notes with a smile, no doubt believing that all the English were not only millionaires but mad as well. (Danbury 1973, 7)

This scene about a silly mistake by the British protagonist becomes an example of understated British generosity, although, as the protagonist warns, the British must be careful in case Canarians think that all the English are rich. Instead of showing the perspective of the Canarian, who generously took the protagonist back to Las Palmas, the author condescendingly focuses on British magnanimity.

CONCLUSION

English readers will have little problem identifying themselves with the British protagonist of these novels, a girl who goes abroad and finds love; better still if, in addition, the man she is infatuated with is dark, attractive, and exotic. The foreign beau allows erotic fantasies of power that do not seem to match those expected of a fellow citizen. In some novels, though, the masculine protagonists are little more than a cliché of what is typically Spanish, according to the English: machismo, haughtiness, and some old-fashioned ideas about women and gentlemanliness.

The Anglo-centric vision agrees with the readers' preconceived ideas about the Canary Islands and with the national image of Spain and the Spanish: *siesta*, lovely weather, good food, *fiesta* and laziness, *machismo* and pride. Once the exotic background is set, the reader can concentrate on the love story. In addition to the most common stereotypes about Spain, these authors showed the situation of women during Franco's dictatorship. In fact, the Spanish woman they portray is usually the ideal woman of the regime. However, when most of these novels were published, Spanish society was changing and moving away from the Francoist guidelines. According to historians, the economic development of the sixties encouraged social change. Urban growth, the increase in the number of working women, the spread of a certain degree of economic well-being, among other factors, favored important transformations in Spain, in the opposite direction to the political, legal, and religious guidelines of the regime. These Anglo-centric texts reveal more about British attitudes towards the Spanish Other than they do about reality. By the same token, British identity is created by contrast to what it is not: in this case Spanish. The protagonist is an independent woman, who usually works and is used to solving her own problems and deciding on her future. Although her beauty is not as obvious as that of Spanish women, her typically British character is usually calm, fairly reserved, modest, and courteous. The British discourse of identity appears in a series of dichotomies: phlegmatic versus extroverted, pure (such as the pure English rose, e.g., the female main character) versus sexual and, although Spanishness has its appeal, and the British protagonist finally recognizes some Spanish qualities as something positive, she succeeds because she does not lose her British identity.

REFERENCES

Airlie, Catherine, 1955. *The Valley of Desire*. Winnipeg: Mills & Boon.

Alzola, Cristóbal. 2017. "70 años del primer intento del turismo aéreo en Canarias." *La Provincia*, December 7, 2017.

Arbor, Jane. 1967. *Golden Apple Island*. Winnipeg: Harlequin Books.

Ashe, Jenny. 1987. *The Surgeon from San Agustin*. Richmond: Mills & Boon.

Danbury, Iris. 1973. *The Silver Stallion*. Richmond: Mills & Boon.

González-Cruz, María Isabel. 2015. "Love in Paradise: Visions of the Canaries in a Corpus of Popular Romance Fiction Novels." *Oceánide* 7 (February).

González Mínguez, María Teresa. 2010. "Who is More Fragile? A Study of Heroes and Heroines in the Twentieth Century Romantic Fiction of Mills and Boon." *Cuaderno Kóre* 2: 179–92.

Goris, An. 2012. "Loving by the Book: Voice and Romance Authorship." In *New Approaches to Popular Romance Fiction*, edited by S. S. G. Frantz and E. M. Selinger, 73–83. Jefferson: McFarland & Company.

Iglesias de Ussel, Julio. 1990. "La familia y el cambio político en España." *Revista de estudios políticos* 67: 235–60.

Jameson, Claudia. 1987. *An Engagement Is Announced*. London: Mills & Boon.

Kamblé, Jayashree. 2014. *Making Meaning in Popular Romance Fiction. An Epistemology*. New York: Palgrave Macmillan.

Lane, Pippa. 1978. *Nurse in Tenerife*. London: Mills & Boon.

Lindsay, Isobel. 2015. "The Uses and Abuses of National Stereotypes." *Scottish Affairs* 20, no. 1 (February): 133–48.

Morales Lezcano, Víctor. 1986. *Los ingleses en Canarias: (libro de viajes e historias de vida)*. Las Palmas de Gran Canaria: Edirca.

Mulligan, Maureen. 2017. "The Representation of Francoist Spain by Two British Women Travel Writers." *Studia Anglica Posnaniensia* 51, no. 4 (February): 5–27.

Oldfield, Elizabeth. 1986. *Beware of Married Men*. Lincoln: Mills & Boon.

O'Reilly, Karen. 2002. "Britain in Europe/the British in Spain: Exploring Britain's Changing Relationship to the Other through the Attitudes of Its Emigrants." *Nations & Nationalism* 8, no. 2 (April): 179–93.

Pérez-Gil, María del Mar. 2018. "Exoticism, Ethnocentrism, and Englishness in Popular Romance Fiction: Constructing the European Other." *The Journal of Popular Culture* 51, no. 4 (August): 940–55.

Philips, Deborah. 2011. "The Empire of Romance: Love in a Postcolonial Climate." In *End of Empire and the English Novel since 1945*, edited by R. Gilmour and Bill Schwarz, 114–33. Manchester: Manchester University Press.

Prieto Arranz, José Igor. 2012. "España vista desde dentro y desde fuera. Una aproximación sociohistórica y cultural a los discursos de identidad nacional." *Oceánide* 4 (January).

Thorpe, Kay. 1973. *An Apple in Eden*. London: Mills & Boon.

Valiente Fernández, Celia. 1996. "Olvidando el pasado: la política familiar en España (1975–1996)." *GAPP* 5–6 (January-August): 151–62.

Wentworth, Sally. 1984. *Dark Awakening*. London: Mills & Boon.

Wodak, Ruth, Rudolf De Cillia, Martin Reisigl, and Karin Liebhart. 2009. *The Discursive Construction of National Identity*. Edinburgh: Edinburgh University Press.

Chapter Three

Cross-Cultural Romance and the Shadow of the Sheikh

Maureen Mulligan

The motif of the heroine apparently held captive in a foreign land achieved its greatest popular success with the publication of E. M. Hull's novel, *The Sheik*, in 1919, and the film version starring Rudolph Valentino two years later. The basic plot, of a "civilized" white woman who is captured and then captivated by an apparently "uncivilized" Arab, became the template for many other popular novels and films. I will analyze two examples of travel books from the 1980s which use the motif of the captivity narrative in a somewhat distorted way in the construction of cross-cultural romance in texts that mix autobiographical and fictional styles. The two travel texts I analyze, both by educated, liberated, and independent women writing in the 1980s, follow the conventions of this tradition of romance fiction to a surprising extent. They are *Nothing to Declare: Memoirs of a Woman Traveling Alone* (1988) by the American Mary Morris and *An Indian Attachment* (1984) by the British writer Sarah Lloyd, set in Mexico and India respectively. Morris (1947–) has written novels and short stories as well as another travel memoir, *Wall to Wall: From Beijing to Berlin by Rail* (1991), and is co-editor of an anthology of women's travel writing, *Maiden Voyages* (1993). Sarah Lloyd, (born London, 1947) is a landscape architect and has written one other travel book, *Chinese Characters* (1987).

Both romantic fiction and women's travel writing are literary genres traditionally viewed by academia as outside or beneath the canon. Rosemary Auchmuty, in her introduction to a study of the fiction of Mills & Boon, says "As 'popular culture' they are fair game for literary dismissal; as books for women they invite condescension and ridicule" (Dixon 1999, ix). Popular romance fiction has been described as "still the most despised and rejected of

41

genres" (Frantz and Selinger 2012, 1). Similarly, the genre of women's travel writing has tended to be ignored by those literary critics who choose to focus on travel writing (e.g., Fussell, 1980; Dodd, 1982; Porter, 1991) or presented by more sympathetic critics as the accounts of eccentric spinsters who are not always to be taken seriously (Blanch, 1954; Robinson, 1991, 1995; Birkett, 1989; Russell, 1986). However, recently there has been a tendency to take both genres more seriously on their own terms, and this chapter attempts to do so by considering the utilization of romance tropes when the female travel writer strays from the lonely path of solitary travel and narrates a romantic encounter with a local man. In Morris's *Nothing to Declare*, the author directly links both genres and connects them with the idea of dreaming, of deferred pleasure and imagined narratives: "Women who travel as I travel are dreamers [. . .] Like readers of romances we think that anything can happen to us at any time" (Morris 1989 [1988], 164). Morris makes explicit the way that travel and romantic relations offer women a vision of escape, however tenuous, from daily routine, that may turn out to be a mirage (as her own experience suggests) but that never quite loses its attraction. Similarly, romance fiction set in distant lands that are unfamiliar to the reader, with heroes from alien cultures, offers endless attractions to many women, as Hsu-Ming Teo comments in her discussion of reader responses to sheikh romances: "Readers also enjoyed the exoticism and Orientalism of the stories" (Teo 2012, 281). The readers are presumably aware they are dealing with fantasies, when it comes to romance fiction: but what happens when the traveler falls in love with the exotic Other in a foreign land in real life?

The popularity of the sheikh hero in the captivity narrative is unrivaled in romance fiction, especially what Hsu-Ming Teo in *Desert Passions: Orientalism and Romance Novels*, categorizes as the "harem historical novel." It is perhaps no coincidence that in the decade of the eighties, when the two travel texts that we are going to discuss were published, many white fictional heroines were adventuring into exotic lands and risking or courting abduction by an attractive dark-skinned foreign local man to the delight of a wide readership. Whether it was packaged as travel writing, romance fiction or autobiographical memoir, the possibilities of engaging with standard orientalist leitmotifs arising from captivity narratives combined with dangerous Byronic heroes were many. According to Teo, "in the late 1970s, American popular culture was suddenly awash with aristocratic blond heroines being abducted by swarthy Barbary corsairs, stripped naked in slave markets, and sold as concubines into the oppressive harems of Oriental potentates, where they tasted the erotic delights of sex and the exotic indulgence of the senses" (Teo 2012, 144). Robin Harders argues, "Of all the motifs in genre romance, captivity is one of the most ubiquitous and diverse. While one of the most popular and enduring romantic captivity scenarios is that made famous in Edith Hull's 1919 novel *The Sheik*, in which the beautiful 'civilised' heroine is captivated body, soul and heart by the 'wild' desert-living sheikh, captivity has many permutations and purposes in the genre" (Frantz and Selinger 2012, 113).

The Sheik sold 1.2 million copies worldwide, outselling every other best-seller of the early 1920s. As a cultural phenomenon, *The Sheik* became even more popular after the film version was released in 1921. The hero is an interesting cultural mix: Valentino, the iconic actor who played the role of Sheik Ahmed Ben Hassan, was originally Italian, while Ahmed turns out to be the son of an English father and a Spanish mother, and educated in Paris: not Arab at all. The heroine, Lady Diana Mayo, is an independent woman who believes that: "Marriage for a woman means the end of independence, that is, marriage with a man who is a man, in spite of all that the most modern women may say. I have never obeyed anyone in my life; I do not wish to try the experiment" (Hull 2015 [1919], 18). When Diana sees a group of Arab women traveling by camel, she reflects on the difference between herself and them. This foreshadows the adventure that is about to befall her, when she is captured by Ahmed Ben Hassan:

> The contrast between them and herself was almost ridiculous. It made her feel stifled even to look at them. She wondered what their lives were like, if they ever rebelled against the drudgery and restrictions that were imposed on them, if they ever longed for the freedom that she revelled in, or if custom and usage were so strong that they had no thoughts beyond the narrow life they led. The thought of those lives filled her with aversion. (Hull 2015, 50)

This moment of self-comparison between the "free" white woman and the "captured" non-white woman is also found in the 1980s travel texts analyzed below and is one of the many motifs they share.

Sheik Ahmed Ben Hassan as romantic hero represents a complex mixture of power in his own society, extreme sexual attractiveness to women, physical bravery and strength, and yet is marked as inferior to the heroine in her condition as British aristocrat and modern white woman. The fact that the character of Diana was seen by many as socially superior in the 1920s is evident from an interview with Valentino: "Asked if Lady Diana would have fallen for a 'savage' in real life, Valentino replied, 'People are not savages because they have dark skins. The Arabian civilization is one of the oldest in the world . . . the Arabs are dignified and keen-brained'" (Leider 2004, 170). Ahmed is described from Diana's perspective in classic orientalist style, full of contrasts between her whiteness and his darkness and heat: "It was the handsomest and cruellest face that she had ever seen. [. . .] He was looking at her with fierce burning eyes that swept her until she felt that the boyish clothes that covered her slender limbs were stripped from her, leaving the beautiful white body bare under his passionate stare" (Hull 2015, 77). When she gets to know him better, contradictions that do not fit in with her simple

categorization of him as a savage are foregrounded: "The evidence of education and unlooked-for tastes [. . .] troubled her. It was an unexpected glimpse
into the personality of the Arab that had captured her [that] was vaguely
disquieting, for it suggested possibilities that would not have existed in a raw
native [. . .] He seemed to become infinitely more sinister, infinitely more
horrible" (Hull 2015, 92). It is more disturbing for Diana to find a complex
individual than it would be merely to be captured by a "raw native," who
would have no connection with her. The rest of the novel describes her
growing appreciation of Ahmed, until she reveals her love for him by writing
his name in the sand.

To summarize, the main traits that we find in the desert romance novels
include firstly what Teo refers to as the "Roxelane" theme (after an early
captive heroine), "whereby the spirited heroine tames the Muslim despot"
(Teo 2012, 154). Secondly, the idea that modern heroes are often "culturally,
if not racially, hybrid [. . .] The English heritage, which is often conveniently
aristocratic, again follows in the footsteps of *The Sheik*, and [. . .] gives the
romantic couple a plausible chance of succeeding in marriage" (Teo 2012,
169). Thirdly, female abduction and captivity; and finally, rescue and further
captivity by the hero who has a standard set of characteristics. Teo describes
the sheikh hero personified in Ben Hassan as "the descendent of the Byronic
hero commingled with the Gothic villain: tall, dark, brooding, mysterious,
marked by his compelling eyes and his cruel streak; a physically powerful
'rogue,' 'brute,' or 'savage' by nature and force of circumstance, he is eventually brought to remorse, repentance, and a change of character by irresis-
tible sex with, if not the love of, a good woman" (Teo 2012, 160); that is, a
complex cultural mixture.

Some of these characteristics, with certain modifications, can be identified in the two travel texts considered below, despite the fact that they were
written several decades later, and after the feminist movement that enabled
the two writers to travel freely around the world with a high degree of
economic independence, and the opportunity to leave whenever they chose.
Surprisingly, we still find in these modern heroines the immediate need to
succumb to the charms of the powerful, inarticulate, brooding, dark, handsome lover whose main attraction seems to be that he comes from another
culture and therefore represents the Other. Both western women are swept
away into the lives of their men, moving in with them and living their lives
through them, despite their cultural differences and the problems that arise.
Both women eventually feel trapped, captive even, and blame the man for
their situation. Both reject offers of settled family life in the host culture and
finally "escape" back to their own countries, leaving their lover behind. This,
of course, is the main difference from the romance novel: the heroes are not
revealed to be secretly partly-white, or aristocratic, or rich, and so according
to the unspoken code of so many captivity novels, they are not potential

marriage material, however much they love their heroines and offer a simple, ordinary life together.

NOTHING TO DECLARE

The initial impulse that leads Mary Morris to leave her comfortable lifestyle in the USA to head for Mexico is a vague search for adventure, in which a romantic relationship soon takes on a great importance. She does not speak much Spanish and like many late twentieth-century women travel writers, she is more interested in her inner journey than in the reality of the country she visits: "Sometimes it is difficult, but I try to read other maps. Maps of my own in the landscape, of dreams" (Morris 1989 [1988], 23). On her first meeting with the working-class Mexican Alejandro, who becomes her lover, she describes him as "dark skinned with pure Aztec features [. . .] He was tall, slender, and striking[. . . .] He had a flat nose and high, sculpted cheek-bones, deep-set dark eyes and thick black hair [. . .] 'they call me "El Ne-gro,"' he said, the dark one" (Morris 1989, 57). The idealized Aztec arche-type she chooses to see in Alejandro, rather than the actual modern Mexican, is emphasized from their first romantic evening together: "His face seemed especially dark and carved in the candlelight, like the stone faces I'd visit among Indian ruins" (Morris 1989, 59). Things do not bode well when she describes Mexicans as being like children: "internal adolescents" (Morris 1989, 64).

Morris initially meets Alejandro in a small town, San Miguel de Allende, in what she describes as a landscape of bandits that could serve as a "back-drop for the classic Westerns, where all you expect the Mexicans to say is 'hombre' and 'amigo' and 'sí, señor," (Morris 1989, 3). She has come with a typewriter and a year of high-school Spanish to live cheaply: "There is no border with greater economic discrepancy in the world than the border be-tween the U.S. and Mexico [. . .] Americans can always do well in Mexico. For a hundred dollars a month we could live like kings in castles" (Morris 1989, 27). She meets Alejandro at a party in San Miguel and he invites her to visit him when she tires of traveling around other parts of Mexico with an American girlfriend. When Morris turns up at Alejandro's address in Mexico City her romantic idyll is somewhat shattered when she sees his basic apart-ment and finds they have to share it with his "fat and ugly" stepmother (Morris 1989, 108). While this character, whose description seems to have been taken from a fairy tale rather than a sympathetic account of a tired family member, settles down to watch her favorite soap opera on television, Morris complains about the dreariness of the rooms and how she could be on a Caribbean beach elsewhere. The reality of working-class Mexican life is a far cry from her romantic fantasy, and Morris is already dreaming of escape to a more idyllic setting. However, she continues to attempt to recreate the exotic fantasy in the figure of Alejandro. On a trip to the Aztec ruins of Teotihuacán she tells how Alejandro "pounded" on his chest at the top of the Pyramid of the Sun:

> "I am an Aztec" he said, "*ciento por ciento* [*sic*]. The history of my people has been a history of conquest, of intervention, of a struggle to survive" [. . .] The wind blew his hair back. His sharply formed features grew more defined. His intensity rose [. . .] "You are a norteamericana. I suppose I will never be good enough for you, will I?" (Morris 1989, 112)

Morris avoids an honest answer to his straight question. The dialogue, which was possibly in Spanish as Morris describes them using Spanish from their first meetings, would fit perfectly in a romantic novel. The dark, morose hero of a doomed race, standing at the top of the pyramid pounding his chest, with his intensity rising, would make a great Mills & Boon cover. At the same time, the mundane reality of contemporary urban Mexican life is presented as something far more sinister by the visitor, who adopts the language of the captivity narrative: "I hated the place where he lived. I could not help it, but it was a dungeon to me and I was a prisoner there. [. . .] we were living in a practically windowless apartment in the city in which I knew almost no one but Alejandro" (Morris 1989, 113). In fact, Morris is in this situation by her own choice, and there is nothing to stop her going out, meeting people, learning the language, adapting. There is a kind of self-pity and dramatic posturing in her description that suggests the attraction of the motifs to be found in romance is greater in fiction than in the reality of a cross-cultural relationship.

Another moment when a classic trope can be perceived, although inadvertently on the part of the author perhaps, is the culture shock experienced by Morris when the "captured" heroine is brought into contact with someone from her own world. In *The Sheik*, when Diana is forced to meet a French gentleman, she tries to run away in order not to experience the shame of him seeing her in the power of Ahmed, wearing Arab clothing (he shows pity, and returns her own clothes to her). In an echo of this moment, Morris introduces Alejandro to an upper-class Jewish-American woman she meets at a gallery. When the woman suspects they are a couple, she calls off a dinner invitation she had offered to them, because of Alejandro's race, and warns the Jewish-American Morris off the relationship. Morris attempts to defend her situation but it causes her great social embarrassment and she denies the truth of the relationship by telling the woman that she and Alejandro are just friends. Not surprisingly, this leads Alejandro to realize she is ashamed of him, and he asks her directly, "Is that why you won't marry me, Maria, because I'm dark?" Mary / Maria tells him, "I really care for you, but marriage has never been an issue" (Morris 1989, 116). Later the attraction of the authentic Indian in Alejandro seems to be wearing thin, when he returns drunk one night: "You're like an Indian when you're drunk," she says as an insult, at which he reverts to his ethnically defined role: "'I am an Indian,' he said pointing proudly at his chest. 'I am an Azteca'" (Morris 1989, 132). His ethnicity is referred to again on a hike into the hills, when Alejandro kicks away a snake to rescue Morris, opens a cactus for her to drink, and spots a rabbit thanks to his great eyesight: "It's in my blood" (Morris 1989, 132). A few weeks later Mexico is losing its attraction: a religious procession reveals "[l]obotomized-looking people, expressionless, dead faces" (Morris 1989, 163). Whenever reality becomes unpleasant, Morris reverts to a dream version of travel mentioned above. This is the prelude to a brief affair with an American man, though eventually she returns to Alejandro's apartment, which she now finds barren and cold. She lies to him about meeting someone else, they argue, and he tells her a few home truths about the way Americans use Mexican culture as a cheap escape route when it suits them.

Morris continues to present her lost love as an Aztec myth: "Like Móctezuma [sic], opening the gates of his city to embrace Cortés, Alejandro welcomed me to break his heart" (Morris 1989, 183). Alejandro takes a new apartment for her sake, but to her it is hell, and another chance to repeat the captivity trope: "The windows had bars on them and it was, for all purposes, the equivalent of a cell block [. . .] My time in that dust-ridden barren tenement dwelling was like solitary confinement to me" (Morris 1989, 233). Eventually she escapes her "captor," promising to see him soon but knowing she will not, and using illness as the excuse for her return to the United States, an ending to the story she documents in the racist words of an American neighbor: "My God, I heard you almost died in Mexico City. Incredible. That's what you get for screwing a spic" (Morris 1989, 238). The romance is over. Alejandro is not mentioned in the final sections of the book, although Morris's superficial fascination with Aztec culture and romantic self-sacrifice offer a final image: "I stand alone, at the top of the Pyramid of the Sun, volcanoes on either side, the wind bearing down. I have come to sacrifice myself as the warrior knights did. To let my heart be plucked out so I can become an eagle and fly closest to the sun" (Morris 1989, 244). The reality is that it was Alejandro's heart that was broken in this story, and his final words reflect what was behind the failed relationship: "You used me. Just like all you gringos. You think you can come down here and use me" (Morris 1989, 237). The colonial relationship between the United States and Mexico is echoed in the inequality between Morris and Alejandro, once the romance is over for her and she has got what she wanted from her travels: another attempt to work out her difficult love life, perhaps with the hope that having a relationship outside her culture would make things easier. It is a recurrent theme in the book: "I do not understand my relations with men. I have searched for love, yet always find those men who cannot love" (Morris 1989, 175).

Morris swings frequently between feelings of loneliness and a need for a romantic partner, and feelings of frustration with her relationship and an equally strong desire to get away and be alone. Travel offers the solution for instant escape when she feels trapped, and provides the mirage of the ideal lover at the next port of call. The travel narrative can reflect this adventure, and the romance narrative similarly can combine its tropes in original ways designed to stimulate the imagination of the reader. The only problem in this symbiotic literary partnership—and morally, it is an insuperable problem if the author does not address it is the way it treats the local people, left behind after the traveler leaves, as expendable, as forgettable, since they do not have the option to keep moving.

AN INDIAN ATTACHMENT

Sarah Lloyd meets her dark romantic hero, "with the eyes of Buddha," on the first page of her narrative:

> He had a powerful face that instantly compelled me: high forehead, long nose, and skin the colour of almonds; but the eyes suggested sadness, a past full of grief. On his head he wore a dome of blue turbans [. . .] in front of him lay a sword [. . .] The clothes he wore, the code he followed and the ideals he lived by had survived unaltered the 300 years of their existence. (Lloyd 1992 [1984], 1)

Almost immediately, perhaps affected by the lump of opium the man feeds her, she falls for him: "Our unspoken attachment deepened. I was moved by his tenderness, his simplicity and his beautiful eyes. Beauty is a great robber of my common sense" (Lloyd 1992, 2). She nicknames him Jungli, meaning unsophisticated, untamed, and he tells her he loves her. For a while she continues her travels but then tracks him down in his village in Amritsar: "I felt I had come home" (Lloyd 1992, 10). The fact that neither speaks more than a few words of the other's language is skimmed over: "Language was never a problem: without understanding, we communicated" (Lloyd 1992, 11), although later she reflects, "Had I understood what Jungli was saying, the words might have dimmed his aura of romance" (Lloyd 1992, 33). Jungli seems to be completely enamored of her; he treats her as if she were a "goddess" but her feelings are more controlled: "I was very much attracted by Jungli, but whereas his emotions were blind and unlimited, my feelings for him could be rationalised. And they were finite" (Lloyd 1992, 14). She adapts to life in the family home, adopting the shalwar kamiz and veil of the local women, living on chapatis and dal, without a toilet or running water or privacy, accepting the limitations of the culture but describing it in Oriental-ist terms: "village taste was the taste of the child" (Lloyd 1992, 54). Soon the question of marriage arises and Jungli suggests they move to England where he could be a househusband while she works. Lloyd is not interested: "I tried to say, as gently as I could, that I wasn't sure if it would work. I was very fond of Jungli and had no wish to leave him. But marriage was another thing. Jungli was wounded to the core [and] feared for his future" (Lloyd 1992, 57). As their common language grows, their cultural differences are more obvi-ous: "I was gradually becoming aware of the enormous gulf between us. I represented the analytical, doubting, educated West; Jungli the innocent, irrational, mystical East" (Lloyd 1992, 69). Elsewhere she describes him as a "sleek black cat" and as a "child." He takes opium every day, and sleeps all day if he can, in order to pass the time, as he does not work: this leaves Lloyd feeling shocked and gradually leads to a loss of respect.

Once again, we find echoes of the classic tropes of captivity narratives in the text: the uncomfortable feelings that arise from contact, however fleeting, with someone from the heroine's own world: that is, in this case, a white woman. A crucial moment in Lloyd's disillusionment with her situation arises when they come across a Sikh soldier with his wife who is dressed in Punjabi clothes but turns out to be a white Westerner. "My instant reaction, appalling though it might sound, was just like most Indians'. I too jumped to the conclusion that the soldier was using the girl for sex and to increase his status. . . . She must live a life of hell, I thought, in that spiritual and cultural graveyard of a military camp" (Lloyd 1992, 102). Lloyd realizes she is iden-tifying herself with the woman:

> Could my horror at the sight of this captive girl have been produced by guilt? Guilt that until that moment I didn't know was there; guilt about my lack of commitment, the suspicion that I was just playacting? Or romanticising? [. . .] Whatever it was, the incident brought home to me, absolutely and finally, that just as I had reacted to the soldier and white girl so the rest of the world probably saw *us*, and that it was no use pretending to be invisible because it just didn't fool people. (Lloyd 1992, 102)

Jungli sees no problem with the couple and certainly does not see the girl as a captive, but for Lloyd it is an epiphanic moment that makes her question her own relationship with him and doubt the very nature of her commitment to their life together in India:

> How could Jungli know just how much a European or North American, com-ing from an educated, liberal and cultured background, has to lose? To commit a Westerner to traditional Indian society for life is like caging a wild bird. That girl had given her soul away. (Lloyd 1992, 103)

The fleeting encounter marks a turning point in the relationship for Lloyd, who realizes she does not see her commitment to life in India as Jungli does, and cannot face a future there.

Despite moving out of the family home and setting up house together in the community of a Sikh saint, the relationship is doomed. Jungli resorts increasingly to drinking and violence, and Lloyd succumbs to frustration and resentment. The final impulse to leave comes when the *dehra* they have joined, a Sikh community led by an autocratic Saint, demands that everyone choose between signing over all personal rights to the Saint or leaving immediately. Lloyd is horrified by the idea of a kind of slavery or voluntary prison for life, while Jungli, knowing the poverty of most of the members and their lack of other options, understands why they would choose to stay and defends them. The moment is represented as a clear cultural difference between the two of them.

Once again, the trope of the captivity narrative is implied. The reality of captivity for so many people who have little other choice in a life of profound poverty breaks the spell for the short-term traveler who can always move on when things get too hard, even if this means destroying the relationship that had been the original reason for the commitment to the foreign culture. What had seemed attractive about the silent, childlike, simple, and irrational hero has become the very reason why the Western woman cannot bear to be with him any longer; she feels trapped and stifled. The romantic idyll is over, and it is only a matter of time before Lloyd leaves a broken man, who continues to write to her after she has left: "I knew with absolute certainty that Jungli would love me until his death" (Lloyd 1992, 244).

CONCLUSION

This chapter has highlighted the use of some tropes of romance fiction in travel writing, typified in the captivity narrative. Examples have been considered of travel texts written by apparently independent women travelers of the 1980s that, consciously or not, invoke the trope of the captured powerless white woman at the mercy of the dark and dangerous foreigner that was created by Hull to such popular acclaim in the 1920s. It is not surprising that such plots and characterizations should be very popular during the late colonial period. However, some of the same narrative structures seem to have been employed by white women traveling abroad, at a time when second-wave feminism was firmly established for educated and relatively wealthy women writers such as Morris and Lloyd. The orientalist topos of the local people as being "childlike" is present in descriptions of both the Mexican and Indian cultures, in contrast to the presumably "adult" American and British travelers. At the same time, these travelers feel confident, on the basis of a brief visit, to assume they know enough to evaluate and ultimately reject what they find. Both texts play on the idea of the dark, brooding, passionate foreign lover who falls hopelessly for the adventurous, liberated white woman traveler, who loves them and leaves them. However, and somewhat ironically, they also focus on the sense of hopelessness both women feel about the prospect of finding a satisfactory relationship with a man: romantic love is still what they both are searching for as part of their inner and outer journey. The texts provide detailed examples of the cultural differences between the lovers, and emphasize the growing sense of the writer that she has become trapped in a hostile world, held there by her lover. Yet the male lover is more a captured victim than the woman: he is socially and economically at a disadvantage compared to the heroine, and does not have the luxury of a ticket out of poverty and another life in a rich country like the United States or Britain when the charms of exotic travel begin to pale. The two men in question do their best to offer a settled home and a stable married relationship, believing that this is what the woman wants. They do not consider their lives as a degrading form of captivity and cannot understand why the woman rejects the offer. They are prepared to travel to the woman's world, but she rejects this possibility, and feels uncomfortable when she is seen by people of her own culture as the man's partner. She, in contrast, is free to continue traveling and living in two worlds, crossing social and geographical boundaries when she chooses, that are impossible to cross for the frustrated hero. In short, this is a degraded form of romantic narrative, when the man is blamed for forcing the woman into a captivity that she has chosen, and when she is capable of leaving him when the romance wears thin without explanation and with little respect for what he has tried to offer. The happy ending of the romance novel is clearly lacking in the travel text: the hero is not revealed as secretly European, or rich, or educated in Paris, and as such is not considered suitable for marriage with the heroine, and the relationship is revealed as less a captivity narrative than a holiday romance turned sour.

REFERENCES

Auchmuty, Rosemary. 1999. *Foreword* in *The Romance Fiction of Mills & Boon 1909–1990s*. (ed. jay Dixon). London: UCL Press Ltd.

Birkett, Dea. 1989. *Spinsters Abroad: Victorian Lady Explorers*. Oxford: Basil Blackwell.

Blanch, Lesley. 2010 [1954]. *The Wilder Shores of Love*. London: Phoenix.

Dixon, jay. 1999. *The Romance Fiction of Mills & Boon 1909–1990s*. London: UCL Press Ltd.

Dodd, Philip (ed.). 1982. *The Art of Travel: Essays on Travel Writing*. London: Frank Cass.

Frantz, Sarah S.G. and Eric Murphy Selinger. 2012. *New Approaches to Popular Romance Fiction: Critical Essays*. Jefferson, USA: McFarland & Co.

Fussell, Paul. 1980. *Abroad: British Literary Travelling Between the Wars*. Oxford: Oxford University Press.

Harders, Robin. 2012. "Borderlands of Desire: Captivity, Romance and the Revolutionary Power of Love" (chapter 10, pp. 133–52). In *New Approaches to Popular Romance Fiction:*

Critical Essays, edited by Sarah S. G. Frantz and Eric Murphy Selinger. Jefferson, NC: McFarland & Co.

Hull, E.M. 2015 [1919]. *The Sheik*. Philadelphia: University of Pennsylvania Press, 2015 [1919].

Leider, E.W. 2004. *Dark Lover: The Life and Death of Rudolph Valentino*. London: Faber & Faber.

Lloyd, Sarah. 1987. *Chinese Characters: A Journey through China*. London: Collins.

Lloyd, Sarah. 1992 [1984]. *An Indian Attachment*. London: Eland.

Morris, Mary. 1991. *Wall to Wall: From Beijing to Berlin by Rail*. New York: Doubleday.

Morris, Mary. 1992 [1988]. *Nothing to Declare: Memoirs of a Woman Travelling Alone*. London: Penguin.

Morris, Mary (editor). 1993. *Maiden Voyages: Writings of Women Travelers*. New York: Vintage Books.

Porter, Dennis. 1991. *Haunted Journeys: Desire and Transgression in European Travel Writing*. New Jersey: Princeton University Press.

Robinson, Jane. 1991. *Wayward Women: A Guide to Women Travellers*. Oxford: Oxford University Press.

Robinson, Jane. 1995. *Unsuitable for Ladies: An Anthology of Women Travellers*. Oxford: Oxford University Press.

Russell, Mary. 1986. *The Blessings of a Good Thick Skirt: Women Travellers and their World*. London: Flamingo.

Said, Edward. 1995 [1978]. *Orientalism*. London: Penguin.

Teo, Hsu-Ming. 2012. *Desert Passions: Orientalism and Romance Novels*. Austin: University of Texas Press.

Chapter Four

Othering and Language

Bilingual Romances in the Canary Islands

María Isabel González-Cruz

Discourse on the Otherness of people is typically based on the binary opposition between alterity and self-identity. These notions are often compared to "two inseparable sides of the same coin. The Other only exists relative to the Self, and viceversa" (Staszak 2009, 43). Defined as "the affirmation of who we are by contrasting nearly every element of our way of life with that of others" (Voesterman 1991, 221), identity is considered to be the result of power relations and is culturally constructed (Castro-Borrego and Romero-Ruiz 2015, 1). Riley put it simply when he wrote: "socially speaking [. . .] 'identity' is a quality which is ascribed or attributed to an individual human being by other human beings" (2007, 86). On the other hand, in Sociolinguistics, the discipline concerned with the study of "how aspects of identity are indexed through language use" (Weston and Gardner-Chloros 2015, 205), Othering could be interpreted as a technical term to describe "the manner in which social group dichotomies are represented via language" (Pandey 2004, 155). Despite the multiple facets of identity construction, language is regarded as one of the most defining attributes of the individual, "an important part of our sense of who we are—of our identity" (Edwards 2009). In fact, David Crystal (2000, 40) recognized language as "the primary index, or symbol, or register of identity," which he defines as "what makes the members of a community recognisably the same. It is a summation of the characteristics which make it what it is and not something else—of 'us' vs. 'them'" (2000, 39).

Following this line of thought, in this chapter I will approach a sample of six romances set in the Canary Islands[1] from a sociolinguistic perspective, examining the way Otherness is constructed and represented linguistically.

53

The study will be shaped by this major sociolinguistic tenet that establishes language as the identity marker par excellence, to the extent that "the entire phenomenon of identity can be understood as a linguistic one" (Joseph 2004, 13). As a sociolinguist, John Joseph (2004, 13) underlines the fact that we tend to "form strong conceptions of each other's identities based on the way we speak," so much so that "language and identity are ultimately inseparable" (2004, 13). Furthermore, as Robert Le Page and Andrée Tabouret-Keller (1985, 14) state, our linguistic behavior or language acts can be described as "acts of identity in which people reveal both their personal identity and their search for social roles." However, while the construction of identity is "in large part established and maintained through language" (Gumperz 1990, 7), identity itself is not static. Actually, recent studies consider identity to be context-dependent and dynamic (Wodak et al. 2009, 3) and, therefore, "highly negotiable in interaction, emergent and largely co-constructed" (Beeching et al. 2018, 6).

My concern, then, will be with the role language and metalanguage play in this process of identity construction in the six romances selected here for study, namely, Arbor's (1967), Ashe's (1987), Britt's (1977), Danbury's (1972), Howard's (1994), and MacLeod's (1990). Focusing on the English/ Spanish contact situations they portray, I will show how through the insertion of metalinguistic comments and Spanish words, phrases, or sentences, the writers recreate more vividly the bilingual context, making readers aware of it. Whenever English and Spanish-speaking characters interact they construct and negotiate their identities by occasionally codeswitching into Spanish within the English discourse of the novels. This is due to the fact that lexical choices can establish in-group solidarity, as many sociolinguists have claimed. In Childs and Mallinson's words, "lexical items may serve a significant indexical function in the social construction of ethnicity," since they work as "symbolic vehicles through which speakers assert and negotiate their ethnic identity" (2006, 3).

Because "language is the writer's raw material" (Chapman 1990, 36), it is precisely through the use of Spanish that this self/other dialectic becomes deeply entrenched in the texts and the opposition between cultures is subtly highlighted. These language switches are useful to "mark closeness, familiarity, to emphasize bonds and to include or, on the contrary, to mark distance, break bonds and exclude" (Jonsson 2010, 1296) so that the characters can be perceived as outsiders, sympathizers or members of the local Spanish-speaking community. Through Spanish, the authors demonstrate their sociolinguistic awareness and provide the reader with a sense of place. This is a crucial strategy for the characters' literary representation and for the construction of the dichotomy "us versus them" since these Hispanicisms generate social allegiances, indicating a sense of attachment. They can even help to "signal shared culture or be used to create it" (Heller 1988, 270–71).

In sum, drawing on this close relationship between language and identity, I will examine the role played by Spanish in the construction of Otherness and in representing the characters' identity. Below I will firstly justify the linguistic analysis of literature and then illustrate each of the sociolinguistic strategies detected in the texts, namely, the insertion of metalinguistic comments, Spanish words (borrowing), and phrases and sentences (codeswitching).

ON LANGUAGE IN LITERATURE

Although the close connection between language and literature (and hence between linguistic and literary studies) is sometimes forgotten, we should bear in mind that literature constitutes an example of language use, and it often includes the representation of language in use (Reyes 2002, 58). With regards to the representation of language or even dialects in writing, Michael Toolan highlighted the "deep and endless division of opinion in literary studies between [. . .] the realist and symbolist viewpoints" (1992, 31). The former considers literature to be "related to the rest of life and discourse," whereas the latter sees it "as more metaphorically related" or, at any rate, as a sort of "non-serious discourse, governed by aesthetic considerations," which seems to conceive the literary as "being far from a faithful record of actual speech" (1992, 31). However, as Sell notes, "language is the material from which literature is made, and [. . .] literary categories are therefore predetermined by, and even coextensive with, hard-core linguistic categories" (1991, xiv).

In fact, literature and language are so closely intertwined that many scholars reject the existence of a specific literary language (Brumfit and Carter 1997; Fowler 1981; Lazar 1993). Rather, the language used in literary texts is just the ordinary language of everyday usage, but with a higher percentage of linguistic features such as metaphors, similes, poetic lexicon, unusual syntactic structures, and so forth. All these elements are not literature-specific, since they can also be found in natural language uses, proverbs, or slogans in advertising, but their frequency of use is much higher in literature, which explains the general tendency to talk about a "literary" kind of language. However, in terms of its linguistic features, there is no special type of language use that could be considered to be "literary" in an exclusive and distinctive manner. When dealing with this stylistic overlap between literary and non-literary texts, Roger Fowler underlines the idea that "literature is language, to be theorized just like any other discourse" (1988, 83). In fact, as Theo D'haen (1986, 1) explains, although attention to the language(s) of literature used to be limited to "philological concerns or to intuitively impressionistic evaluations of 'style'" it was in the late 1950s that "the systematic study of literature with the aid of tools and concepts borrowed from linguistics [came] into being."

Likewise, applying a sociolinguistic perspective to the analysis of literary texts is not new. Following Fowler's (1981, 21) suggestion, many scholars have examined how literary authors achieve the social characterization of their protagonists (Culpeper 2014; Fennel and Bennett 1991; Galván Reula 1983; Hewitt 1992; Montes-Alcalá 2001; Montes-Granado 1991, 2012; Sarangi 2005). Mainly, they do it through the written representation of their speech and via the inclusion of dialectal forms or foreign languages, often for humorous purposes (Gardner-Chloros and Weston 2015, 186).

Regarding the ways in which speech is represented in fiction, Geoffrey Leech and Michael Short affirm: "fictional speech may aspire to a special kind of realism, a special kind of authenticity, in representing the *kind* of language which a reader can recognize, by observation, as being characteristic of a particular situation" (1981, 160). This explains why an author's ability to reproduce in writing the distinctive features of any spoken language as it is used in conversation is so highly valued. As David Lodge (2002, xiii) claims in the preface to his work on the language of fiction, "[t]he novelist's medium is language: whatever he does, *qua* novelist, he does in and through language," which means that a writer, whether a novelist or a poet, is always expected to be a verbal artist, above all. For this, they must be aware of how rooted the language of fiction is "in ordinary discourse and situations," so much so that using a sociolinguistic perspective certainly "adds a dimension to the reading of literature," as Black (2006, 157) put it. The reason is simply that

> [t]he moment we open our mouths we situate ourselves sociolinguistically: our lexis, pronunciation and the syntactic choices we make allow our interlocutor(s) to make inferences about our education, our geographical and social origins. Our choice among the options available to us in the language will also be influenced by the activity we are engaged in. Every speaker has unique features of language use: these are termed idiolect. (It should be noted here that few fictions provide sufficient evidence of a character's lect to enable an identification of idiolectal features which would satisfy a sociolinguist. Rather, what happens is that features of language are used contrastively with the language of the narrator, and so function to suggest idiolectal features of the character.) All of this means that the speech of fictional characters can make a most useful contribution to their characterisation: they can indicate what they are doing, suggest their relations with other characters, and mark their educational and social status. (2006, 63)

These observations reveal some of the underlying motivations and implications of the usage of Spanish words, phrases, and sentences in our literary texts: they stand as powerful identity markers that can also indicate the characters' awareness of—and attitudes towards—the Other culture. Before addressing these issues, in the following section I will describe the kind of metalinguistic references that help our writers to set the stage for their bilingual romances.

SETTING THE STAGE:
OTHERING THROUGH METALINGUISTIC COMMENTS

The protagonists of each of the love stories narrated in the selected novels form a bilingual couple, invariably an English-speaking heroine, while the heroes are all Spanish or have Spanish origins, as in MacLeod (1990). This poses a literary problem when it comes to representing the way they communicate and deal with the language barrier. Obviously, linguistic realism is usually restricted in literature since "the more languages one uses in a work, the more one limits the audience that will have access to the work" (Traugott and Pratt 1980, 377). To solve this puzzle, literary authors often resort to a variety of strategies.[2] One of the most frequent ones in our sample has to do with inserting metalinguistic comments, that is, using language to talk about language, either through the narrator's or the characters' voices. This metadiscourse, which Hyland defines as the "writer's awareness of the reader and his or her need for elaboration, clarification, guidance and interaction" (2005, 17), contributes to the depiction of the linguistic context in which the plot develops. In these novels metadiscourse manifests in different ways, namely, by making reference to the fact that a particular language is being spoken, by describing the particular features of that language, by expressing the characters' concerns about the need to learn it or improve their skills, or simply by highlighting the protagonist's linguistic features, abilities or difficulties, as in the examples below:

- After a few moments' conversation in Spanish and English, Lorian excused herself (Danbury 1972, 34)
- He muttered something in Spanish (Howard 1994, 146–47)
- He raised a thick silky brow, for they were conversing in English (Britt 1977, 118)
- [. . .] began to talk quietly in his beautiful accent [. . .] (Ashe 1987, 37)
- Although Lorian could not understand every word, she gathered the gist of the sharp staccato sentences (Danbury 1972, 56)
- "And soon all our errors in your difficult English language will be swept away!" (MacLeod 1982, 50)
- She admitted she had only a smattering of Spanish (Danbury 1972, 5)

In addition, the writers often represent orthographically the speech features of some characters, showing, for instance, the typical errors of non-native speakers of English, or by making comments on Spanish speakers' pronunciation of English, and occasionally indicating a specific regional accent, as the examples below respectively illustrate:

- "He slow and he no kick out." (MacLeod 1990, 42)
- [. . .] then Lucia said, "Our dinner-guest tonight is English, a Señor—Jervis"—making a long roll of the "r" and breathy sound of the "J" [sic] (Arbor 1967, 28)
- "You closed, love?" he asked, in a broad Liverpool accent [. . .] "OK, I'll come back *termorrer*. It's me jaw" (Ashe 1987, 45)

OTHERING AND SPANISH VOCABULARY

The British protagonists of our romances have traveled to (or live in) the Canaries,[3] a reputedly exotic location far away from their British hometowns, off the West coast of Africa, a place with a very different climate and landscape, where people have their own distinctive culture and language. As Romaine explains, "when moving to a new setting, speakers will encounter a variety of things which are specific to the new environment or culture and will adopt readily available words from the local language to describe them" (1995, 55). Obviously, the use of part of the Spanish vocabulary inserted in the texts is inevitable since certain terms, mainly those related to the local culture, do not have an equivalent in English, or can only be matched artificially because "they reflect and pass on ways of living and ways of thinking characteristic of [. . .] [the other] speech community" (Wierzbicka 1999, 4), or simply because "they refer to different entities or activities or [. . .] express divergent perspectives" (Bonvillain 2008, 320). No wonder then that the English discourse in these novels is frequently sprinkled with words and expressions taken from the variety of Spanish spoken in the islands. These words both reflect and enable readers to feel the sociocultural and linguistic differences, letting them "taste all the connotations and echoes accompanying the words," as Galván Reula notes by reminding us that each language provides words with "a different colour," which constitutes "a very sensitive index of the culture of a people" (2007, 62). Some Spanish words are followed up within the narrative by short explanations or by their English equivalents, so as to avoid any kind of semantic loss for the reader, as shown below:

- Ricardo reached the *parador*, the national tourist inn. (Danbury 1972, 153)

- [. . .] at the next *bodegon*—a cross between an eating-house and a bar (Arbor 1967, 116)
- [. . .] spooning up her gazpacho, a delicious chilled soup (Britt 1977, 118)
- "*Salud, chiquita* (little girl)." (Ashe 1987, 95)
- [. . .] to the new *autopista*, the motorway. (Danbury 1972, 81)
- [. . .] blown on the *levante*, the east wind. (Arbor 1967, 120)
- "[. . .] noticed this *tristeza* in you—an incomprehensible sadness." (Britt 1977, 54)
- [. . .] a monster. *El diablo.* The devil. (Howard 1994, 9)
- "Then soon. *Lo antes posible.*" (Ashe 1987, 35)
- "*Hasta la vista!*" she said. "We will meet again." (MacLeod 1982, 45)

Following Lamy-Vialle's (2015, 107–8) line of thought, I assume that the Spanish vocabulary introduced into the texts is generally meant to convey an effect of foreignness, as emphasized by the frequent use of italics which "maintain the distance between the two languages and, ostensibly, tell the reader that the value of such [Spanish] words is different from the rest of the narrative texture, [. . .] thus contributing to Barthes's 'effect of reality.'" Occasionally, however, those Hispanicisms the readers are expected to be more familiar with are neither glossed nor italicized, as "patio," "Marquesa," and "siesta" below:

- [. . .] pots which surrounded the *estancia* and the patio itself. (MacLeod 1990, 34)
- "You'll like the Marquesa [. . .]" (Britt 1977, 110)
- [. . .] their afternoon siesta together. (Britt 1977, 76)

There are exceptions, though, since many Hispanicisms with dictionary-status are often italicized, as can be observed in the following quotes:

- "[. . .] he's the *árbitro* of our fate." (MacLeod 1982, 19)
- In the quiet *siesta* hour the *patio* lay peacefully [. . .] (MacLeod 1982, 68)
- "There is *mañana* and all the *mañanas*," was the suave reply. (Britt 1977, 139)
- [. . .] skirted the *hacienda* wall, passing tiny *adobe* houses (MacLeod 1982, 60)
- "You are right, *señorita* [. . .]" (Ashe 1987, 36)
- "[. . .] attended *fiesta* in a white mantilla [. . .] to captivate all the local *caballeros* " (MacLeod 1990, 75)

Weston and Gardner-Chloros consider this option to be "a visual clue as to how foreign the writer perceives a given word to be, or how foreign s/he wishes it to be perceived" (2015, 197). Apart from providing more realism and enriching the narrative with some local color, another possible interpretation for the insertion of Spanish words which could easily have been translated into English is one proposed by Cronin (2000, 41) in his monograph on travel language. He believes that their role is to give the impression that conversations are held in Spanish. Similarly, Spanish honorifics, such as *Señor, Señora, Marquesa,* or *Don,* tend to be preserved and they play a function that is unique to literature: reminding the reader "that a conversation is actually taking place in a language that is not that of the text" (Weston and Gardner-Chloros 2015, 198). In turn, Silva-Corvalán (1989, 174) points out that certain words may be transferred as a result of their being more expressive, hence, more useful for the writer's communicative aim. On the other hand, from a merely linguistic perspective, the reason for using Spanish terms is simply that "using ready-made designations is more economical than describing things afresh" as Weinreich (1979, 57) explained. The words that are taken over in the receiving language are *loanwords* and the process is called *borrowing.*

Technically speaking, loanwords have officially been incorporated into the lexical repertoires of the English language, which legitimizes their use. In fact, many of the Hispanicisms employed in our romances are already registered in the *Oxford English Dictionary.* This is the case with *adiós, adobe, alpaca, amiga, árbitro, autopista, barranco, caballero, dueña, estancia, fiesta, flamenco, Guanches, hacienda, macho, mantilla, mañana, mirador, palomino, parador, patio, pesetas, pico, plaza, playa, querido, quinta, señor, señora, señorita, siesta, sombrero, tango, tapas, torero, tristeza.* It is difficult, though, to determine to what extent all these and other officially adopted words may have already lost their Spanish flavour, despite their frequency of use.

However, a considerable number of the Spanish words the writers themselves use (as narrators) or put into their characters' mouths are not real borrowings as they do not have dictionary-status. Apparently, they cannot be justified by any lexical need as there are suitable equivalents in English to refer to the meanings they convey. The following are some examples:

- "She is her true *nieta*" (MacLeod 1982, 74)
- [. . .] drink cheap *cerveza* every night (Ashe 1987, 13)
- [. . .] wide tree-lined *avenidas* (Arbor 1967, 46)
- "You are indeed *bienvenida!*" (Danbury 1972, 122)
- "[. . .] they are *guapa* [. . .]" (MacLeod 1982, 17)
- "[. . .] on speaking terms with his *novia*" (Britt 1977,47)
- "You would like to be her *novio*" (Arbor 1967, 63)
- "[. . .] sweet and *delicada* [. . .]" (MacLeod 1982, 93)
- "A *medico* should always have the Mercedes [. . .]" (Ashe 1987, 31)
- [. . .] with a large *limonada* (Arbor 1967, 66)

Although the inclusion of these Spanish words may seem totally unnecessary, they must respond to some aim since, as Page asserts, "every work of literature possesses in every word that composes it a selective and purposive nature" (1988, 1). By choosing these particular terms the writers show that they know not only their referential meanings but also all their communicative potential and the pragmatic information encoded in them (Jiménez-Hurtado 2001; Wotjak 2006, 68). As underlined by Quirk, "[t]he effectiveness of every communication depends on the selection of specific lexical items from the hundreds of thousands that are available to us as speakers and writers" (1986, 10–11).

Since bilinguals (people or characters) enjoy more linguistic resources, they "often employ strategies for maximizing the potential expressiveness of their linguistic repertoire" (Bonvillain 2008, 320) but their choices will always be motivated by specific communicative needs and serve a number of discourse functions (cf. González-Cruz 2018). These include an affiliative function for constructing in-group solidarity between the characters, in such a way that this Spanish vocabulary that "we" understand helps "create or generate a cohesive identity" (Cortés-Conde and Boxer 2002, 139). Thus, by using *cerveza, limonada, nieta,* or *novia,* instead of their equivalents ("beer," "lemonade," "granddaughter," "girlfriend"), the English-speaking characters make cordial nods to their Spanish hearers, tacitly acknowledging and somehow indicating appreciation of the Spanish culture and language. In other words, through these linguistic choices, the characters are able to express whether they feel "closer to or further apart from individuals with a different linguistic and cultural background" (Jackson 2014, 142). In sum, Spanish proves to be a "powerful [marker] of In-group identity, contributing to create boundaries that define the group," although of course it might also be used to "exclude 'strangers' to it," as Allori (2011, 9) put it.

OTHERING AND CODESWITCHING

The term *codeswitching* (henceforth, CS) refers to the act of "shifting from one dialect or language to another" (Black 2006) and involves alternation between two linguistic codes in the same stretch of discourse mainly at the syntactic but also at the lexical level (single words). In fact, borrowings and CS are two of the most salient manifestations of multilingualism in literature. Kniaz (2017) outlines neatly the distinction between borrowing and lexical CS, highlighting the fact that CS has been approached differently in the sociolinguistic literature, either as a continuum (Myers-Scotton 1992) or as a discrete process (Poplack 1980). However, the classification of lone items as cases of borrowing or CS is not always easy, as Lipski (2005) shows. In Heath's (2001, 432–33) words, a borrowing is (ideally) a historically transferred form, usually a word (or lexical stem), that has settled comfortably into the target language, while code-switching is (ideally) a spontaneous, clearly bounded switch from sentences of one language to sentences of another, affecting all levels of linguistic structure simultaneously. However, if actual speech patterns in bilingual environments are observed, one finds that borrowing and code-switching are not always so clearly distinct.

This debate still continues but, for the purposes of this study, suffice it to say that whereas loanwords or borrowings have become lexicalized and are used consistently in the recipient language that has adopted and adapted them, "the most telling feature of all codeswitching material is its relative lack of predictability" (Myers-Scotton 1992, 37). Admittedly, as Weston and Gardner-Chloros maintain, "[a]ny approach that attempts to subdivide bilingual phenomena based on spontaneity of production is bound to be less applicable in literature, where production involves a process of reflection" (2015, 196). However, these authors also prove that CS serves "as a literary resource in its own right, conveying liminality or states of transition" (2015, 209). In fact, they underline the fact that, as a sociolinguistic phenomenon, literary CS is "complex and multi-layered, reflecting the multiple motivations which characterize CS in all its forms" (2015, 209). In addition to portraying the speech of bilingual characters in plays or novels, literary CS can perform an indexing function "for which there is no precise equivalent in conversational CS" (2015, 198). As Black explains, "CS may be perceived as promoting solidarity, and this reaction will presumably be shared by readers who come from the same community, though the promotion of solidarity often carries with it the exclusion of others" (2006, 89). Paraphrasing Black (2006, 89) I conclude that the insertion of Spanish words and expressions into these novels may generate a range of "weak implicatures," such as promoting a sense of community, of being members of an in-group who can appreciate its effects. These also include "promoting solidarity with some readers, while possibly alienating others." In short, just like using Spanish borrowings, switching into Spanish words, phrases or sentences serves to characterize or identify the characters sociolinguistically and may indicate a positive attitude and closeness to the Other. Yet, as Black noticed, "readers may react in unpredictable ways, partly on account of the dialect chosen, and perhaps with our familiarity (or ignorance) of it. It makes the reader consider why a particular encoding has been chosen, and what effects it might have" (2006, 89). This is the case in the following excerpts:

- [. . .] a *pequeña prima* coming over from England (Arbor 1967, 32)
- "*Buenas noches, señorita!*" she added with a small, mocking laugh. "*Usted habla español muy bien!*" (MacLeod 1982, 30)
- "*Está bien,*" he said softly [. . .] (Howard 1994, 53)

- "He will not cheat you, *lo prometo*" (Ashe 1987, 31)
- "Buenos dias, Señor Marques, señorita," she said in a soft voice (Britt 1977, 74)
- "Another time," he said, opening the door for her. "*Es tarde.*" (MacLeod 1990, 94)
- "*Para la linda señorita pelirroja!*" he proclaimed (Howard 1994, 124)
- "*Buenas noches,* everyone! *Velocidad moderada, Ramon!*" (MacLeod 1982, 134)
- "*Desde cuando está allí?*" "I really don't know, Señor Riviero" (Ashe 1987, 47)

Admittedly, we cannot always be certain about the authors' intentions whenever they decide to use Spanish words and expressions in the English discourse of their novels. As Zentella argues, "pinpointing the purpose of each codeswitch is a task as fraught with difficulty as imputing the reasons for a monolingual's choice of one synonym over another, and no complete accounting may ever be possible" (1997, 99). Yet, I believe readers can perceive and interpret some of the effects of this technique within each context of use. After all, the words authors employ in any text always create an impression in the readers' or the audience's minds (Culpeper 2014). In Montes-Granado's words, CS "conveys pragmatic meta-messages, such as showing some type of subjective assessment, changing the interpersonal connection with the interlocutor or contrasting a 'we' code with a 'they' code" (2012, 130).

CONCLUSION

This chapter has examined the way Otherness is constructed and represented linguistically in a sample of romances set in a Spanish-speaking archipelago, the Canaries. One common feature of these novels is the authors' tendency to insert metalinguistic comments and Spanish borrowings as well as to codeswitch into Spanish words, phrases, and sentences. By resorting to these sociolinguistic strategies, the writers manage to portray the bilingual context and relationships among the characters and to establish a self/other dialectic.

My conclusion is twofold. Firstly, these texts demonstrate the consolidation of a considerable number of Hispanicisms into the English lexical repertoire, while working as channels for their diffusion. Secondly, this Spanish vocabulary performs a variety of functions (cf. Gonzalez-Cruz 2018), including an affiliative or indexical one. These linguistic choices work as symbolic vehicles that indicate not only an awareness of the other culture and language, but can also be interpreted as markers of in-group identity which, in these novels, mostly tend to emphasize sociocultural closeness, creating affective bonds with the Other.

NOTES

1. The sample selected for analysis in this chapter belongs to the corpus of thirty-four romances compiled for Research Project FFI2014-53962-P, a grant hereby gratefully acknowledged.

2. Weston and Gardner-Chloros (2015, 198) refer to three specific strategies, namely, *referential restriction, homogenizing convention* and *vehicular matching*. The first simply consists of confining the literary work to "monolingual characters whose speech patterns are fully comprehensible"; the second includes "bilingual discourse, characters and settings, all of which are, however, represented monolingually," whereas in the latter "the literary work does not shy away from multilingual characters or themes, and multilingual or multidialectal speech is represented without apology."

3. Although lying less than sixty miles off the West coast of Africa, the Canaries are a Spanish archipelago since their incorporation into the Crown of Castile in 1493. The Spanish-speaking colonists from the continent settled on the islands readily imposing their language and culture on the native Guanche aborigines, who are mentioned in several romances in the corpus. Due to its strategic position in the middle of the maritime commercial Atlantic routes, the archipelago soon became a point of linguistic and socio-cultural contact. For centuries it was seen politically as a remote, rather isolated, colony of Spain. Socially and culturally their dependence on the continental government was strong, but the islanders soon established commercial contacts with the Anglo-Saxon world, firstly through the wine trade with English merchants from Bristol since 1519. In fact, Shakespeare acknowledged the quality of Canarian wine, *canary* or *sack*, in works like *Henry IV, Twelfth Night,* and *The Merry Wives of Windsor*. In contrast to continental Spain, where the influence of English did not filter through until the 1960s, the people in the Canary Islands have been in close contact with the English language and culture since the last decades of the nineteenth century. The impact of the British was strongly felt, as the islands' economy was completely dominated then by British money and in practice they were almost considered a British territory until World War II (Cf. González-Cruz 2012).

REFERENCES

Allori, Paola E. 2011. "Discourse and Identity in the Professions. Corporate, Legal and Institutional Citizenships. An Introduction." In *Discourse and Identity in the Professions. Corporate, Legal and Institutional Citizenships,* edited by Vijay Kumar Bhatia, Paola Evangelisti Allori, 9–24. Bern: Peter Lang.

Arbor, Jane. 1967. *Golden Apple Island.* Winnipeg, Canada: Harlequin Books.

Ashe, Jenny. 1987. *The Surgeon from San Agustin.* Richmond: Mills & Boon.

Beeching, Kate, Chiara Ghezzi, and Piera Molinelli, eds. 2018. *Positioning the Self and Others.* Berlin: John Benjamins Publishing Co.

Black, Elizabeth. 2006. *Pragmatic Stylistics.* Edinburgh: Edinburgh University Press.

Bonvillain, Nancy. 2008. *Language, Culture and Communication. The Meaning of Messages.* New Jersey: Prentice Hall.

Britt, Katrina, 1977. *The Villa Faustino.* Toronto: Harlequin Books.

Brumfit, Christopher and Ronald Carter. 1997. *Literature and Language Teaching.* Oxford: Oxford University Press.

Castro-Borrego, Silvia Pilar and Maria Isabel Romero-Ruiz. 2015. "Introduction." In *Identities on the Move. Contemporary Representations of New Sexualities and Gender Identities,* edited by Silvia Pilar Castro-Borrego and Maria Isabel Romero-Ruiz, 1–10. Lanham, MD: Lexington Books.

Chapman, Raymond. 1990. *The Language of Thomas Hardy*. Hampshire: Macmillan.
Childs, Becky and Christine Mallinson. 2006. "The Significance of Lexical Items in the Construction of Ethnolinguistic Identity: A Case Study of Adolescent Spoken and Online Language." *American Speech* 8 (1/1): 3–30.
Cortés-Conde, Florencia and Diana Boxer. 2002. "Bilingual Word-Play in Literary Discourse: the Creation of Relational Identity." *Language and Literature* 11 (2): 137–51.
Crystal, David. 2000. *Language Death*. Cambridge: Cambridge University Press.
Culpeper, Jonathan. 2014. *Language and Characterization. People in Plays and Other Texts.* London / New York: Routledge.
Danbury, Iris. 1972. *Jacaranda Island*. London: Mills & Boon.
D'haen, Theo. 1986. "Introduction." In *Linguistics and the Study of Literature,* edited by Theo D'haen, 1–6. Amsterdam: Rodopi.
Edwards, John. 2009. *Language and Identity*. Cambridge: Cambridge University Press.
Fennel, Barbara A. and John Bennett. 1991. "Sociolinguistic Concepts and Literary Analysis." *American Speech* 66 (4): 371–79.
Fowler, Roger. 1981. *Literature as Social Discourse. The Practice of Linguistic Criticism.* London: Bastford.
Fowler, Roger. 1988. "Studying Literature as Language." *Alicante Journal of English Studies* 1: 81–90.
Galván Reula, Fernando. 1983. "Caracterización sociolingüística de Charlie Thornton y Paul Morel." In *Héroe y antihéroe en la literatura inglesa. Actas del V Congreso de AEDEAN,* edited by Patricia Shaw, 169–78. Madrid: Alhambra.
Galván Reula, Fernando. 2007. "Sobre bilingüismo, multiculturalismo y traducción en los Estados Unidos: Doris Sommer y Gregory Rabassa." In *En/clave de frontera. Homenaje al Profesor Urbano Viñuela Angulo,* edited by Esther Álvarez López, Aurora García Fernández, and Martín Urdiales Shaw, 57–67. Oviedo: Universidad de Oviedo.
Gardner-Chloros, Penelope and Daniel Weston. 2015. "Code-Switching and Multilingualism in Literature." *Language and Literature* 24 (3): 182–93.
González-Cruz, María Isabel. 2012. "English in the Canaries: Past and Present." *English Today. The International Review of the English Language,* 109 (1): 20–28.
González-Cruz, María Isabel. 2018. "Hispanismos en el discurso romántico de *Harlequin* y *Mills & Boon.* Ámbitos temáticos y funciones socio-pragmáticas." *Moderna Sprak* 1: 157–78.
Gumperz, John Joseph. 1990. *Language and Social Identity*. Cambridge: Cambridge University Press.
Heath, Jeffrey, 2001: "Borrowing." In *Concise Encyclopedia of Sociolinguistics,* edited by Rajend Mesthrie, 432–42. Kidlington, Oxford: Elsevier.
Heller, Monica, ed. 1988. *Codeswitching: Anthropological and Sociolinguistic Perspectives.* Berlin: Mouton de Gruyter.
Hewitt, Lindsay Ann. 1992. *A Sociolinguistic Approach to the Study of Literary Dialect in the Work of John Galt and Christian Johnstone*. PhD Thesis, University of Glasgow.
Howard, Stephanie. 1994. *Beware a Lover's Lie*. Richmond: Mills & Boon.
Hyland, Ken. 2005. *Metadiscourse. Exploring Interaction in Writing*. London: Continuum.
Jackson, Jane. 2014. *Introducing Language and Intercultural Communication*. London and New York: Routledge.
Jiménez-Hurtado, Catalina. 2001. *Léxico y pragmática*. Frankfurt am Main: Peter Lang.
Jonsson, Carla. 2010. "Functions of Code-Switching in Bilingual Theater: An Analysis of Three Chicano Plays." *Journal of Pragmatics* 42: 1296–1310.
Joseph, John E. 2004. *Language and Identity. National, Ethnic, Religious.* New York: Palgrave Macmillan.
Kniaz, Malgorzata. 2017. "English Lexical Items in Egyptian Arabic." *Alicante Journal of English Studies* 30: 185–210.
Lamy-Vialle, Elisabeth. 2015. "Foreign Languages and Mother Tongues: From Exoticism to Cannibalism in Katherine Mansfield's Short Stories." In *Katherine Mansfield and Translation,* edited by Claire Davison, Gerri Kimber and W. Todd Martin, 106–18. Edinburgh: Edinburgh University Press.

Lazar, Gillian. 1993. *Literature and Language Teaching: A Guide for Teachers and Trainers.* Cambridge: Cambridge University Press.

Le Page, Robert Brock and Andrée Tabouret-Keller. 1985. *Acts of Identity: Creole-Based Approaches to Language and Ethnicity.* Cambridge, UK / New York: Cambridge University Press.

Leech, Geoffrey N. and Michael H. Short. 1981. *Style in Fiction. A Linguistic Introduction to English Fictional Prose.* London / New York: Longman.

Lipski, John M. 2005. "Codeswitching or Borrowing? No sé *so* no puedo decir, *you know.*" In *Selected Proceedings of the Second Workshop on Spanish Sociolinguistics,* edited by L. Sayahi and M. Westmoreland, 1–15. Somerville: Cascadilla Press.

Lodge, David. 2002. *The Language of Fiction. Essay in Criticism and Verbal Analysis of the English Novel.* London: Routledge.

MacLeod, Jean S. 1982. *Meeting in Madrid.* London: Harlequin Books.

MacLeod, Jean S. 1990. *Flame of Avila.* Richmond: Mills & Boon.

Montes Alcalá, Cecilia. 2001. "Oral vs. Written Code-Switching Contexts in English-Spanish Bilingual Narratives." In *La lingüística aplicada a finales del siglo XX. Ensayos y propuestas,* edited by Isabel de la Cruz et al., vol. 2, 715–20. Madrid: Universidad de Alcalá de Henares.

Montes-Granado, Consuelo. 1991. "El dialecto en la literatura inglesa: notas diacrónicas de sus usos y estudio sincrónico de la aportación de D.H. Lawrence." *Revista Canaria de Estudios Ingleses* 22/23: 37–49.

Montes-Granado, Consuelo. 2012. "Code-Switching as a strategy of brevity in Sandra Cisneros' *Woman Hollering Creek* and other stories." *DQR Studies in Literature* 49: 125–38.

Myers-Scotton, Carol. 1992. "Comparing codeswitching and borrowing." *Journal of Multilingual and Multicultural Development* 13 (1–2): 19–39.

Page, Norman. 1988. *Speech in the English Novel.* London: Macmillan.

Pandey, Anjali. 2004. "Constructing Otherness: A Linguistic Analysis of the Politics of Representation and Exclusion in Freshmen Writing." *Issues in Applied Linguistics* 14 (2): 153–84.

Poplack, Shana. 1980. "Sometimes I'll start a sentence in Spanish Y TERMINO EN ESPAÑOL: Toward a typology of code-switching." *Linguistics* 18 (7–8): 581–618.

Quirk, Randolph. 1986. *Words at Work. Lectures on Textual Structure.* London: Longman.

Reyes, Graciela. 2002. *Metapragmática. Lenguaje sobre lenguaje, ficciones, figuras.* Valladolid: Universidad de Valladolid.

Riley, Phillip. 2007. *Language, Culture and Identity.* London and New York: Continuum.

Romaine, Suzanne. 1995. *Bilingualism.* Oxford: Blackwell.

Sarangi, Jaydeep. 2005. *Indian Novels in English. A Sociolinguistic Study.* Bareilly: Prakas Book Depot.

Sell, Roger, ed. 1991. *Literary Pragmatics.* London: Routledge.

Silva-Corvalán, Carmen. 1989. *Sociolingüística. Teoría y análisis.* Madrid: Alhambra.

Staszak, Jean-François. 2009. "Other/otherness." In *International Encyclopedia of Human Geography,* edited by Rob Kitchin and Nigel Thrift, 43–47. Amsterdam: Elsevier.

Toolan, Michael. 1992. "The significations of representing dialect in writing." *Language and Literature* 1: 29–46.

Traugott, Elizabeth Closs and M. Louise Pratt. 1980. *Linguistics for Students of Literature.* San Diego, CA: Harcourt Brace Jovanovich Publishers.

Voesterman, Paul. 1991. "Alterity/Identity: A Deficient Image of Culture." In *Alterity, Identity, Image: Selves and Others in Society and Scholarship,* edited by Raymond Corbey and Joep Leersen, 219–249. Amsterdam: Rodopi.

Weinreich, Uriel. 1979 [1953]. *Languages in Contact. Findings and Problems.* New York: Mouton.

Weston, Daniel and Penelope Gardner-Chloros 2015. "Mind the Gap: What Codeswitching in Literature Can Tell Us about Codeswitching." *Language and Literature* 24 (3): 194–212.

Wierzbicka, Anna. 1999. *Understanding Cultures through Their Key Words: English, Russian, Polish, German and Japanese.* New York: Oxford University Press.

Wodak, Ruth, Rudolf de Cillia, Martin Reisigl, and Karin Liebhart. 2009. "Introduction." In *The Discursive Construction of National Identity,* edited by Ruth Wodak et al., 1–6. Edinburgh: Edinburgh University Press.

Wotjak, Gerd. 2006. *Las lenguas, ventanas que dan al mundo. El léxico como encrucijada entre morfosintaxis y cognición: aspectos semánticos y pragmáticos en perspectiva intra e interlingüística.* Salamanca: Ediciones Universidad de Salamanca.

Zentella, Ana Celia. 1997. *Growing up Bilingual: Puerto Rican Children in New York.* Oxford: Basil Blackwell.

Chapter Five

Language Awareness in Four Romances Set on the Island of Madeira

Aline Bazenga

This chapter studies the way language awareness is presented in four romance novels set wholly or partially in Madeira, Portugal, proposing a sociolinguistic approach with a quantitative and qualitative analysis of the representation of language contact. Published in the UK between 1977 and 1990 for an English-speaking audience, the novels are the following: Elizabeth Hunter's *Pride of Madeira* (1977) (henceforth, POM), Katrina Britt's *The Silver Tree* (1977) (henceforth, TST), Betty Neels's *Last April Fair* (1980) (henceforth, LAF), and Sally Wentworth's *Illusions of Love* (1990) (henceforth, IOL). In each romance, the story is developed in a bilingual context which involves interactions between Portuguese and English-speaking characters. This chapter will analyze the instances of *written codeswitching or code-switching* (WCS), *metalinguistic discourse* (MD), *language representation* (LR), and *forms of address* (FA) strategies present in the novels and the sociopragmatic functions they fulfill. This analysis will reveal not only authorial attitudes toward language, but also attitudes toward cultures and the Other.

These four romances are a representative sample of the contemporary romance novels set in Madeira Island in the last quarter of the twentieth century. The stories they tell are centered on love, always with a happy ending (Vivanco 2011). In some cases, the characters involved in the love story share the same nationality when both the hero and the heroine are British citizens, who may or may not have family ties to the island. In other cases, the plot involves a "mixed" couple with different nationalities, and hence with differing cultures and mother tongues. When one of the protagonists is an islander, the English male or female protagonist always moves to the island to live or to stay temporarily. As a result, both the narrator and the characters are usually aware of being immersed in a sociocultural and linguistic contact situation, which favors the analysis not only of the typical phenomena of language contact situations, such as single or extended written language switches, but also the study of issues such as identity and Otherness, both as a concept and as a practice, in the terms defined in Stuart Hall's seminal work, "The Spectacle of the 'Other.'" According to Hall, "difference" is represented by stereotyping, because it allows classification of social groups while also establishing binary oppositions (Hall 1997, 236). These binary oppositions are "crucial for all classification, because one must establish a clear difference between things in order to classify them" (Hall 1997, 236). For instance, "we know what it is to be 'British,' not only because of certain national characteristics, but also because we can mark its 'difference' from its 'others'" (Hall 1997, 234–35). Thus, "Britishness" is defined in terms of its binary opposite: all forms of not-Britishness.

The aim of this chapter is to show the authors' language awareness by describing the strategies which they use to recreate the bilingual environment of the novels' settings, following the lines suggested by González-Cruz (2017a, 2017b) in her studies of a corpus of romances set in the Canaries. These strategies include metalinguistic references, the orthographic representation of characters' speech, and the representation of codeswitching through the insertion of single words or several phrases and expressions in foreign languages in the English texts. In the first section of the chapter, the theoretical framework used to analyze the results is presented, with comments on how the study may be considered from a sociopragmatic perspective. This section also includes a brief description of the methodology applied to the samples selected for investigation. Then, in the second section I will offer the results obtained, followed by some final remarks in the third section.

THEORETICAL FRAMEWORK AND METHODOLOGY

The concept of *language awareness* is defined by Van Lier (1995) as explicit knowledge about language, more specifically, the ability to understand the different forms and functions of language. Carter (2003, 63) refines this definition, stating that it is the ability to understand the different forms and functions of language in cultural and social life. Anna Verschik has contributed to the theoretical understanding of language awareness in language contact situations, pointing out that it may be applied to both metalinguistic awareness and multilingualism. She explains the issue as follows:

> "language awareness," "metalinguistic awareness," and "knowledge about language" are used as synonyms [. . .]. In a recent publication, Jessner [. . .] suggests that metalinguistic awareness can be defined as "an ability to focus

on linguistic form and to switch focus between form and meaning." This understanding is also valid for language contacts because, in a sense, the process and outcome of language contacts is about innovation and restructuring of forms and meanings under the co-influence of several language systems in a multilingual's cognition." (Verschik 2017, 99–100)

In this study, the concept of language awareness will be considered from the perspective of Sociolinguistics, a discipline that deals with the study of language as a social and cultural phenomenon. Sociolinguistic awareness must, therefore, be understood as the ability to perceive linguistic and cultural diversity, as well as the social value of language, culture, and identity in intercultural contexts. As will be demonstrated, linguistic and sociocultural perceptions and evaluations can be seen in the comments, descriptions, and representations of the languages in contact that appear in the novels.

Language contact awareness may construct Otherness by producing differences and marking out distinctions. A binary of "Us" and "Them" is socially constructed, according to perceptions of difference in social identity (e.g., racial, geographic, linguistic, ethnic, economic, ideological). In Jean-François Staszak's words:

> The creation of otherness (also called othering) consists of applying a principle that allows individuals to be classified into two hierarchical groups: them and us. The out-group is only coherent as a group as a result of its opposition to the in-group and its lack of identity. This lack is based upon stereotypes that are largely stigmatizing and obviously simplistic. (Staszak 2008, 43)

Many scholars have applied a sociolinguistic approach to literary works in order to understand the social representation of the characters, by analyzing the orthographic representation of the characters' speech, the use of different dialects, and sometimes the use of foreign accents for humorous or satirical purposes (see, among others, Hewitt 1992; Callahan 2004; Gardner-Chloros 2009; Gardner-Chloros and Weston 2015). Recently, Jonathan Culpeper and Carolina Fernandez-Quintanilla investigated "how characters are constructed in the interaction between top-down knowledge from the reader/perceiver's head and bottom-up information from the text" (Culpeper and Fernandez-Quintanilla 2017, 93). According to these authors, there are three dimensions in the process of characterization:

> narratorial control, the presentation of self or other, and the explicitness or implicitness of the textual cue. It elaborates on narratorial filters (point of view [. . .] and the presentation of speech and thought), character indexing (through, for example, speech acts) and inter-character dynamics (through, for example, the manipulation of social relations). (Culpeper and Fernandez-Quintanilla 2017, 93)

This research demonstrates the validity of applying sociolinguistic concepts to the study of all kinds of texts and, of course, to literary analysis, as has been done by González-Cruz on romance novels (2017a, 2017b), which will be considered as a model.

This chapter utilizes three major sociolinguistic concepts to analyze the texts. The first is linguistic alternation or *codeswitching* (CS). It is a type of code-mixing (Poplack 1980; Milroy, Lesley, and Pieter Muysken, 1995; Auer 1998; Bullock and Almeida, 2009; Gardner-Chloros 2009, Lipski, 2014, among others) and it consists of the alternating use of two or more languages within the same piece of discourse, either at the lexical or syntactic level, both in speech and in writing (Sebba, Mahootian, and Jonsson 2012). While spoken or conversational codeswitching makes reference to "the idea of a 'now' in Language A and an immediate 'next' in Language B," *written codeswitching* (WCS) is mostly characterized by its permanency (Sebba 2012, 6). Two main types of CS are generally identified in the literature: intersentential CS, which involves "switches from one language to the other between sentences," and intrasentential CS, which occurs "within the same sentence, from single-morpheme to clause level" (Myers-Scotton 1995, 4). Generally, CS reveals knowledge about languages in contact that is distinctive among competent bilinguals and multilinguals who switch languages according to the people in the conversation, the topic, and the context in which the conversation occurs.

In literature, WCS has proved to be a useful narrative resource which has attracted increasing interest in recent decades because of its recognized ability to express social, discursive, and referential meaning, as Penelope Gardner-Chloros and Daniel Weston (2015) show. In fact, many researchers have noticed how writers use language as a marker to highlight the different cultural or social attributes of their characters (Jonsson, 2010; Montes-Alcalá 2012, 2015; Jackson 2014).

Another significant sociolinguistic concept studied here is metalinguistic discourse (MD), a term which covers a variety of phenomena that demonstrate the fundamentally interactional nature of all texts. According to Hyland, the term *metadiscourse* is "based on a view of writing (and speaking) as a social and communicative engagement" (Hyland 2005, 14) and refers to the "writer's awareness of the reader and his or her need for elaboration, clarification, guidance and interaction" (Hyland 2005, 17). This idea also underpins this research, together with strategies such as the representation of specific patterns of speech (Young 1999; Page 1988; Nash 1990). Language representation (LR) strategies include the representation of specific patterns of speech. Finally, under the label FA (forms of address), I will refer to address terms in use and related to bicultural systems represented in the novels, and also to the differentiated ways in which names are given to the characters and the forms of address used for them.

The analysis of all these strategies will show how these novels present language contact situations, concerning Portuguese and English as spoken by the characters and considering their difficulties or abilities when using both of these languages. As will be shown in the next section, the four novels in this study provide a rich source of material for the analysis of the previously described strategies: WCS, MD, LR, and FA. The use of the Portuguese language (words, idiomatic expressions, and, to a lesser extent, phrases and sentences) is likely to attract the attention of the reader. However, due to the limits that literature imposes on linguistic realism, these forms do not neces-sarily reflect real linguistic use, as González-Cruz (2017a) explains.

All these concepts relating to language awareness may be subsumed into the broader field of sociopragmatics. This is a term coined by Geoffrey N. Leech to describe the ways in which pragmatic meanings reflect "specific 'local' conditions on language use" (Leech 1983, 10) since "communication of pragmatic meaning involves speakers' presentation of their identities" (Leech 1983, 159). Sociopragmatic knowledge refers to the ability to judge the contexts in which particular forms and strategies of language use are appropriate (Lillis 2013). In this study, the four strategies mentioned above (WCS, MC, LR, and FA) will be analyzed using a sociopragmatic approach in order to show how they contribute to the bilingual mode and multicultural-ity presented in the four selected romance novels set in Madeira.

As stated, our sample is composed of four romance novels published in the UK, between 1977 and 1990, whose heroines are British women who travel to Madeira. In two of them (POM and IOL), the two protagonists are English native speakers. In both of these novels, the male protagonists are British citizens who have been living in Madeira for a long time, while the female protagonists are British visitors. TST is the only novel in which one of the main characters is a local, a highly educated Madeiran man with a high social status. Finally, in LAF, where only half of the plot is set on Madeira, the lovers are also of different nationalities, but in this case the hero is Dutch.

A reading of the selected novels reveals the use of four main strategies that demonstrate the sociolinguistic awareness of the authors. The first of these is WCS, whenever Portuguese is inserted into the English texts. The use of Portuguese for single words (mostly nouns) and phrases or expres-sions is marked by italics, except in the case of toponyms or the proper names of the Portuguese characters. The use of a different font functions as a visual device that "provide[s] contextualisation cues" (Sebba 2012, 12), which highlight the situation of language contact for the reader.

The second strategy involves MD about Portuguese or English, that is, the inclusion of metalinguistic comments about the language or languages spok-en or about the skills or linguistic difficulties of the characters. The third and fourth strategies relate respectively to LR (the orthographic representation of non-native English spoken language) and to the FA used for both Portuguese and British characters. The analysis of all these *sociopragmatic* strategies used by the authors and listed above reveals the important role they play in the novels, displaying their general view of Otherness.

ANALYSIS AND DISCUSSION OF RESULTS

The most frequent strategy in the texts is WCS with the use of different Portuguese words, idioms and, to a lesser extent, phrases inserted into the English text, followed by the other three strategies mentioned above.

Written Codeswitching (WCS) Strategies

A total of 129 Portuguese tokens (occurrences) can be found in the selected novels, inserted in italic font. These include words (117) and phrases and sentences (12). Table 5.1 below shows the Portuguese loanword tokens identified in the samples, at the lexical level of WCS, corresponding to a total of 27 different lexical items. The most frequently repeated words, which are inserted in three of the four novels, represent 36 percent of the data.

As expected, TST, the novel in which one of the protagonists is Portuguese, includes a much higher number of Portuguese words (72/117), equivalent to 61.5 percent of the total. Below, some examples of other WCS materials in Portuguese, where more than one word is inserted, are presented:

- "Chame uma ambulância" [*Call an ambulance*] (IOL, 36)
- "minha querida" [*my dear*] (IOL, 186)
- "Faz favor de sentar se" [*Please, sit down*] (POM, 157)
- "Parabéns, senhora!" [*Congratulations, Madam!*] (POM,157)
- "Desculpe, senhora" [*Excuse me, Madam*] (POM, 159)
- "Bom dia, minha menina" [*Good morning, Miss*] (TST, 49)
- "Boa noite" [*Good night*] (TST, 118)

This WCS data above can be analyzed as formulaic expressions, related to Routine Speech Acts which are used to request (examples 1, 3), to address (example 2), to congratulate (example 4), to apologize (example 5) or to salute (examples 6, 7). This kind of syntactic WCS represents only 9 percent of the data. Out of the total number of WCS identified (single words, phrases and sentences) in the four romance novels (LAF, IOL, POM and TST), in terms of percentage, 57 percent of the data is found in TST, the novel with a mixed couple—a Portuguese man and a British woman. The next highest proportion (25 percent) of occurrences appear in POM, in which one of the protagonists, though British, is a long-term resident on the island. Only 16.7 percent is to be found in IOL, whose protagonists are both British, the British woman visiting the island and the British citizen living on the island. The

Table 5.1.   Lexical WCS: Portuguese Loanwords in the Four Novels Set on the Island of Madeira

LAF Mixed couple		IOL Both British		POM Both British		TST Mixed couple		TOTAL
bifes de	1	Armazém	1	Levadas	2	Duque	5	
atum	1	Espada	1	Recomeçar	1	Quinta	28	
pudim		Estufas	1	Gasolina	2	Fado(s)	2	
Madeira		Enfermeira	1	Senhor	5	Sala	12	
		Olá	1	senhora	11	Bailinho	1	
		Escudo	1	Senhorita	4	Pequena	4	
		Vinho	1			Barriga de	1	
		verde	1			freira	2	
		Levadas	1			Senhor	3	
		Caldo	1			Senhora	12	
		verde	2			Senhorita	1	
		sim	1			Boa noite	1	
		Querida	1			Obrigado		
		Obrigado	1					
		Tio	1					
		Senhor	2					
		senhora						
		senhorita						
	2		18		25		72	117

novel containing the lowest number of WCS is LAF (1 percent), which is understandable because only a portion of the plot occurs in Madeira.

Given that the novels are aimed at mostly English-speaking monolingual readers, the texts are written primarily in English with isolated words and expressions in Portuguese serving as ethnic and cultural markers rather than being part of an integrated bilingual grammar as Lipski (1982, 195; 2014) explains in his proposed typology for language codeswitching in speech and literature. As a result, the Portuguese switches are not very important in terms of quantity and only a few words are used in each. A similar pattern can be observed in some of the romance novels set in the Canary Islands (González-Cruz 2017a, 338).

When considering the codeswitchers represented in three of the sample novels (POM, IOL and TST), different strategies can be observed. In TST, the narrator is the most important codeswitcher (55 percent), responsible for forty-one switches, which can be seen as a sign of a better knowledge of the island by the author, followed by Alonso, the Portuguese hero (19 percent) and Diane, the British heroine (14 percent). Six Portuguese minor characters are responsible for the remaining switches.

In the two novels characterized by the presence of both a British hero and heroine, different strategies are observed. In IOL, British characters are the most prominent codeswitchers, responsible for 91 percent of WCS: Stella, the heroine (36 percent), Lennox, the hero (27 percent), Christopher, Lennox's cousin (14 percent), and the narrator (14 percent). Some minor characters, representing the native speakers, also produce switches: a man (5 percent) and a receptionist (4 percent). On the other hand, in POM the opposite strategy appears: the Portuguese characters Reinalda (31 percent), Alfonso (24 percent), Tio Luis (21 percent), and Ana (6 percent) are the main codeswitchers. The British codeswitchers are Matthew, the hero (24 percent), Candida, the heroine (21 percent), and the narrator, who only produces 3 percent of the inserted Portuguese words and expressions. In TST, 72 percent of the switches correspond to a lexical WCS category, and the remaining data (28 percent) relates to the insertion of more than one word (i.e., phrases and/ or sentences). Under the lexical WCS category, few words are used but with considerable frequency, such as the word *quinta* (villa) (37 percent), repeated 28 times (see table 5.1), *sala* (living room) (16 percent) and address terms such as *senhor/senhor(a),* (Sir or Mr./ Madam or Mrs.) and *senhorita* (Miss), which represent 19 percent.

The Portuguese loanwords in the sample can be divided into two main categories according to their topic and discursive function:

> (i) cultural items with referential function, which are used to refer to objects or concepts that do not have an adequate equivalent in English, like types of building, music, or local food, such as *barriga de freira* (or nun's belly, in TST), *bifes de atum* (tuna stake, in LAF) or *caldo verde* (green broth, in IOL); and
>
> (ii) for pragmatic reasons, that is, as a way to represent language contact in use, as González-Cruz (2017a, 2017b) has pointed out in the use of Spanish words in similar novels located in the Canary Islands. There is no apparent referential need for their use and an English word could have been employed, but the insertion of those words contributes to creating a sense of place and emphasizes the bilingual context of the fictional world. This is the case with vocative function items, which include terms of address (*senhora, tio, menina, etc.*) and also terms of endearment (*querida, pequena*).

Metalinguistic Discourse (MD) Strategies

The metalinguistic discourse (comments about language) found in the texts is usually made by the narrators. They mention the fact that a character is speaking in a certain language, as in the following examples:

- She spoke in English because she was too mad to get the words out fast enough in Portuguese (IOL, 28)

- They spoke Portuguese the whole evening and got on very well (IOL, 122)
- Alonso's brilliant dark eyes [. . .] said something quick and teasing in Portuguese. Then he spoke in English (TST, 92)
- They spoke to one another in Portuguese, excluding Candida from their moment of intimacy (POM, 49)

There are also evaluative comments on the ability of the characters to speak either language, as exemplified in the following quotes:

- "I don't even speak Portuguese," she managed to say (POM, 40)
- "Come," she said in *passable* English. "Come and become clean. We talk!" (POM, 50)
- She chatted in *simple* Portuguese with Diane learning, nodding and making deprecating gestures (TST, 44)
- "I shall send my wife to you, though she speaks *little* English—only what she learned from an English woman a long time ago, who came to the island and taught all the young girls how to do the embroidery for which they are now famous." (POM, 160)

The adjectives are italicized in the original texts, pointing out that fact and helping the readers to notice it.

Language Representation (LR) Strategies

In this category, the representation of non-native English spoken in the novels is considered. As noticed in González-Cruz's studies, the authors of these novels do not only describe the speech features of the characters or comment on aspects of their pronunciation. In many cases they also resort to spelling as a means of representing some islanders' pronunciation or their non-standard morphosyntactic features as speakers of English as L2 or foreign language. This is what can be seen below in the example taken from POM; it depicts the pronunciation errors made by a Madeiran character when expressing himself in English.

> 'Zen I take you to Senhor 'Eron! 'E 'as lived 'ere in Madeira for the 'olidays all 'is life. We are proud of the Senhor in Madeira. Many great Englishmen 'ave come to Madeira, but the only one I have known is Senhor 'Eron! [. . .] "That is the 'ouse," he announced. (POM, 10–11)

As outlined by González-Cruz (2017a, 2017b), this kind of linguistic representation is almost always reserved for servants, and their errors contribute to characterizing them socially. This example reproduces the speech of a taxi driver and represents the Portuguese accent when speaking in English, especially the difficulty Portuguese speakers have when pronouncing English words beginning with "h." This is the only occurrence of this type of strategy in our sample.

Naming Characters and Forms of Address (FA) Strategies

The process of naming characters and the FA strategies used in the texts also exhibit the authors' multicultural awareness. However, some names given to the Portuguese characters are not currently in use in Portuguese society (*Reinalda*, for example), while others reveal a confusion between Portuguese and Spanish usages, such as *Alfonso* or *senhorita*, for which the Portuguese equivalents are respectively *Afonso* and *menina*. In addition, the use of honorifics such as *duque*, in TST, is not appropriate in Portugal's contemporary social landscape, because all honorifics were banned by Constitutional Law in 1911, during the 1st Republic. This shows a lack of knowledge on the part of the author of this novel.

The strategies for addressing characters, or FA strategies, are realized according to their social status (lower vs. upper class) with an added ethnic perspective. Portuguese characters of a low social status are only referred to by their first name. This is the case with the servants in POM: *Reinalda* (the housekeeper), *Alfonso* (a young man who is Reinalda's son), *Ana* (a Portuguese woman who was in service with Matthew's grandparents before her marriage). In addition to the use of their first name alone, lower class characters can be characterized by the following vocative variants: first name preceded by *senhor/tio/tia*, that is, Sir or Mr./Uncle/Aunt (e.g., *tio Luís*, and *tia Rosa*), or followed by their occupation, such as the *taxi driver*, *the chauffeur*, *the gardener*, *the receptionist*. For upper class Portuguese characters, beyond first name as vocative, the noun *senhor* with a patronym (*Senhor Pedro Ornelas*, *Senhor Ornelas*) and /or an honorific (*duque*, as *Alonso*, the *Duque de Valmardi*, in TST) are used. In contrast, all British characters—living in or visiting the island—are characterized by the fact that they all belong to the same social class, which seems to be middle class. The English-speaking characters receive a patronym: in POM, for example, *Matthew Heron* (a Nobel Prize recipient and the hero), *Jessica Heron* (Matthew's mother), *Candida Mansell* (the heroine and journalist), *Mary Hutchins* (Candida's aunt), or, in TST, *Dwight Rogan* (an American visitor), *Diane McNair* (from the UK, and the heroine). Some of them are addressed by both their full name, first name and the corresponding short name: *Matthew Heron/Matthew/Matt* and *Candida Mansell/Candida/Candy*, in POM, and *Christopher Brodey/Christopher/Chris*, in IOL.

These different naming processes are correlated to different social, ethnic, and cultural parameters, showing how characters are positioned in the social and cultural space, following patterns of the colonial / postcolonial island landscape, historically characterized (Bazenga et al. 2012) by the British presence and influence.[1] However, the FA used for native characters reveal the writers' poor knowledge of Portuguese address terms, which constitute a highly coded and complex system (Cintra, 1972; Carreira 1997, 2002). Its uses are regulated by social norms according to gender, degree of power and intimacy, or distance between speakers in interaction.

CONCLUSION

The strategies described above seem to be used both to highlight the fact that the narrated story takes place in a bilingual and bicultural context and to preserve distinctiveness among characters since some protagonists have mastered the two languages and others have not. These strategies are therefore used to characterize and portray the different characters according to their language competence.

The data provided in table 5.1 confirms that most of the Portuguese material used in the works is made up of nouns that serve a referential function and are limited to particular situations related to local culture. They typically refer to some local cultural features and are related to the world of leisure: food (*caldo verde, espada*), music (*fado, bailinho*), geography (*levadas*). They can be considered to be "travel words," within the more general process of making meaning and shaping experience through language, the so-called *languaging*, which Gloria Cappelli uses to refer to "the use of foreign words to provide local color or to flatter the pseudo-abilities of the reader" (2013, 353). This seems to be an important function which explains the lack of diversity of Portuguese used in the sample of novels analyzed (few words and several repetitions). Portuguese culture is viewed superficially, using stereotyped cultural forms (music, food, and geography), as indicated by the lack of knowledge of the local culture, the incorrect use of forms of address and the confusion between Portuguese and Spanish.

With the data presented, I can confirm that the sociolinguistic approach used provides a valuable insight into situations of language contact in novels. The strategies described (WCS, MD, LR, together with characters' names and FA) highlight the sociolinguistic differences between characters, while also emphasizing the fact that the story takes place in a bilingual / multicultural context which the novel recreates, either directly through the characters' speech or indirectly through the narrator. These strategies demonstrate the authors' sociolinguistic awareness, transmitted through the narrator and the protagonists. They contribute "to making readers aware of the sociolinguistic and sociocultural differences between characters [. . .] and [. . .] recreate the bilingual context in which the plots are developed" (González-Cruz 2017a, 338). In these four novels, while the bilingual context is clear, the knowledge of the Other, in this case the Portuguese inhabitants of Madeira, is superficial and often inaccurate. Therefore, these novels may contribute to the diffusion of a stereotyped image of Madeira as a tourist paradise. In fact, "tourism has been the dominant sector of the economy and enjoys a centenary tradition as Madeira is one of the oldest touristic destinations in the world" (Almeida 2016, 146). Despite inaccurate representations, these strategies allow readers to perceive and make social and cultural inferences about the narrated language contact situation, stimulating their curiosity about Madeira. The authors' awareness of language differences may also help promote the vision of this Atlantic island as a site of language and cultural contact. Last, but not least, the novels provide a vision of Madeira and the world which is marked through signifying processes of stereotyping and dichotomization.

NOTE

1. The *Elucidário Madeirense*, first published in 1921, quoted the Portuguese historian Dr. Álvaro Rodrigues de Azevedo, who wrote in 1873, "Madeira is largely anglicized in race, costume, ownership of land, as well as in its trade and money; English (after Portuguese) is the language spoken most frequently . . . [and] it is only national pride which contrives to keep us Portuguese" (1945, vol. II, 322). The foundational legend of Machim reinforces the idea of the mythical and historical connection of Madeira to the English culture, which has been explored mainly in British literature. According to this legend, Madeira was first discovered on the 8th of March 1344 by a couple of English lovers, Roberto Machim and Ana de Arfert (or Harfert), who landed at a port which they named Machico, after stormy weather drove their vessel out into the ocean for thirteen days. Both died there, and the other surviving members of the stranded group on the island made a cross out of cedar wood and placed it upon Roberto's grave. Upon this cross they inscribed the word MACHIM. The legend also tells us that, a few years after the Portuguese discoverers came in 1419, they built the first chapel of the island near the graves of the two English lovers, giving it the name of Machico in honor of that inscription. The British colony in Madeira developed as early as the fifteenth century and enlarged itself considerably during the eighteenth and nineteenth centuries. This community contributed significantly to the development of the island economy, in its different periods (with sugar, wine, embroidery trade, and tourism). In addition, the study of the island's natural heritage is also largely indebted to the scientific activity conducted by British naturalists who lived on the Island, collecting data that integrate several scientific taxonomies (botany, fauna, geology, etc.). However, it should be noted that, despite the influence of the English community on the island, their contact with Portuguese islanders was superficial. As David Hancock states, "The Portuguese had a strong aversion to the British, particularly to British Protestants, and the British had a similar, symmetrical view" (2009, 18).

REFERENCES

Almeida, António Manuel Martins de. 2016. "Modelling Tourism Demand in Madeira since 1946: And [sic] Historical Overview Based on a Time Series Approach." *Journal of Spatial and Organizational Dynamics* 4 (2): 145–56.
Auer, Peter, ed. 1998. *Code-switching in Conversation. Language, Interaction and Identity.* London/New York: Routledge.
Bazenga, Aline, João Adriano Ribeiro, and Miguel Menezes de Sequeira. 2012. "The British Presence in Madeira Island: Historical Overview and Linguistic Outcomes." https://www.researchgate.net/publication/273203537_The_British_presence_in_Madeira_Island_historical_overview_and_linguistic_outcomes.

Britt, Katrina. 1977. *The Silver Tree*. London: Mills & Boon.
Bullock, Barbara E. and Jacqueline T. Almeida. 2009. *The Cambridge Handbook of Linguistic Code-Switching*. Cambridge: Cambridge University Press.
Callahan, Laura. 2004. *Spanish/English Codeswitching in a Written Corpus*. Amsterdam: John Benjamins.
Cappelli, Gloria. 2013. "Travelling Words: Languaging in English Tourism Discourse." In *Travels and Translations: Anglo-Italian Cultural Transactions*, edited by Alison Yarrington, Stefano Villani, and Julia Kelly, 353–74. Amsterdam: Rodopi.
Carreira, Maria Helena Araújo. 1997. *Modalisation linguistique en situation d'interlocution: proxémique verbale et modalités en portugais*. Louvain-Paris: Peeters.
Carreira, Maria Helena Araújo. 2002. "La désignation de l'autre en portugais européen: instabilités linguistiques et variations discursives." In *Instabilités linguistiques dans les langues romanes*, organized by M. Helena Araújo Carreira, *Travaux et Documents* n° 16, 173–84, Paris: Université Paris 8.
Carter, Ronald. 2003. "Language Awareness." *ELT Journal* 57 (1): 64–65.
Cintra, Luís Filipe Lindley. 1972. *Sobre "Formas de Tratamento" na Língua Portuguesa*. Lisboa: Livros Horizonte.
Culpeper, Jonathan. 2014. *Language and Characterisation. People in Plays and Other Texts*. London/New York: Routledge.
Culpeper, Jonathan and Carolina Fernandez-Quintanilla. 2017. "Fictional Characterization." In *Pragmatics of Fiction*, edited by Miriam A. Locher and Andreas H. Jucker, 93–128. Berlin: De Gruyter.
Da Silva, Fernando Augusto and Carlos Azevedo de Meneses. 1945. *Elucidário Madeirense*. Vol. II. Funchal: Typographia Esperanca.
Gardner-Chloros, Penelope. 2009. *Code-Switching*. Cambridge: Cambridge University Press.
Gardner-Chloros, Penelope and Daniel Weston. 2015. "Code-Switching and Multilingualism in Literature." *Language and Literature* 24 (3): 182–93.
González-Cruz, M. Isabel. 2017a. "Exploring the Dynamics of English/Spanish Codeswitching in a Written Corpus." *Alicante Journal of English Studies* 30: 331–55.
González-Cruz, M. Isabel. 2017b. "Conciencia Sociolingüística e Hispanismos en un Corpus de Novela Rosa Inglesa." *Sociocultural Pragmatics* 5 (2): 125–49. DOI 10.1515/soprag-2017-0014.
Hall, Stuart. 1997. "The Spectacle of the 'Other.'" In *Representation: Cultural Representations and Signifying Practices*, edited by Stuart Hall, 225–39. London/Thousand Oaks, CA/New Delhi: Sage.
Hancock, David. 2009. *Oceans of Wine. Madeira and the Emergence of America Trade and Taste*. New Haven: Yale University Press.
Hawkins, Eric W. 1984. *Awareness of Language. An Introduction*. Cambridge: Cambridge University Press.
Hewitt, Lindsay A. 1992. *A Sociolinguistic Approach to the Study of Literary Dialect in the Work of John Galt and Christian Johnstone*. PhD Thesis, University of Glasgow.
Hunter, Elizabeth. 1977. *Pride of Madeira*. Toronto: Harlequin.
Hyland, Ken. 2005. *Metadiscourse. Exploring Interaction in Writing*. London: Continuum.
Jackson, Jane. 2014. *Introducing Language and Intercultural Communication*. London/New York: Taylor & Francis Group.
Jonsson, Carla. 2010. "Functions of Code-Switching in Bilingual Theater: An Analysis of Three Chicano Plays." *Journal of Pragmatics*, 42 (5): 1296–10.
Leech, Geoffrey N. 1983. *Principles of Pragmatics*. London/New York: Longman.
Lipski, John M. 1982. "Spanish-English Language Switching in Speech and Literature: Theories and Models." *Bilingual Review / La Revista Bilingüe* 9 (3): 191–12.
Lipski, John M. 2014. "Spanish-English Code-Switching among Low-Fluency Bilinguals: Towards an Expanded Typology." *Sociolinguistic Studies* 8 (1): 23–55.
Milroy, Lesley and Pieter Muysken, eds. 1995. *One Speaker, Two Languages. Cross-Disciplinary Perspectives on Code-Switching*. Cambridge: Cambridge University Press.
Montes-Alcalá, Cecilia. 2012. "Code-Switching in U.S. Latino Novels." In *Language Mixing and Code-Switching in Writing: Approaches to Mixed-Language Written Discourse*, edited

by Mark Sebba, Shahrzad Mahootian, and Carla Jonsson, 68–88. New York / London: Routledge.

Montes-Alcalá, Cecilia. 2015. "Code-Switching in US Latino Literature: The Role of Biculturalism." *Language and Literature* 24 (3): 264–81. https://doi.org/10.1177/0963947015585224

Muysken, Pieter. 2000. *Bilingual Speech. A Typology of Code-Mixing*. Cambridge: Cambridge University Press.

Myers-Scotton, Carol. 1992. "Comparing Code-Switching and Borrowing." *The Journal of Multilingual and Multicultural Development* 13 (1–2): 19–39.

Myers-Scotton, Carol. 1995. *Social Motivations for Codeswitching. Evidence from Africa*. Oxford. Clarendon Press

Nash, Walter. 1990. *Language in Popular Fiction*. London: Routledge.

Neels, Betty. 1980. *Last April Fair*. New York, Toronto: Harlequin.

Page, Norman. 1988. *Speech in the English Novel*. London: Macmillan.

Poplack, Shana. 1980. "Sometimes I'll Start a Sentence in Spanish Y TERMINO EN ESPAÑOL: Toward a Typology of Code-Switching." *Linguistics* 18 (7–8): 581–18.

Sebba, Mark. 2012. "Researching and Theorising Multilingual Texts." In *Language Mixing and Code-Switching in Writing: Approaches to Mixed-Language Written Discourse*, edited by Mark Sebba, Shahrzad Mahootian, and Carla Jonsson, 1–26. New York and London: Routledge.

Sebba, Mark, Shahrzad Mahootian, and Carla Jonsson. 2012. *Language Mixing and Code-Switching in Writing: Approaches to Mixed-Language Written Discourse*. New York and London: Routledge.

Staszak, Jean-François. 2008. "Other/otherness." In *International Encyclopedia of Human Geography*, 2008, edited by Rob Kitchin and Nigel Thrift, 43–47. Oxford, Elsevier, vol. 8.

Van Lier, Leo. 1995. *Introducing Language Awareness*. London: Penguin English.

Verschik, Anna. 2017. "Language Contact, Language Awareness, and Multilingualism." In *Language Awareness and Multilingualism*. (3rd ed.), edited by Jasone Cenoz, Durk Gorter,and Stephen May, 99–100. Cham, Switzerland: Springer International Publishing.

Vivanco, Laura. 2011. *For Love and Money. The Literary Art of the Harlequin Mills and Boon Romance*. Penrith: Humanities Ebooks.

Wentworth, Sally. 1990. *Illusions of Love*. Richmond, Surrey: Mills & Boon.

Young, James O. 1999. "Representation in Literature." *Literature and Aesthetics* 9: 127–43. http://openjournals.library.usyd.edu.

Chapter Six

Archipelagoes of Romance

Decapitalized Otherness in Caribbean Trash Fiction

Ramón E. Soto-Crespo

This chapter proposes that the category of trash is an essential component of Caribbean cultural production. More specifically, I argue that Anglophone Caribbean literary traditions are shaped not only by literary norms and canonical works but also by an understudied stream of pulp fictions whose narratives are set in the Caribbean. In order to make this argument, this chapter traces a boom in representations of lesser forms of white otherness in Anglophone Caribbean romance novels published in the 1970s, such as British Guyanese Christopher Nicole's *Mistress of Darkness*, part of the Hiltons saga (1974–1978), two of the novels in Jamaican Jeanne Wilson's *Vane* family saga, *Weep In the Sun* (1976) and *Troubled Heritage* (1977), and Jamaican Rosalind Ashe's *Hurricane Wake* (1977). These writers find sustenance in the history of the Lesser Antilles when writing their narratives of archipelagic romance. In their works we encounter motifs such as human trafficking, shipwrecks, the appearance of monstrous white trash entities, and the violent actions of privateers. Because their narratives are set in ocean sounds, straits, channels, and whirlpools, these writers find inspiration in the lesser-known histories of local archipelagoes. Their novels substantiate a greater history of the Leeward and Windward Islands by becoming literary reservoirs of archipelagic thought. Like Ann Laura Stoler's (2009) understanding of the archive in the global south as including works that have left "barely a historiographic trace" (5), my chapter elucidates a transnational Caribbean body of narratives that have been largely ignored, thanks to their being considered lesser works of West Indian fiction.

In *The Other America* (1998), J. Michael Dash rethinks Caribbean otherness as a link to subaltern "literary relationships" (Dash 1998, 20). For Dash, otherness signifies a subterranean "field of relations" (Dash 1998, 164). That is to say, otherness in the Caribbean is not a "kind of reductive polarity, but the recognition of a field of relations" (Dash 1998, 164). Another way of putting this is that, in the Caribbean, binaries such as self and other are not fixed entities but rather are diluted in the geographic area's "intense cultural flux" (Dash 1998, 14). For Dash, there is no capital "O" in other because in the "creolizing incompleteness" of the Caribbean there is a continuous inde-terminate relation to multiple forms of otherness (Dash 1998, 14). This con-ceptualization is different from the sharp separation between self and other found in European history. And, for Dash, this is precisely the point, because he wants to reveal the hidden connections to subterranean otherness that remain occluded after the writing of Caribbean national literary histories. He understands nation-building and canon formation as manufacturing a reduc-tive idea of self against the reality of a diverse Caribbean otherness. In the context of the mid-to-late twentieth century Anglophone Caribbean, decolo-nization coincided with the creation of national literary canons that were ideologically Afrocentric. Dash finds this historical construction of the liter-ary canon incompatible with the diverse relational reality of otherness in the Caribbean: "To force a national model onto a literature that often identifies itself with larger regional and ideological entities would be a misleading simplification" (Dash 1998, 3). Following Dash's ideas of relatedness and otherness against narrow nationalisms, the present chapter studies a series of overlooked literary texts of decapitalized Caribbean otherness. Accordingly, I examine here the relationship among literature, trash subjects, and trash fictions because, in the context of literature produced in the Americas, trash forms refer to a group of texts and entities that are other to the Caribbean literary canon, such as popular romance novels, pulp fictions, and white trash characters.[1] Trash forms, trash subjects, and literary works of trash challenge the reader to rethink how we read racialized class otherness across the liter-ary field.

I first discuss Nicole's *Mistress of Darkness,* in order to show how other-ness is constructed, looking closely at the narrative's proliferation of shades of whiteness and of lesser white subjects. I then discuss cultural processes of decapitalization—that is, the loss of wealth and status—in Wilson's novels of plantation romance between mixed-race protagonists. Lastly, I examine Ashe's *Hurricane Wake* and the tropes of decapitalization/decapitation in a novel that echoes Jean Rhys's *Wide Sargasso Sea* (1966) with its narrative of failed transnational / transatlantic romance. The 1970s novels analyzed here generated a rich literary vein of trash characters and decapitalized subjects.

ROMANCING LESSER ARCHIPELAGOES:
CHRISTOPHER NICOLE'S *CARIBEE* SAGA

Consisting of five plantation novels—*Caribee* (1974), *The Devil's Own* (1975), *Mistress of Darkness* (1976), *Black Dawn* (1977), and *Sunset* (1978)—the Hilton saga is Nicole's rendition of Lesser Antillean history from the early decades of European colonization in the 1600s to West Indian independence in the mid-twentieth century. That is to say, as historical novels this saga tells the history of the Lesser Antilles from the perspective of the Hilton family. The third installment, *Mistress of Darkness,* is especially relevant to examining the relationship between representations of lesser white subjects and themes of inter-island travel, because its narrative chronicles a journey among multiple islands and exemplifies the complexity of racialized class in a Caribbean setting. *Mistress*'s narrative action takes place in the 1790s; in its opening pages readers become acquainted with Gislane Nicholson, a mustee slave from the island of Nevis. Gislane is described as having a "sixteenth part of African blood" and as being the "bastard daughter of a white planter and an octoroon slave" (Nicole 1976, frontispiece). The novel begins with a series of romantic scenes in the port city of Bristol, showing Matt Hilton, heir to the Caribbean Hilton plantation fortune in Antigua, with Gislane during the days before their wedding. However, before the ceremony can take place, Gislane is kidnapped, sold into bondage, and immediately shipped to the West Indies. This initial sequence of events situates the narrative in an Odyssean-like journey, where Matt embarks on a decades-long search for Gislane. Traveling from Nevis to the Guyanas, and from there to Haiti, inter-island travel propels the narrative action and dislocates the traditional genre conventions that favor single nation settings.

The dislocation of a narrow understanding of the nation-state from the story's center is consistent with the decentering of whiteness as a uniform entity. These two narrative techniques work together in Caribbean trash fictions. In *Mistress*, the fact that Gislane is "too white"—that is, she has unblemished white skin—alerts others to her racial otherness as a "near-white girl" (Nicole 1976, 29, 109). The narrator explains that, in a West Indian context, her too-perfect whiteness is cause for suspicion since it indicates more readily that she has "tar in her veins" (92). Paradoxically, it is Gislane's impeccable whiteness that unveils her racialized class position as a lesser form of white subjectivity—one that legally is other than white (29). The novel's categorization of white skin as potentially duplicitous makes readers aware of a new meaning being given to white skin, emphasizing that in a Caribbean society white skin can now indicate the trashing of its position of privilege.

The large number of white subjects in the novel intensifies the cultural complexity of white skin. *Mistress*'s narrative is peppered with numerous examples of not-quite-white subjects, often referred to as "poor whites" or "petit-blancs." This collection of lesser white characters is brought together with the overarching rationale that white skin can lose its value and that its "inherent" privilege can be trashed. Instead of the transparent clarity that is customarily associated with whiteness, trashed white skin becomes a repository of opaque otherness. In Nicole's account, the petit-blancs assume monstrous characteristics as they publicly show their envy of, and hatred for, wealthy planters. For instance, the petit-blancs "might be resentful of their betters, but still were unable to resist the temptation to gather beyond the white palings of the garden and watch the wealth from which they were forever excluded" (Nicole 1976, 3). In *Mistress,* one of the petit-blancs argues openly: "Is it not reasonable for someone in my position to hate everything and everyone which is purely white?" (390).

Unlike the archipelago of Greek islands where Odysseus encounters all sorts of monsters (Cyclops, sirens, Scylla), the Caribbean archipelago is rich with monstrous shades of white skin that elude visual detection of real—or less than real—whiteness. It is in this context that Gislane's white skin fails to disguise the minor percentage of black blood in her veins. In Nicole's world, otherness and lesser forms of white subjectivity have merged into one. However, Gislane represents an even more complex otherness since her white skin reveals that she is less than white, but at the same time conceals the fact that she is a *mamaloi*, a voodoo priestess who can channel the "great serpent *Damballah Oveddo*," and who triggers the beginning of the Haitian revolution (248). In her case, white skin becomes multivalent since it reveals her lesser status yet grants her a perfect cover for clandestinely developing a radical agency. With Gislane, Nicole proposes transnational origins for a national revolutionary movement, thus challenging the historical account of the Haitian revolution as a purely local insurrection. Moreover, Nicole inserts lesser forms of whiteness at the heart of the revolution, thereby dislocating any claims of pure black or pure white origins for the uprising. Cloaking her multi-layered otherness, the narrator tells readers that Gislane "is innocent of anything save her beauty and her white skin" (152). In this novel where shades of whiteness proliferate, the narrative makes it impossible for the protagonists to find love. Without love there is no unified multiracial nation. Matt and Gislane are both living in the Caribbean, but their white skins have acquired different meanings. Still, in these trashy Caribbean fictions, lack of love does not mean lack of sex: *Mistress* ends with Gislane's rapturous sexual intercourse with one of the leaders of the Haitian Revolution. A euphoric Gislane says: "You appeal to the bitch in me. . . . You bring out my bitch desires" (395). Nicole's examples of Caribbean otherness now remind readers of the prejudices against lesser whites who are perceived to compromise their whiteness when their behavior crosses the boundary between human propriety and lustful animality. The plot closes with themes of violence and renewal, a trashy sex scene and the portrayal of a lesser white Caribbean subject in ecstasy.

DECAPITALIZATION, OTHERNESS, AND ROMANCE
IN A SEA OF CANE

Jeanne Wilson's *Vane* family saga consists of three installments: *Weep in the Sun* (1976), *Troubled Heritage* (1977), and *Mulatto* (1978). These novels' convoluted stories are centered on three sugar-producing estates in the British colony of Jamaica: Vane, Lonsdale, and Wells. The saga begins in 1662 with the arrival in Jamaica of a "white indentured bond servant" named Robert Vane (Wilson 1976, 3). Sold for "twenty-one pounds" (48), Vane joined the poor white hordes being forcibly transported to the Indies. He describes this wretched mass of humanity as having "faces grown hard in a life of poverty or from spending years in prisons" (41). Their stories were all similar; for instance, the narrative mentions Jem Marston's tale, the story of a subject who "had stolen a hen to make broth for his sick child; for this he was sentenced to be hanged, then the sentence had been commuted to transportation for life" (49). The forced exodus of poor whites overseas was part of Oliver Cromwell's famous Western Design; his plan to "wrest all the West Indies from the Spanish" (42). Cromwell intended to displace the Spanish hold on the islands by injecting a massive influx of poor whites from the British Isles. In this historical context, Vane's indentured servitude is characterized by cruelty and being subjected to "the sting of the overseer's lash" (3). Once on the island he was forced to work in what he describes as a "sea of cane" (3). Although written as a love story between the mixed-blood sons and daughters of the Vane, Lonsdale, and Wells families, the saga emphasizes the ever-growing diversity of decapitalized whites that is produced at a time of great racial and class upheaval.

I understand decapitalization in Caribbean trash fiction as the loss of wealth and status—in Vane's case by a newly impoverished full white subject, and in other cases by white subjects who, having been born into poverty, are continually impoverished.[2] Accordingly, two types of lesser whites are described in the opening scenes: a recently indentured subject and a formerly indentured subject, one bonded and the other free from bondage. The overseer, Jez Davis, had been an indentured bondservant in Barbados for five years. He came from "humble, oppressed stock living in the warrens of Bristol" (Wilson 1976, 4). For his part, Vane is recruited to fight French and Spanish forces in the island of St. Christopher, located in the Caribbean archipelago known as the Lesser Antilles, and becomes a war hero. Given his new status, he marries into the sugar plantocracy. These two characters represent two types of decapitalization: those born into poverty (e.g., Jez) and those whose white privileges have been trashed either by themselves or others (e.g., Vane). Vane's trashed white subjectivity makes it easy for him to decide to have his mixed-blood son inherit the plantation.

If the saga starts with a theme of white indentured servitude, subsequent installments develop the theme of decapitalized whiteness in three families: Vane, Wells, and Lonsdale. Matt Wells is labeled white trash because of his propensity for sexually abusing the black female slaves. One of the servants describes his decapitalized position with a brief statement: "Mas' Matt white trash" (Wilson 1977, 55). Disinherited by his father in his living will, Matt is envious of his mixed-blood half brother Seth, who inherits Wells's plantation. It should be noted that the ghastly disposal of the decapitalized subject is a popular convention in this group of trash fictions. Therefore, it does not come as a surprise when Matt is poisoned and his gruesome death by oleander powder represents one of the most horrific scenes in the multivolume saga. Other installments in the saga use the phrase "base born" to indicate subjects who, unlike Matt, were born poor white and are therefore understood to be less-than-full white.

Wilson's most significant contribution to this topic is her account of a major realignment in society initiated by formerly decapitalized subjects. In this world of less-than-full white types of otherness, full whiteness is slowly being left behind and a mixture of degrees of white blood eventually becomes highly desirable. Neither full white nor black, this mixture dominates the recapitalized subjects of Vane's heritage. Although the oldest members of the plantocracy held on to full whiteness as an unquestionable proof of their right to rule, other members welcomed new cultural trends that positioned the local plantocracy at odds with aristocratic metropolitan values: "These planters had a new-found pride in the growing plantocracy, rooted in money and position in the island, rather than on a distinguished heritage" (Wilson 1977, 14). This is due to the fact that, as the narrator clarifies, "[m]any of the now respected planters' ancestors had been of that ill-fated rabble that served under Penn and Venables who took Jamaica from the Spanish, or men of doubtful background: petty thieves, desperadoes fleeing from Newgate, reformed buccaneers or pirates, impressed reluctant bondsmen, with here and there a scion of good family, forced to settle in the young colony" (14). The metropolitan-born and educated members of the local plantocracy, residing on the island due to marriage or inheritance, "scorned the Vanes and the Lonsdales for their recognition and acceptance of mixed blood" (15). But the King of England, recognizing these families' great wealth, granted them a title of nobility thus making Alan Lonsdale a fifth Baronet. This development takes place notwithstanding their "shameful quarter of Negro blood swamped by generations of aristocratic English blood" (1).

Considered mulattoes, the new generation of Vanes and Lonsdales represented a shift in local racial distribution of power where "a swelling core of coloureds," rejected by the full whites and despised by the blacks, became "too numerous to ignore" (Wilson 1977, 15). Lady Deborah, an English dowager, states plainly: "I did not see the consequences of a mixed marriage or how the coloured population would swell and so threaten the whites' supremacy" (46). Her niece adds to the dowager's concerns that "the proportion of white to coloureds and negroes dwindles daily" (185).

Former decapitalized subjects, in this case white indentured servants, had overturned the plantocracy. Their revenge consisted in replacing full whiteness with a new class of mixed-race subjects. Referred to in the saga as the "growing power" of non-full whites, this outcome frightens full white metropolitan members of the local upper class who uphold white skin as the repository of ultimate value in a slave society. The realization of an impending change leads Lady Deborah to ponder openly: "I don't have a problem with my white skin. Not now but in the years to come, I wonder. . . ." (Wilson 1977, 22).

THE OTHER SIDE OF A LOOKING GLASS

When a sheet of metal flying from a roof in the middle of a hurricane decapitates Maurice, the poor white character in Rosalind Ashe's *Hurricane Wake* (1977), it provides textual evidence of decapitalization's ugly turn in 1970s Caribbean fiction. There, it assumes macabre dimensions that threaten to possess other types of white subjects. From decapitalization to decapitation, Maurice's death portrays a development in which decapitalized whiteness has become a haunting specter.

The powerful hurricane that dominates the narrative of *Hurricane Wake* symbolizes a storm raging over the novel's white protagonists. Set in the Caribbean island of Jamaica, the novel narrates the dramatic events that take place in an old plantation house when an unnamed hurricane makes landfall. The novel is structured in twelve chapters, each chronicling the events of a single hour from six o'clock in the evening to six o'clock in the morning. The narrator, Miss Liz, confides about this narrative structure: "I must be strict: twelve hours of storm, described in sequence. Twelve parts, carefully labeled: it must be well ordered" (Ashe 1977, 8). Miss Liz is writing after the fact from a room in the mansion's turret where she had been locked up. Describing "my imprisonment in this turret," Miss Liz decides to write an account of the hours that led to her confinement (14). As she accuses her captors of claiming that her captivity is a measure necessary for her safety after suffering a nervous breakdown, Miss Liz's rationale for writing her narrative is twofold. Not only is it a chronicle of events that led to her imprisonment but also a document intended to disprove claims of insanity leveled against her.

In this narrative, otherness is structured according to types of racialized class subjectivity within whiteness, and not in terms of the typical white-black axis that conditions otherness in mainstream Caribbean narratives. Categories such as poor white, decapitalized planter white, and metropolitan (or full) white mark the difference between white characters in this novel. Four characters take precedence in this psychologically driven account of decapitalized whiteness: Miss Liz, Tom, Edward, and Maurice. Miss Liz and Tom are twins. Edward, who is Miss Liz and Tom's British cousin, is depicted as smart, unquestionably white, and adventurous. Miss Liz describes Maurice and Tom as characters from *Huckleberry Finn*, thus making a close connection between poor whites in the Caribbean and poor whites in the U.S. South. But whereas Miss Liz and Tom were born into the Jamaican planter class and are now decapitalized whites, Maurice is a poor white of European (German) stock.

In the Caribbean context, Maurice is described as an anomaly within whiteness: "Maurice was that anomaly, a poor white, the last of a family of immigrant Germans who had come over to help fill the labor gap left by the slave emancipation" (Ashe 1977, 12). Maurice's anomalous racialized class position assumes a physical dimension that points to genetic differences within whiteness: "He had none of the pallor and physical narrowness of most white men, but the strong build . . . of [his] own menfolk" (Ashe 1977, 135). Because Maurice's place in the local class strata is anomalous, it had been explained to Miss Liz since her childhood years that: "You must remember Maurice is blessed by the Master's favour always, but even your good father, Miss Liz, can't make him an equal to Mars Tom and youself" (55). In the novel there are moments when Maurice needs to be reminded of his place in the local hierarchy of whiteness. For instance, during the hurricane he is told to weather the storm in the lower-level room where the non-white servants are sheltered.

Maurice is but one of many decapitalized subjects. In archipelagic novels, decapitalizations are as diverse as the descriptions of differing shades of white skin. At the time of the story, Miss Liz and Tom have become members of a growing decapitalized class of their own. They have joined the ranks of many formerly wealthy planter families that have fallen on hard times and who are desperately trying to retain the last remnants of their lost economic status. Tom, who inherited the plantation, has severely mismanaged its finances. Being more interested in gambling than accruing capital, Tom neglected the main house, the crops, and accumulated an increasing amount of debt. Miss Liz describes this state of decapitalization in the following way: "There was no escaping the sad alteration in the house and yard, the neglect and seediness. It started quite slowly, I think, dating from

Father's illness, but now I could tell it had accelerated. The tufted roofs and courtyard, the broken panes, the unpolished expanses of cedar floor . . . an anachronism almost untouched by progress and change" (Ashe 1977, 64).

In this novel, the planter's economic downfall is connected to shifts in trade affecting post-slave societies, problems caused by the families' financial mismanagement, and also to the depraved character associated with decapitalized subjects. Miss Liz's romantic involvement with Maurice and Edward is complicated by Tom's incestuous feelings for her. Here we encounter a narrative of romance and decapitalization in the global south where incestuous relations between twins remind the reader of William Faulkner's *The Sound and the Fury* (1929) where we find the incestuous relationship between Quentin and Caddy. But whereas in Faulkner's narrative Quentin ends up committing suicide, in Ashe's novel fatal accidents and murder predominate. Edward is killed when his plane crashes on the way to Jamaica from Cuba, yet the novel's most dramatic event is Maurice's gruesome decapitation.

Evoking the status of lesser whites who are asked to enter through the back door, Maurice is beheaded as he "knocks" on the front door (Ashe 1977, 130). His body falls through the door frame with his head missing. Decapitalized since birth and newly decapitated, Maurice becomes the source of the novel's main drama. The story's suspense is built not on whether but on when the poor white's head is coming to fetch his body: "Head must find body, seeking unity . . . If head come look for body, will come soon" (Ashe 1977, 140, 142). No other Caribbean trash fiction has developed the trope of the decapitation of a white trash subject. As Maurice's head "rolled out" of a bag, it unleashes "a pandemonium of terror" (187). Ashe's novel marks a significant moment when Caribbean romance takes a turn for the worse. With the two suitors dead, romantic love gets lost in a "conflux of wild and evil forces" (208).

It is at this moment of ultimate horror that the novel unexpectedly focuses on its insular location. The horror of a headless decapitalized white monster merges into the terror associated with being isolated from the other islands during a hurricane: "We were on an island, cut off from the rest of creation by the spinning wall of wind and water as surely as if we had fallen through a fault in Time" (Ashe 1977, 201). Isolation and horror become one in a tale where the heroine is perceived to have become mad. Not only is Maurice's white trash severed head and headless body haunting the storm-ravaged dilapidated mansion, but Edward's ghost appears, adding another layer to the house's disruption. Edward's spirit comes back from the dead to seduce Miss Liz to join him in the afterlife. Miss Liz's decision to join him entails crossing the boundary between this world and the next.

Her crossing to the other side of what she calls "the looking glass" has echoes of Lewis Carroll's *Through the Looking Glass, and What Alice Found*

There (1871)—the sequel to *Alice's Adventures in Wonderland* (1865)—and of Jean Rhys's *Wide Sargasso Sea* (1966). In Rhys's novel, Antoinette/Bertha Mason stares at the looking glass in Thornfield Hall and finds a moment of clarity. In *Hurricane Wake,* Miss Liz's crossing of the spiritual divide coincides with the advent of the eye of the storm. This ominous coincidence of natural and supernatural forces seals Miss Liz's fate. The appearance of Maurice's decapitated head and the surprising visit by Edward's spirit become for the narrator a psychological and psychic crossing. Moving from this world to an upside-down world, Miss Liz loses her chance for love and romance. Instead she gets lost in "a wild topsy-turvy world [on] the other side of the looking-glass" (Ashe 1977, 218). Miss Liz's tale of home imprisonment revisits literary tropes from the postwar Caribbean literary tradition such as the one developed in *Wide Sargasso Sea.* In many ways, Miss Liz's imprisonment in the turret evokes Rhys's protagonist, Antoinette, and her confinement in the attic of an English manor house.

To be clear, *Wide Sargasso Sea* is inspired by Charlotte Brönte's *Jane Eyre* (1847), and the confinement of the white Creole in the attic stems from Bronte's novel. *Wide Sargasso Sea* is actually Rhys's revision of Brönte's unfair characterization of a decapitalized white Caribbean subject. By telling the story of how Antoinette Mason becomes Bertha, Rhys gives Bertha's place of Otherness in the British literary tradition a new meaning. No longer simply a madwoman in the attic, Antoinette's/Bertha's story provides an account of a failed love in a Caribbean tale of romance. Like Rhys's story of Antoinette, Ashe writes Miss Liz's story of how she became imprisoned/mad. Similar to Rhys's novel, Ashe's narrative is organized and clear, but more importantly it delivers what it sets out to tell in a precise and cogent style. As a gripping and straightforward account of a lost romance, Ashe writes a version of the events that is dramatically different from what the protagonist's captor may tell or write about her condition. Potentially an unreliable narrator, Miss Liz's account relies on the reader's judgment of whether she is mad or not. Although we don't have her brother's account, readers are aware that the protagonist's captivity depends on his official narrative justifying her confinement. Like Rhys's use of the African religion of obeah in her novel, Miss Liz's tale shifts from romance to the supernatural and, from there, to the macabre. What becomes clear in *Hurricane Wake*, as well as in Rhys's novel, is that the decapitalization of whiteness seems to be incompatible with romantic love.

CONCLUSION

The 1970s Caribbean archipelagic narratives of romance develop a racialized class dimension of otherness associated with the dislocation of a single idea of whiteness. These narratives contest conventions in the representation of white subjects by complicating racialized class within whiteness and by making it a highly diverse category. As a result, these fictions heterogenize whiteness. In these romance narratives, otherness becomes antithetical to the narrowing nation. For Rhys, the Sargasso Sea represents a new allegory of a space where debris finds a home and where plant life thrives without being rooted.[3] In *Wide Sargasso Sea*, Rhys looked to a Sargasso-like cohabitation of lesser forms. In a similar way, the 1970s novels of white trash types produced narratives that do not fit the decolonized nation building project, but which nevertheless suggest other types of cohabitation. Like Rhys, 1970s trash fictions look outward to relations of otherness outside the narrowing horizon of a mid-to-late twentieth-century nationalist literary canon. Their narratives capture the "cultural flux" and sense of cultural "incompleteness" that Dash proposes to be the guiding coordinates of an aggregate Caribbean literary history.

NOTES

1. In *Not Quite White* (2006), Matt Wray explains that in the United States "white trash" refers to low breeding and, during particular historical periods, to those who have polluted whiteness by mixing the races (Wray 2006, 23). By contrast, West Indian literature uses "white trash" to refer to newly poor whites, that is to say, individuals who have lost their wealth and status, and also to generational impoverished whites (Andrews 1996, 490). By the 1970s both definitions are present in "trash fiction." I use the term "trash fiction" to refer to those works of literature where white trash or decapitalized white characters are represented.

2. For decapitalization in circum-Atlantic literature, see Soto-Crespo 2016, 112–13.

3. For a more detailed analysis of Rhys's *Sargasso Sea* as a model of political cohabitation for trash forms, see Soto-Crespo, "Archipelagic Trash," 309–12. See also, Soto-Crespo, *The White Trash Menace*, 2020.

REFERENCES

Andrews, Gordon H. 1996. "'White Trash' in the Antilles." 1934. In *Negro: An Anthology*, edited by Nancy Cunard, 488–92. London: Bloomsbury Academic.

Ashe, Rosalind. 1977. *Hurricane Wake*. London: Hutchinson and Co.

Dash, Michael J. 1998. *The Other America: Caribbean Literature in a New World Context*. Charlottesville: The University Press of Virginia.

Nicole, Christopher. 1976. *Mistress of Darkness*. New York: St. Martin's Press.

Soto-Crespo, Ramón. 2016. "Trash Travels: White Cockroaches and Decapitalization in Circum-Atlantic Literature." *Atlantic Studies* 14, no. 1: 112–26. https://doi.org/10.1080/14788810.2016.1219090 .

Soto-Crespo, Ramón. 2017. "Archipelagic Trash: Despised Forms in the Cultural History of the Americas." In *Archipelagic American Studies: Decontinentalizing the Study of American Culture*, edited by Michelle Ann Stephens and Brian Russell Roberts, 302–19. Durham: Duke University Press.

Soto-Crespo, Ramón. 2020. *The White Trash Menace and Hemispheric Fiction*. Columbus: The Ohio State University Press.

Stoler, Ann Laura. 2009. *Along the Archival Grain: Epistemic Anxieties and Colonial Common Sense*. Princeton: Princeton University Press.

Wilson, Jeanne. 1976. *Weep in the Sun*. New York: Pocket Books.
Wilson, Jeanne. 1977. *Troubled Heritage*. London: Macmillan.
Wray, Matt. 2006. *Not Quite White: White Trash and the Boundaries of Whiteness*. Durham: Duke University Press.

2

Tensions and Transformations

Chapter Seven

Public Conflicts and Private Treaties in Kathleen Eagle's *Fire and Rain*

Johanna Hoorenman

Anglo-Americans' images of Native Americans serve and respond to white interests, desires, and anxieties. They reflect very little, if anything at all, about the wide and varied group of peoples categorized together as Native Americans or American Indians. Such images speak to Anglo-American anxieties about national identity and desires for an aboriginal American belonging that are formed through a continuous interplay of Othering and identifying with (an imagined version of) "the Indian": as Vine Deloria Jr. observed, "Underneath all the conflicting images of the Indian one fundamental truth emerges—the white man *knows* that he is an alien and he *knows* that North America is Indian—and he will never let go of the Indian image because he thinks that by some clever manipulation he can achieve an authenticity that cannot ever be his" (1980, xvi). Published in 1978, Robert F. Berkhofer's seminal study *The White Man's Indian* explored the development (and continuity) of these White images of Native Americans throughout the history of contact and conflict between European Americans and Native Americans. He states that "the essence of the White image of the Indian has been the definition of Native Americans in fact and fancy as a separate and single other. Whether evaluated as noble or ignoble, whether seen as exotic or degraded, the Indian as an image was always alien to the White" (xv) and calls attention to what he terms "the metaphysics of White Indian-understanding" (xv). Berkhofer adapts this phrase from *The Confidence Man* (1857)—in which Herman Melville speaks of "the metaphysics of Indian-hating"—in order to account for the fluctuating levels of hate and love expressed in white images of Native Americans (224).

However, Berkhofer's study appeared before North America was exposed to the passionate levels of Indian-loving that would come to be expressed in hundreds of romance novels since 1980. From that year onwards, American popular fiction was awash with book covers depicting bare-shouldered white women entangled in a lurid clinch with long-haired men dressed (scantily) in buckskins and feathers. Such books imagine love affairs between (predominantly) white women and Native American men as exotic fantasies of what romance blogger Alexa Day characterized as "life-changing Othersex" (Day, 2014). Amongst what has become a sizable corpus of romance novels categorized as "Indian historical romance fiction," romance author Kathleen Eagle is hailed as a writer in the romance genre who avoids exoticizing Native American characters and obfuscating the dark history of conflict between Native and Anglo American peoples.

This chapter explores the narrative strategies and the engagement with history and voice in Eagle's novel *Fire and Rain*. This work, a nominee for the Romance Writers of America's 1994 RITA Award for Best Historical Single Title Romance, stands out for its extensive and overt engagement with the Lakota Sioux history of territorial conflict, treaties, land rights, and the 1980 Supreme Court ruling over the land rights to the Black Hills (*United States v. Sioux Nation of Indians*, 448 U.S. 371). The novel's foregrounding of these historical circumstances permits it to serve as an example of the potential of historical romance fiction to engage with complex histories rather than sidestepping them, and forms a useful counterpoint to the majority of Native American themed romance fiction. However, Eagle's own position as an Anglo-American author engaging with Native American experiences also poses questions of authorship and "own voices" in writing Native American romances.[1]

The scholarly debate surrounding the white conceptualization of Native Americans tends to be located in a distinctly gendered version of the concept. In *The White Man's Indian*, the Indian is male, and the white person who invents him is also, clearly, male. Vine Deloria Jr.'s description quoted above is overtly gendered male, as are the discussions by Philip J. Deloria in *Playing Indian* (1998), Shari Huhndorf in *Going Native: Indians in the American Cultural Imagination* (2015), and Daniel Francis in *The Imaginary Indian: The Image of the Indian in Canadian Culture* (1992).[2]

But imagining Indians is not, of course, a solely male pursuit. Certainly, "Indian" seems to be interpreted most often as a male term, and "playing Indian" or "going Native" are also typically associated with a white male freedom to abandon (Western) society, domesticity, and/or civilization. However, white women's engagement with imagined Indianness is, in fact, likewise abundant and follows similar (but not the same) patterns as that of their male counterparts. One place in which this engagement is most visible is in American popular romantic fiction. Native American–themed romance novels form a consistent and significant subgenre within the popular romance market. This uniquely North American subgenre is published at an average of 20 new novels per year since 1980. This amounts to a corpus of nearly 800 titles. The website Goodreads offers a list of 776 novels shelved by multiple readers as Native American Romance, which corresponds with that estimate (Goodreads). The novels are overwhelmingly written by non-Native female authors for a predominantly non-Native readership, and their plots and character types have long roots in the American imaginary. They can be traced back to the first type of American popular literature: Indian captivity narratives of the Early American period such as those of Mary Rowlandson and Mary Jemison, early sentimental novels such as Lydia Maria Child's *Hobomok* (1824), Catherine Maria Sedgwick's *Hope Leslie* (1827), and most recognizably to James Fenimore Cooper's *The Last of the Mohicans* (1826).

The Native-themed romance subgenre has been discussed in a number of shorter scholarly publications, including Beidler (1991), McCafferty (1994), Castiglia (1996), Wardrop (1997), and MacDonald et al. (2000). These publications all tend to focus on typical examples of the subgenre in order to come to a coherent analysis of this type of book. By contrast, I choose to focus on Eagle because various readers (academic and non-academic) signal her work as somehow different from the type.[3] Eagle's work is generally (but not always) hailed as less problematic than the bulk of the "Indian Romance" subgenre. As such it provides a stimulating starting point for considering the variation within this seemingly monolithic corpus, and for imagining how the subgenre could look were it to cease the Othering of Native Americans.

Kathleen Eagle was born in 1947 in Virginia and holds a BA from Mount Holyoke College and an MS from Northern State University. She taught at Standing Rock High School on the Cheyenne River Reservation for seventeen years and published her first romance novel in 1984. She is married to Clyde Eagle, an enrolled member of the Lakota Sioux tribe, and they have three children who are also enrolled with the tribe. She has published fifty-two romance novels, most of which include Native American characters. I include Eagle's biographical circumstances here specifically to draw attention to her position as an Anglo-American woman closely affiliated with the Lakota Sioux via her teaching career, her marriage, and her children. The nature and range of her affiliations are significant because they set her apart from the many Anglo-American authors of Native-themed romance who claim some type of connection to a Native identity in interviews or marketing materials. For instance, Cassie Edwards invokes a "full-blooded" Cheyenne grandmother (though at some points this is a great-grandmother), and Karen Kay a Choctaw great-great grandmother. Catherine Anderson claims Shoshone heritage. Rosanne Bittner's grandmother was half Potawatomi. Georgina Gentry is married to an "Irish-Indian" husband. Sheri Whitefeather is mother to two children who are enrolled in the Muscogee Creek Nation.

These claims tend to serve to legitimize the author's engagement with Native American characters in their work, and are often phrased specifically as the occasion for their interest in Native American cultures and histories. [4] The Native connections are heralded in interviews, the author's notes to their books, on their websites or their Goodreads profile pages. The claims are generally tenuous at best, and thus aside from the difficult debate around identity, blood quantum laws, and tribal citizenship, the key point is that not only are these authors not Native but that their claims to a distant connection function to support their legitimacy and authority as writers of Native American stories in a way that white readers will find credible, but that many Native readers may well find objectionable. The "Native" romance subgenre does not (yet) have well-known "own voices" authors. That is not to say such authors do not exist. Pamela Sanderson (Karuk), Mardi Oakley Medawar (Cherokee), and Evangeline Parsons-Yazzie (Navajo) are three authors with tribal enrollment who write romance novels featuring Native American protagonists, but their work is not as well-known as that of Cassie Edwards, Karen Kay, or Catherine Anderson. As a consequence, the subgenre perpetuates and re-inscribes a pattern in which Native American cultures are depicted by non-Native auteurs, be it in fiction, film, history, anthropology, or any other field.

Eagle's position is thus relevant in this respect. While she is also an Anglo-American author writing about Native characters, her association with the Lakota Sioux is much closer than that of the other Anglo-American authors mentioned above. In the essay "Indians without Cowboys" that she wrote for *Writing Romances: A Handbook by the Romance Writers of America* (1997), Eagle addresses this explicitly:

> I've been asked what background I had that qualified me to write about "the Indian experience." That's it. I'm a mother, a neighbor, a wife, a family member. I'm also a first-hand observer. But I am still non-Indian. I don't write about the Indian experience so much as I write about the experience of a non-Indian sojourning in the Indian world. One of the primary viewpoint characters in my books is always non-Indian, usually female. That's me. For the most part, that's my reader. That character is a touchstone for writer and reader, and my book becomes a bridge between the world I grew up in and the world that adopted me as an adult. No, I don't claim to be an "adopted member of the Sioux tribe." (181)

In the essay, she also carefully distances herself from the typical style of "Indian romances," stating that "Generally, they were white captive fantasies—I've heard them referred to as 'pirates in buckskins'—and they are just as popular now as they were in the early 1980s. Very early on, I deduced that my own writer's vision did not lend itself to that kind of book" (181). One of the most marked ways in which Eagle's work differs from the type is that her romances are typically set in the present rather than the past. However, her historical books also deviate from "that kind of book" in significant ways.

By contrast, Cassie Edwards also wrote an entry on her Indian romance novels, in *How to Write a Romance and Get It Published* (1990). Her essay reveals a good deal of naivety on the subject and points out that she specifically avoids certain tribes and time periods to sidestep the history of conflict. Edwards indicates that she tries to focus on tribes that co-existed peacefully with the white settlers, "to make the point that the Indians were not the savages that many people thought they were" (455). She explains that she avoids the late 1800s because most tribes were confined to reservations by that time, since "they had generally lost their pride because they were no longer able to fight for their rights" (457). Finally, she states that she has also rarely written about the 1700s, because there was "no understanding at all between the Indian and the white man" (457). Edwards specifies that it is only after more understanding was possible that there was at least "some measure of peace" between them, and then concludes:

> It is this measure of peace I choose to write about, because I like to write romances that make people feel good. The slaughter and violence can be left for the blood-and-guts men's books. (457) [5]

I have quoted from this essay fairly extensively because it reveals much about the fundamental investment of the majority of "Indian Romance" authors in stories of peace, co-existence and harmony between Native Americans and Anglo-Americans. While Edwards is by no means the only Indian Romance writer, she is one of the best-known and more prolific authors in the subgenre with more than ninety "Indian Historical Romances." Although part of Edwards's high profile comes from the 2007 plagiarism scandal uncovered by the blog *Smart Bitches, Trashy Books*, she was already hailed as the "queen of Indian romance" well before this inglorious episode in her writing career.[6]

In the 1996 study *Bound and Determined*, Christopher Castiglia examines the development of women's captivity narratives from the early Puritan-edited autobiographical narratives, through the highly popular fictional narratives that followed, up to present-day historical romance novels that use the captivity plot. Castiglia argues that captivity narratives (historical and fictional) offer female authors space for investigating the relative freedom of Indian "captivity" from Anglo-American patriarchy, both in a historical context and in the contemporary context (191). Moreover, he notes that "these contemporary romances, in retaining the trope of captivity, imply that white women still need an excuse for investigating their whiteness and their womanhood, particularly in relationship to one another: women cannot simply choose to have adventures outside their cultural 'homes'" (193). Castiglia's careful research demonstrates that white female authors (both past and present) use Indian captivity plots to imagine adventures otherwise realistically closed off to female characters, as well as to interrogate and criticize the position of women within Western patriarchy through a comparison with the Otherness of Native American cultures.

While Castiglia does not further engage with the notion that authors use these narratives to investigate their whiteness, I would argue that in addition to imagining sites of freedom from Western patriarchy, Anglo-American female authors use Native American–themed romance novels to negotiate their own desires for an American aboriginal identity, their own place in American wilderness adventures, and their own culpability or innocence in America's dark history of colonization and genocide. Edwards's preference for writing stories of peace and understanding between the races reveals a desire to distance herself from the "slaughter and violence" of white men's histories, while simultaneously satisfying a desire for a wilderness adventure and an escape from Western patriarchal constraints through an exotic fantasy of Native Otherness. This is a significant contrast to the work performed by Eagle's historicals. While her heroines are also white women who (learn to) disavow racism, oppression, and colonialism, thus distancing themselves from the "savagery" of Anglo-American men, her historical novels foreground the question of conflict and violence and her double plots emphasize the difficulty of a "happily-ever-after ending" in a historical setting.

In a 2014 post for the blog *Lady Smut*, Alexa Day proposes Kathleen Eagle as an author of "good" Native American romance that dispenses with "the shop-worn figure of the Noble Savage" and heroines who engage in "life-changing Othersex" with a man who looks "about as Native American as [Johnny Depp's] Tonto." Jackie Horne wrote a similar short post about Eagle in a 2013 blog for *Romance Novels for Feminists* called "Rethinking Columbus Day: Native American Romance."[7] MacDonald et al. (2000) make similar assessments of Eagle's work.[8] It seems, therefore, that Eagle succeeds in writing a different kind of Native American romance fiction.

However, when Elizabeth Cook-Lynn singles Eagle out for attention in her critical discussion of the representation of Native Americans in popular fiction, "American Indian Intellectualism and the New Indian Story" (1996), she does so much less approvingly. Criticizing the long-standing practice of non-Natives appropriating Native voices, she argues that "[m]uch as the title to Indian land is still held by the white American government, the major Indian story is held in non-Indian enclaves though not, like the land, by overt congressional mandate. [. . .] This means that the works of non-Indians invade every genre, and they can't be written fast enough, it seems" (60). She singles out Kathleen Eagle as an author who works in the romance market and who "seems to be attempting to lead the way toward harmony and assimilation between the races, with interracial love her major theme" (60).

This, she makes clear, should be regarded with a great deal of caution and skepticism. While Cook-Lynn does not discuss the content of Eagle's work, she points to the historical references in Eagle's forewords and epilogues to several novels and takes issue with what she terms Eagle's "'do-gooder' approach to history and fiction" (61). Cook-Lynn takes Eagle to task for appropriating Sioux history to build a successful career as a writer, and she expresses a good deal of skepticism about Eagle's claims of historical verac-ity and cultural sincerity. She also formulates her dismay with Native American–themed romance fiction in terms of the practice of Native people's cultural assimilation or erasure through white women's bodies. However, her discussion does not engage with the content of Eagle's books beyond their paratextual information about the historical events referenced in the books.

A closer reading of Eagle's *Fire and Rain* reveals a number of ways in which her work does indeed differ from the majority of the "Indian Ro-mance" subgenre. The most important of these are two strategies which I outline below: Eagle's explicit inclusion of the history of Sioux-Anglo con-flict embedded in the plot, and the book's thematic foregrounding of ques-tions of memory, historiography, and voice.

While Edwards notes that she leaves stories of Native and Anglo-American "slaughter and violence" to male authors, Eagle explicitly fore-grounds the history of conflict between Sioux tribes and Anglo-Americans in *Fire and Rain* and embeds this history firmly in her plot. This is a marked difference from the bulk of the Native-themed historical romances, since the majority sidestep this history or ignore it altogether. It is also a deviation from Eagle's general approach, as she has written many more contemporar-ies than historicals: five of her fifty-two novels are historicals, the rest are contemporaries. Two of those five have a double plot with a historical and a contemporary couple. By far most of the novels feature an Anglo-American heroine and a Lakota (sometimes mixed-race) hero. Eagle's contemporaries predominantly revolve around horses: set on a ranch, horse sanctuary, or on the rodeo circuit, Eagle's heroes combine the Indian and the Cowboy in one character.[9]

For almost two decades, Eagle was the only author writing contemporar-ies with Native heroes.[10] In 1999 Sheri Whitefeather began to publish novels with Native heroes in contemporary settings, and in the mid-2010s Jenna Kernan began publishing romantic suspense novels set on Western Apache reservation lands in a present-day setting. These exceptions draw attention to the general practice of setting Native-themed romances in the past. This practice cumulatively reinscribes the stereotypical depiction of Native people in historical settings, in keeping with the harmful myth of the Vanishing Indian. This myth constitutes a common trope in literature and popular cul-ture, with Cooper's depiction of *The Last of the Mohicans* as its most familiar instance. In short, it suggests that there are no more Native Americans, or at least no more "Real Indians" and that they have become extinct during the westward expansion of the United States, in keeping with the doctrine of the Manifest Destiny. This myth both avoids examining the causes of this mythical extinction, and conveniently obviates any consideration of the position of Native peoples in present-day USA. It is reinscribed by repetitive depictions of Native peoples in historical settings, which work to override any notion of Native peoples as existing in the present.[11] Eagle's deviation from this pattern and her writing of Native American–themed love stories in contemporary settings thus form a marked antidote to that myth. These romances set in the present are effectively a third strategy with which Eagle deviates from the problematic patterns of Native-themed romances.

However, for a useful comparison with the more typical historicals, this chapter focuses on those books in her oeuvre that are set in the past. I look at these not because they are the most representative of her body of work, but because they are representative of the ways in which Eagle negotiates the tensions of writing historicals while avoiding reinscription of harmful patterns. One of those ways is her use of the double romantic plot. Eagle's two novels with a double plot each follow a couple in a historical setting whose courtship mirrors that of a couple in a contemporary setting. In *Fire and Rain*, the historical plot revolves around the love story of the white daughter of the Indian Agent to the Sioux territory and a Lakota man (Priscilla Twiss and Whirlwind Rider).[12] The narrative is set between 1871 and 1876, and framed mostly by the heroine's diary entries (the diary is later found by the contemporary heroine, who uncovers this history). The framing places most of the emphasis on the white heroine's point of view, though the narrative is occasionally focalized through the Lakota hero. The setting of the narrative and the connection to the Indian Agent foregrounds the ongoing conflicts and treaty negotiations between the U.S. government and the various bands of the Sioux. And while the historical plot ends with a Happy For Now of the interracial couple, the reader learns more of their fate in light of the ongoing conflicts in the course of the novel: the heroine ultimately dies at the Massacre of Wounded Knee but their baby survives.

The contemporary love plot between Lakota hero Kiah and Anglo-American heroine Cecily takes place between 1971 and 1980, and foregrounds significant historical events in that period, including the occupation of Wounded Knee in 1973 and the 1980 Supreme Court ruling over the Black Hills. Kiah is a Vietnam veteran who eventually becomes a member of the Lakota tribal council, and Cecily is a college girl who volunteers at the reservation for a summer, and who returns ten years later as a journalist in search of a story about the court ruling. Not only is the history of conflict thus firmly embedded in both plots, but this particular strategy also encourages the reader to see all the events in the book as interrelated. The period between the end of the historical plot and the beginning of the contemporary plot is covered by the memories of the elders of the contemporary Lakota hero. The elders reminisce in various settings, including the contemporary hero's grandmother's house, and a powwow. The contemporary couple's search for what happened to the historical couple drives part of the contemporary love plot and facilitates an extensive engagement with the importance of elders as keepers of the history of the tribes, and of extended family connections as a way of locating oneself in a time and place. The following exchange takes place between Kiah and his grandmother, in the presence of Cecily:

> "They were right not to talk about him. It's not a good thing to talk about the dead." Grandma Emma gave a dry chuckle. "But I'm too old to worry about ghosts. I'm close to being one myself."
>
> "Jeez," Kiah scolded. "What a thing to say, Grandma."
>
> "You should know these things about your Oglala relations, *takoja*. Pretty soon there will be no one left who can tell you." (321–22)

A few days later, Cecily returns to grandmother Emma on her own:

> Emma's voice drifted with her focus, to another time, another talk between women.
>
> "they lost three, my grandmother said."
>
> "Three babies? You mean [. . .] Whirlwind Rider and Priscilla," Cecily insisted.
>
> "The fourth time they thought she might be too old, and everyone was worried, but that time it finally went okay. They had a son." She smiled wistfully. "He was a big one, my grandmother used to tell him." (345)

Via several relatives and elders, the contemporary hero begins to uncover his family's history. But the contemporary heroine specifically returns to ask more of grandmother Emma. The example above illustrates the specific role that elders have in passing on family history, but also suggests that much of that history, which is also tribal history, is transmitted by generations of women: conversations between women, overheard by girl children who, when they are elders, pass them on to other women, in this case to the non-Lakota Cecily. The book suggests that the connection between these women established through the common experience of childbirth and marriage transcends racial boundaries and gives Cecily access to particularly female facets of family history that Kiah has no access to. The book's focus on oral narratives in addition to the written diary narrative also stresses the complementary nature of different forms of cultural transmission. Passing on history, especially in times of conflict and war, is a communal effort rather than an individual one. Moreover, different versions of history are recorded in written accounts such as official (Anglo-American) documents and personal diary entries, and oral histories within the tribe.

The novel foregrounds the question of who records history, in what medium, for which audience—and whose voices are relevant—throughout the double plot, and makes it explicit in the contemporary heroine's professional vocation: as a journalist, Cecily is sent to the Pine Ridge Sioux reservation, where she volunteered one summer during her college years, to cover the 1980 Supreme Court ruling over the land rights to the Black Hills. She renews her connection with Kiah, the contemporary Lakota hero who is now on the Tribal Council, to report on the deliberations of the Sioux Nation on whether to accept the ruling. Kiah's considerations regarding this renewal reveal his mistrust of mainstream journalists' reporting on Native American issues. The Supreme Court affirmed that the United States' taking of property from the Great Sioux Nation had been unlawful and awarded "just compensation," including interest, to the Sioux in the amount of $105 million. After deliberations, the Sioux Nation declined to accept the money and renewed their claim to the land.

Kiah expresses his dismay with the kind of attention such a ruling brings, from lawyers, investors, and reporters alike: "he gave a long sigh. 'Follow the money. Money is power. The lawyers get their ten percent, and Cecily Metcalf gets her story'" (305). Cecily believes she has a good and reliable angle from which to tell the story of the Black Hills because she has the diary of historical heroine Priscilla Twiss, who recorded the events she witnessed in the period in which the treaty between the United States and the Sioux was signed. The uniqueness of Priscilla's diary is located by the novel both in its status of an eyewitness account, and in the fact that it was written by a woman: "[Priscilla] had been [. . .] an eyewitness to the taking of the Black Hills, and she offered a unique perspective on the background of the story Cecily intended to write. But it was a personal perspective. It was a woman's life" (301). In assessing the value of Priscilla's story, Cecily prioritizes the historical heroine's gender over her ethnicity, and Cecily repeatedly stresses her commitment to telling an "honest" story herself, by focusing on the "facts" and presenting them "objectively." She has faith in her own abilities as a reporter and asserts herself confidently to the skeptical hero.

Her sense of integrity is so central to the heroine that, upon finding that her editor is only interested in stories that perpetuate existing stereotypes, Cecily quits her job. Her comments and considerations in this process can be read like an assessment of the romance genre itself. This is visible in the debate with the editor over what kinds of stories audiences want versus the story Cecily has to tell:

> "Well, look, in your next version of this thing, let's get some local color. You know, you can't leave out the drunks, you can't leave out the poor little kids. You've got to *show* that stuff because that's what people—"

> "That's what people expect," she finished for him. "You give them what they expect, Harold. I'd rather give them surprises."
> "What kind of surprises?"
> "Anything that's not a stereotype is usually a surprise. Sometimes it's even a *pleasant* surprise. You think the readers could stand that, Harold?" (365)

Cecily's emphasis on providing stories that deviate from the stereotypes, and her confidence that there is a readership for them, reads like a metacommentary on the types of deviations Eagle makes from the conventions of the Indian romance subgenre in an echo of her carefully worded essay quoted above.

At the end, however, the novel intimates a less confident stance about who should be telling these stories. When Cecily reveals to the hero that she has quit her journalism job, he asks:

> "Really?" I saw you taking notes. What's going to happen to your story?"
> "One way or another, I'll see that it gets told. [. . .] I've applied for a teaching job at the Indian community college. Maybe one of my students will tell the story better than I could." She risked a glance at him. "Or maybe I'll tell it myself some other way. I'll keep writing. I'd like to help with the newspaper here." (369)

This conversation reveals a more conflicted position on whose story this is, and who is best placed to tell it. While the hero calls it "her story" in a serious question, he refers to the heroine's "story" more ironically throughout the book, and with a good deal of suspicion over how well the "newspaper lady"—as Kiah calls her repeatedly—is placed to tell it (290). Instead of "her story" in this final conversation it becomes "the story," as Cecily imagines her role as an educator or facilitator rather than narrator. The book seemed confident that its heroines were able to provide accurate accounts of Native stories but the ending reveals some anxiety about this.

One cannot discount Eagle's own position as an educator turned romance writer in this regard: there are similarities between the author's biography and the contemporary heroine, which strongly indicate that this romance novel itself may be her choice of strategy to tell this story "some other way." Aside from a question of voice, this is also a question of audience and medium: the stories of historical heroine Priscilla Twiss are recorded in her diary, ostensibly for her Indian Agent father but found by Cecily. Cecily's stories were originally intended to become a series of newspaper articles aimed at an Anglo-American audience, while the elders of the Lakota are focused on sharing their memories specifically with Kiah as a young Lakota man.

The ending does not indicate to whom Cecily envisions her future students telling the story of the Lakota: to the Sioux, to Anglo-Americans, or to both. The novel itself, however, is clearly aimed at an Anglo-American audience, and its careful strategies in narrating the history of the conflict over the Black Hills strongly suggest an educational objective.

With the novel's foregrounding of these two issues—the history of (ongoing) conflict between the United States and the Sioux Nation, and the question of who writes or tells that history, in what medium and to what audience—*Fire and Rain* illustrates some of the ways in which Eagle's writing indeed differs from the majority of the Native-themed historical romance subgenre. The high predominance of contemporaries over historicals in Eagle's oeuvre provides further evidence of her commitment to writing romance stories that depict Native heroes as real and appealing characters living in the present rather than in the past, and Eagle's focus on the Lakota rather than changing tribe with each novel or series signals her commitment to writing from personal experiences rather than relying on textual sources. While these strategies do indeed set Eagle's work apart and warrant her special status among Native American themed romances, the fact remains that her books do not change the dearth of "own voices" published in Native-themed romance. It is likely that this is at least in part a consequence of systemic racial bias in Romancelandia, which is well documented elsewhere and currently under serious and necessary scrutiny.[13] While Eagle's novels are engaging, one of her writing tips is also worth following: "Read American Indian writers. Pay attention to the voice" (184). Eagle gives her personal favorites (Simon Ortiz and Louise Erdrich, among others); I offer my own suggestions for romance readers here: Evangeline Parsons-Yazzie (*Her Land, Her Love*) and Pamela Sanderson (*Heartbeat Braves*).

NOTES

1. Corinne Duyvis is the originator of the phrase "own voices" as a hashtag on Twitter.

2. Philip Joseph Deloria states: "The groups I have chosen to pursue are by and large white American men. Although riven along class lines and differentiated by historical crises, they have been the primary claimants of an American cultural logic that has demanded the formulation and performance of national identities" (8).

3. See Cook-Lynn, Macdonald et al., Cremant, Horne, Day.

4. Cassie Edwards, Georgina Gentry, Karen Kay, Sheri Whitefeather on their Goodreads page. Rosanne Bittner on her website's "About me" page, Catherine Anderson in the Author's Note to *Comanche Heart*: "As I wrote *Comanche Heart*, my mother informed me that I am part Shoshone, which explained my interest in and my affinity with the Comanche people, who were actually Shoshones who left their parent tribe to seek a warmer climate and better hunting on the plains" (2009).

5. I am deeply indebted to Laura Vivanco for bringing these *Handbook* entries to my attention.

6. The synopsis to the reprint of three Edwards novels by Rhapsody press in 2003 reads: "Passion rages across the wild frontier in this exclusive 3-in-1 Rhapsody edition from the queen of Indian Romance" (Edwards 2003). In an article on the plagiarism scandal, *The Telegraph* calls Edwards "the world's most successful author of American Indian historical romance

novels" (Leonard 2008). The posts concerning Cassie Edwards on *Smart Bitches, Trashy Books* were collated by Candy Tan (Tan 2008).

7. Both authors refer to an earlier post by Janga on *Heroes and Heartbreakers* that highlighted Eagle as an author of a different kind of Native American Romance. Janga's blog itself is no longer online, but Horne quotes: "Truthfully, when I think of Native American characters in romance fiction, the first image that comes to mind is a bodice ripper from the 1980s with a bare-chested Native American hero on the cover and a distressing use of stereotypes between the covers. Then, I remember the books of Kathleen Eagle and am reminded that my first image is not the whole of Native American romance" (Janga, qtd in Horne).

8. The book by MacDonald et al. entitled *Shape-Shifting: Images of Native Americans in Recent Popular Fiction* (2000) includes a chapter on Native Americans in romantic fiction, and the authors similarly hail Eagle for her work. The chapter itself, however, contains problematic elements, including the claim that "Indian Romance" novels are ahistorical because Native Americans did not have romance traditions. The authors state: "The relationship of men and women differed from tribe to tribe, but overall the European tradition of romantic love and 'falling' in love has never been a part of the Native American tradition" (117). I will therefore make no further use of this text, other than to note my awareness of it.

9. One representative example is *This Time Forever*, which won the 1993 RITA for Single Title Contemporary Romance: the hero is a Lakota rodeo rider battling false legal charges, the heroine an Anglo-American nurse hoping to adopt a disabled Lakota baby. In addition to romance, the plot explicitly addresses alcoholism, systemic racism, land rights, and Sioux tribal adoption laws.

10. Eagle has stated that when she began "writing contemporary series romance, there was a subgenre of Indian romance, but they were primarily historicals" (1997, 181). Even as late as 1999 Kristin Ramsdell, in her guide to the romance genre, could only claim that "books including Native American characters in contemporary settings (e.g., those by Kathleen Eagle) are appearing more often" (Ramsdell 1999, 292).

11. For further reading on this subject, see for instance Berry (1960), Dippie (1982), and Banerjee (2016).

12. The other is *Sunrise Song* (1996), which has a historical plot that revolves around a Lakota man imprisoned in a mental institution and an Anglo-American nurse, and a contemporary plot that centers on an Anglo-American niece of the owner of the institution, and the Lakota son of the historical couple.

13. See for instance Beckett (2019) and Vivanco (2019).

REFERENCES

Anderson, Catherine. 2009. "Author's Note." *Comanche Heart*. New York: Signet.

Banerjee, Mita, ed. 2016. *Comparative Indigenous Studies*. Heidelberg, Germany: Universitaetsverlag Winter.

Beckett, Lois. 2019. "Fifty Shades of White: The Long Fight Against Racism in Romance Novels." *The Guardian*. https://www.theguardian.com/books/2019/apr/04/fifty-shades-of-white-romance-novels-racism-ritas-rwa. Accessed 27 May 2019.

Beidler, Peter. 1991. "The Contemporary Indian Romance: A Review Essay." *American Indian Culture and Research Journal* 15: 97–125.

Berkhofer, Robert F. 1978. *The White Man's Indian: Images of the American Indian from Columbus to the Present*. New York: Knopf.

Berry, Brewton. 1960. "The Myth of the Vanishing Indian." *Phylon* 21 (1): 51–57.

Carter, Jimmy. 1978. "American Indian Religious Freedom Statement on Signing S.J. Res. 102 Into Law." *The American Presidency Project at UC Santa Barbara*. https://www.presidency.ucsb.edu/documents/american-indian-religious-freedom-statement-signing-sj-res-102-into-law. Accessed on 27 May 2019.

Castiglia, Christopher. 1996. *Bound and Determined: Captivity, Culture-Crossing and White Womanhood from Mary Rowlandson to Patty Hearst*. Chicago: The University of Chicago Press.

Child, Lydia Maria. 1824. *Hobomok: A Tale of Early Times*. Boston: Cummings, Hilliard & Co.

Cook-Lynn, Elizabeth. 1996. "American Indian Intellectualism and the New Indian Story." *American Indian Quarterly* 20 (1): 57–76. Special Issue: Writing about (Writing about) American Indians.

Cooper, James Fenimore. 1826. *The Last of the Mohicans: A Narrative of 1757*. Philadelphia: Carey & Lea.

Cremant, Laurel. 2015. "Let's Talk Romance: Native American Heritage Month 2015." *Romance Novels in Color*. http://romancenovelsincolor.com/2015/11/lets-talk-romance-native-american-heritage-month-2015/. Accessed 27 May 2019.

Dailey, Janet. 1980. *Night Way*. New York: Pocket Books.

Day, Alexa. 2014. "The Savage Past: The Evolution of Native American Romance." *Lady Smut*. https://ladysmut.com/2014/10/12/native-american-romance/. Last accessed 1 June 2017.

Deloria Jr., Vine. 1980. "Forward: American Fantasy." In *The Pretend Indians: Images of Native Americans in the Movies*, edited by Gretchen M. Bataille and Charles L. P. Silet, ix–xvi. Ames: Iowa State UP.

Deloria, Philip Joseph. 1998. *Playing Indian*. Yale Historical Publications. New Haven: Yale University Press.

Dippie, Brian W. 1982. *The Vanishing American: White Attitudes and U.S. Indian Policy*. Middletown, CT: Wesleyan University Press.

Duyvis, Corinne. n.d. "#ownvoices." http://www.corinneduyvis.net/ownvoices/.

Eagle, Kathleen. 1994. *Fire and Rain*. New York: Avon.

Eagle, Kathleen. 1996. *Sunrise Song*. Memphis, TN: Bell Bridge Books.

Eagle, Kathleen. 1997. "Long Contemporary—Indians without Cowboys." In *Writing Romances: A Handbook by the Romance Writers of America*, edited by Rita Gallagher and Rita Clay Estrada, 180–185. Cincinatti, OH: Writer's Digest Books.

Eagle, Kathleen. "About Kathleen." https://www.kathleeneagle.com/bio.html. Accessed 27 May 2019.

Edwards, Cassie. 1990. "Indian Romance." In *How to Write a Romance and Get It Published*, edited by Kathryn Falk, 455–458. Signet.

Edwards, Cassie. 2003. *Wild Ecstasy; Wild Rapture; Wild Embrace*. Rhapsody. https://www.amazon.com/Wild-Ecstasy-Rapture-Embrace/dp/073943926X. Accessed 27 May 2019.

Edwards, Cassie. "About Cassie Edwards." Goodreads.com https://www.goodreads.com/author/show/29440.Cassie_Edwards. Accessed 27 May 2019.

Francis, Daniel. 1992. *The Imaginary Indian: The Image of the Indian in Canadian Culture*. Vancouver, B.C.: Arsenal Pulp Press.

Gentry, Georgina. "About Georgina Gentry." Goodreads.com. https://www.goodreads.com/author/show/53337.Georgina_Gentry. Accessed 27 May 2019.

Goodreads. "Popular Native American Romance Books." https://www.goodreads.com/shelf/show/native-american-romance. Accessed 13 July 2019.

Horne, Jackie C. 2013. "Rethinking Columbus Day: Native American Romance." *Romance Novels for Feminists*. http://romancenovelsforfeminists.blogspot.com/2013/10/rethinking-columbus-day-native-american.html. Last accessed 1 June 2017.

Huhndorf, Shari M. 2015. *Going Native: Indians in the American Cultural Imagination*. Ithaca: Cornell University Press.

Kay, Karen. "Biography." https://novels-by-karenkay.com/biography/. Accessed 27 May 2019.

Leonard, Tom. 2008. "Romantic novelists out of love over plagiarism." *The Telegraph*. https://www.telegraph.co.uk/news/worldnews/1575381/Romantic-novelists-out-of-love-over-plagiarism.html. Accessed 27 May 2019.

Macdonald, Andrew, Gina Macdonald, and MaryAnn Sheridan. 2000. *Shape-Shifting: Images of Native Americans in Recent Popular Fiction*. Westport, CT: Greenwood Press.

McCafferty, Kate. 1994. "Palimpsests of Desire: The Re-Emergence of the American Captivity Narrative as Pulp Romance." *Journal of Popular Culture* 27 (4): 43–56.

Melville, Herman. 1857. *The Confidence Man*. New York: Dix, Edwards & Co.

Ramsdell, Kristin. 1999. *Romance Fiction: A Guide to the Genre.* Englewood, CO: Libraries Unlimited.

Regis, Pamela. 2003. *A Natural History of the Romance Novel.* Philadelphia: University of Pennsylvania Press.

Sanderson, Pamela. 2016. *Heartbeat Braves* (Crooked Rock #1). Createspace Independent Publishing Platform.

Sedgwick, Catharine Maria. 1987 [1827]. *Hope Leslie, or, Early Times in the Massachusetts.* Ed. Mary Kelley. New Brunswick: Rutgers University Press.

Tan, Candy. 2008. "A Centralized Document for the Cassie Edwards Situation." *Smart Bitches, Trashy Books.* https://smartbitchestrashybooks.com/2008/01/a_centralized_document_for _the_cassie_edwards_situation/. Accessed 27 May 2019.

Vivanco, Laura. 2019. "Race and the RITAs." *Teach Me Tonight.* http://teachmeto-night.blogspot.com/2019/03/race-and-ritas.html. Accessed 27 May 2019.

Whitefeather, Sheri. 1999. "Bio." http://www.sheriwhitefeather.com/bio.html. Accessed 27 May 2019.

Yazzie, Evangeline Parsons. 2014. *Her Land, Her Love* (Their Land, Their Love #1), Salina Bookshelf Inc.

Chapter Eight

Changing Attitudes to Others

Meljean Brook's Riveted *(2012) and Its Context*

Laura Vivanco

Meljean Brook's *Riveted* (2012) is part of an as yet rather small subgenre of novels which first appeared around 2007 (Pagliassotti 2013, 65): steampunk romance. Steampunk is "essentially historical science fiction" (Brook 2009): "the majority of works belonging to this category have taken the conventions of fantasy and science fiction and relocated them in worlds that run on steam power" (Jagoda 2010, 47). In *Riveted* steam-powered airships are used to travel between Europe (some of which has only recently emerged from the domination of an Asian empire which employed nanoagents to control the population) and the various states across the ocean in the New World, which was colonized hundreds of years prior to the start of the novel by those fleeing the Old World. The book's hero, David, is a scientist, descended on his father's side from native New Worlders. Having been seriously injured as a child in an explosion caused by new technology, he has altered his body with nanoagents and the latest metal prosthetics. Annika, the heroine of the novel and an engineer on an airship, may have been born in Manhattan City in the New World but she knows nothing of her birth parents and was brought up in Iceland, a part of the Old World which remained free yet which, apart from Hannasvik, the secret, women-only village where Annika lived, was largely uninhabited.

The geography and history of *Riveted*'s world exemplify steampunk's ability to "fuse familiar convergences and strange divergences that invite a rethinking of potential historical paths and [. . .] defamiliarise both the [. . .] past and the globalising present, isolating facets of both eras to make them more susceptible to analysis" (Jagoda 2010, 48) and in this novel Brook has chosen to focus on facets of past and present which relate to Otherness. The skill and thoroughness with which she explores the topic and renders it "susceptible to analysis" led to *Riveted* being hailed as a particularly noteworthy romance novel.[1] The romance review site *Dear Author*, for example, selected *Riveted* as one of the "Best of 2012," with the reviewer stating that "What Brook does with disability and otherness in her stories is unmatched" (Jane 2012). On her own site "Mrs Giggles" stated that

> it is actually amazing to see how well Ms Brook included all these affirmative action sentiments in this story without coming off as too preachy, at least to me. This is a multicultural romance that also contains positive messages concerning homosexuals, women, and physically disabled people, but I never felt as if I was being bludgeoned in the head by Ms Brook with a giant RESPECT sign. These elements are part of the story, and in many ways, they are the story. (n.d.)

The reviewer at *Smart Bitches Trashy Books* commented that she "ended up with a lot to think about including issues of gender, sexuality, equality" (Carrie 2012) while at *Clear Eyes Full Shelves* the reviewer observed that "*Riveted* stands out [. . .] because of the exploration of difference. [. . .] In grad school we would have called this 'Otherness'" (Moon 2012).

The types of Otherness in *Riveted* vary both in their source and in the severity of their consequences for those who feel, or are judged to be, Other. One kind of Otherness is experienced by many people, simply because each of us is unique: it makes Annika Fridasdottir doubt she will ever "fit in. Only at home—and even there, not in every way [. . .] Sometimes I think it would be nice to be normal somewhere" (Brook 2012, 155).[2] Annika is also aware of the existence of severe, institutionalized forms of Othering, such as those which are enforced via the "identifying papers" (Brook 2012, 9) required of travelers, and those which may cause people to be "sent to insanitariums" or "be beaten bloody by a crowd" (Brook 2012, 131). People can, of course, fall into more than one category of Otherness: Annika knows that she herself is "marked [. . .] by the darkness of her skin" (Brook 2012, 13). Another possible source of Otherness is place of origin. According to Annika, New Worlders have an "obsession" (Brook 2012, 100) with it:

> That is always the first thing someone asks: Where are you from. Not "What do you like?" or "What do you believe?" or even "What is your mother like?" which all have more bearing on the person I am [. . .] but what does my coming from Hannasvik tell you? Nothing at all. (Brook 2012, 251)

Whereas José Ortega y Gasset would argue that "yo soy yo y mi circunstancia" (1914, 43), which can be translated as "I am myself and my context," Annika appears to be denying the influence of place and, in effect, arguing that "yo soy yo" (I am me). The novel itself, however, seems to suggest that, in this comprehensive rejection of a type of Otherness which is forced upon her, Annika is erring on the side of overstating individuality. For example, David begins to suspect Annika's place of origin precisely because of certain similarities he perceives between her and his mother, who came from the same Icelandic village. Although they are physically dissimilar they share an unusual accent (Brook 2012, 20) and a lack of awareness of the social conventions of his community (Brook 2012, 22). Furthermore, the fact that she comes from an all-woman village where same-sex couples are common has shaped Annika's expectations about the roles women are capable of filling and means she is entirely free of the homophobia which permeates the New World. Clearly her *circunstancia*, or context, has indeed played a part in making her who she is.

Annika's position with regard to the balance between individuality and membership of a group is more nuanced with respect to other aspects of identity. She states quite clearly that sexual orientation *"does* matter. It matters to [...] all the women of Hannasvik, whether they lie with other women or not—and it must matter to many New Worlders, because they'd done their damnedest to stop women from loving each other" (Brook 2012, 166). Similarly, she says of David's scars and prosthetics that "They *do* matter, because they are a part of you. But I don't see them in the same way that I think many others do" (Brook 2012, 313). Annika does not appear to question the binary categories of "men" and "women" and does generalize that men are, "when part of a group, stupider" (Brook 2012, 8) but she nonetheless avoids Othering on the basis of gender because she minimizes its importance in shaping personality: men are, she thinks, "much like women" (Brook 2012, 8). Annika is thus a protagonist who recognizes that people can be grouped according to certain characteristics, but who nonetheless resists the processes by which those groupings become the basis for Othering. This critical approach to Othering is one which was increasingly being adopted in the early twenty-first century romance reading and writing community, the *circunstancia* in which the novel itself was produced.

Historically, however, it has been common, as romance authors Linda Barlow and Jayne Ann Krentz have stated, to find "plot devices [. . .] based on paradoxes, opposites, and the threat of danger. The more strongly emphasized the contrasts between hero and heroine are, the more the confrontations between the two take on a sense of the heroic. [. . .] She is light, he is darkness; she is hope, he is despair" (1992, 17).[3] To emphasize the contrast between the protagonists, multiple markers of Otherness have often been overlaid on one another, to intensify their emotional and erotic impact. Stephanie Burley, for example, has drawn attention to

the standard description of the "tall, dark, and handsome" hero, in distinction to the seemingly paler heroine [. . .]. While "tall" usually connotes the hero's

physical power, [. . .] darkness symbolizes the hero's danger, mystery, sensu-
ality and otherness. [. . .] For the most part, race [. . .] is not explicitly
addressed in these texts; but when it is, it most often appears in stereotypical
depictions. (2000, 328)[4]

Nonetheless, as Amy Burge's study of romances featuring Middle Eastern
sheikh heroes demonstrates, there have tended to be limits placed on acceptable Otherness in romance fiction: the unstated "rules of [. . .] modern romance require a flattening of difference—an elision of strangeness—rather
than an embracing of otherness. The audiences [. . .] might enjoy the way
these texts play with motifs of difference, but the possibility of breaking
cross-cultural, interracial or interreligious boundaries is never really considered" (2016, 179–80). Of course, the genre is extremely large so it is possible
to find exceptions to such rules, but it is certainly the case that for many
years romances featuring African American protagonists were, with a few
noticeable exceptions, published in separate imprints marketed to African
American readers rather than being integrated into the mainstream of romance publishing.[5]

Romance author Monica Jackson, herself African American, acknowledged the role of publishers but, she argued, "readers define the market. If a
black romance broke out to majority readers, there would have been a stam-
pede to make books by black authors more available to the white dollar. But
the fact is the white dollar has never been spent on black popular fiction with
any great significance. The reader's dollars are what ultimately leads the
publishers" (2005).[6] After Jackson died in May 2012 one romance blogger
wrote of her that,

> Long after Romance Land had tired of the Racism in Romance discussion, she
> was always there, ready to bring this conversation that many readers and
> authors alike found uncomfortable, to the fore. She loved this discomfort,
> because it was proof to her that at last the issue was in the psyche of those
> readers, who subconsciously avoided those otherly books.
>
>   She was passionate about the Racism in Romance issue, and her tenacity
> and willingness to fight the long and good fight was inspiring. (Karen 2012)

Meljean Brook's *Riveted* was published in September 2012, just months after
Jackson's death, and was dedicated to this author who "fought to turn the
world around" and "flipped some of us" (2012, i). This image of the world
being inverted is repeated in the text of the novel itself when David confides
to Annika that "now and again, something comes along to change the way I
think. [. . .] You completely turned the world about [. . .] you tipped me over"
(Brook 2012, 318–19). This tipping occurred, he says, after Annika revealed
the same-sex nature of the relationships of the majority of Hannasvik's residents and told him he would have to decide what he thought about this.

Although he quickly responded that the information didn't make him think worse of them (Brook 2012, 166), the revelation forced him "to reorder everything he'd learned about his mother's people" (Brook 2012, 158). His experience therefore parallels the "flipping" of a white romance author forced to think deeply about Otherness as the result of an insight into racism in the romance community.

RIVETED IN ITS CONTEXT

Len Barot, an author and publisher of lesbian romances, has observed that "Fiction both reflects the current sociopolitical nature of the community that it represents (and seeks to reach) and portends the emerging forces shaping the future direction of that same community" (2016, 389). By 2012 many in the romance reading and writing community had been taking a critical look at its norms concerning a variety of forms of Otherness. In addition to the discussions about racism there had been debates about heteronormativity and portrayals of disability. One of the most notable debates about Otherness involved the highly influential Romance Writers of America and the very definition of popular romance fiction. As they stated on their website:

> At the November 2015 Board of Directors meeting, one of the issues discussed was an RWA survey conducted in 2005. Though this occurred eleven years ago, the ill effects of that survey still linger for many members. The survey was included in the Romance Writers Report and asked RWA members to vote on whether romance should be redefined as being between one man and one woman. The survey responses were never acted upon, and RWA's definition of romance was not changed.
>
> The survey, however, sparked a discussion that compelled our LGBT+ members to justify their existence to others and to participate in debates about their humanity and their capacity to love. This incident was a low point from which RWA's reputation has never recovered. (RWA 2016)[7]

No such controversies emerged with regards to disability, but significant discussions of this topic were taking place in the romance community in the years prior to the publication of *Riveted*. In 2011 for example, Ridley, "the self-appointed Spokesperson for Disability in Romance," commented on a thread at *Smart Bitches Trashy Books* that "romance does terrible things with disability themes as a rule" and in May 2012 another of the largest romance review sites, *Dear Author*, published a list of romances which Ridley considered exceptions to that rule (Ridley 2012). Also, 2012 was the year in which disability activist Stella Young popularized the term "inspiration porn" to refer to pictures "of a person with a disability, often a kid, doing something completely ordinary—like playing, or talking, or running" which serve "as feel-good tools, as 'inspiration', [. . .] based on an assumption that the people in them have terrible lives, and that it takes some extra kind of pluck or courage to live them" (2012).[8] A literary example of a similar situation can be found in *Riveted* when Lorenzo di Fiore, the villain of the novel, says of David, who has "lost his legs, an arm, and part of an eye" (Brook 2012, 38) and had them replaced by prosthetics, that "Men like him have had to fight harder than all of us, every day [...] It should be a lesson to the rest of us, to remember how our lives could be much more difficult. We need to be thankful for what we have" (Brook 2012, 145). David, however, does not want to be considered either "a hero, or a lesson. [...] People treating him like less or more than one made his life more difficult than losing his legs ever had" (Brook 2012, 145). *Riveted,* then, was written, published and first read in the context of an increasing awareness within the romance community of problematic issues related to Othering, and this awareness is reflected in the text itself.[9]

THE LANGUAGE OF ROMANCE

In addition to addressing Othering explicitly in its plot and dialogue, *Riveted* also seems to address Otherness more subtly in its rejection of common expressions of eroticized Otherness. The extent to which these are embedded in the genre is evident from their presence in Zoë Archer's *Warrior* (2010). It is precisely because this text is so similar in other respects to *Riveted* that it reveals the thoroughness of Brook's rejection of Othering. *Warrior* resembles *Riveted* not just in being a romance with both a female and male protagonist, an adventurous plot, a dangerous villain and "some steampunk-like elements" (Archer 2012) but also, most importantly, in explicitly addressing Otherness. As a historical fantasy romance set in a world containing an alternative version of the Victorian British Empire, it too is able to "fuse familiar convergences and strange divergences that invite a rethinking of potential historical paths and [. . .] defamiliarise both the [. . .] past and the globalising present, isolating facets of both eras to make them more susceptible to analysis" (Jagoda 2010, 48). *Warrior*'s protagonists are assisting a diverse group known as "The Blades of the Rose" who are engaged in a struggle for magical supremacy with the aristocratic "Heirs of Albion." The Blades' embrace of difference and rejection of Othering is in stark contrast to the beliefs espoused by the elitist Heirs, one of whom, Henry Lamb, is representative of them all in his conviction that

> his country [. . .] had the best of everything—land, food, language, monarchy [. . .]. He honestly could not fathom why anyone [. . .] would ever knowingly and deliberately hinder the work of the Heirs of Albion. Every Briton stood to benefit from their nation's global advancement, though the ruling class— Lamb's class—benefited more than most. [. . .]

> The Blades of the Rose were dangerous subversives, anarchists, probably reformers. [. . .] A strange and motley collection of men from all walks of life. Worse, they even allowed *women* in their ranks[. . . .] And Lamb would not allow himself to think of Catullus Graves [a black member of The Blades of the Rose] and his whole blighted family. A shame, really, [. . .] the singular problem of their skin's pigment. (Archer 2010, chap. 9)

By placing these ultra-nationalistic, classist, sexist, and racist sentiments in the mouths of the arch-villain of the novel, Archer is clearly condemning them. Despite all this, and the fact that Archer has striven "to make sure that her heroines were just as kick-ass and capable as the heroes, and that the heroes loved them for it" (Archer n.d), her novel nonetheless eroticizes Otherness in the manner identified by Mary M. Talbot: "eroticised difference is [. . .] encoded in [. . .] masculine aggression, muscularity and physical strength [. . .] contrasted, with varying degrees of explicitness, to feminine passivity, flaccidity and weakness" (1997, 109). Archer's heroine, Thalia, has admittedly not been "trained to serve, docile and obliging" (Archer 2010, chap. 9), nor is she "pale and delicate. Thalia failed on both counts" (Archer 2010, chap. 2); there is a "small bunching of muscles" in her "slim arms" (Archer 2010, chap. 5) and she is shown to be capable of killing in self-defense. However, although in absolute terms Thalia is neither passive, weak, nor lacking in aggression she, with her "sweet soft femaleness" (Archer 2010, chap. 9), must be judged so when compared to a hero who is "the essence of Man, a warrior who would possess his woman" (Archer 2010, chap. 13),

> the mythic Warrior [. . .]. His body was a weapon [. . .].
> Every year he had spent as a soldier showed. Each of his muscles were developed to their apotheosis, the ideal of form and use. (2010, chap. 11)

His sheer size is sexually attractive to Thalia because she associates it with masculinity: even when "his chest was hidden from her sight [. . .] there were his hands, his feet, capturing her attention. Large, capable, unmistakably masculine, and so powerfully suggestive that Thalia felt herself spellbound" (2010, chap. 6). Archer's language thus associates the hero's greater size, muscularity, and potential for aggression with his masculine Otherness, which is in turn shown to be powerfully erotic to the heroine.

Unlike in *Warrior*, in which we are told that "Thalia had been intrigued by male bodies" because they were "so unlike her own" (Archer 2010, chap. 11), *Riveted* highlights physical similarities between male and female bodies. Admittedly *Riveted*'s hero, like *Warrior*'s, is physically more powerful than his heroine: David's hand is a metal prosthetic and, as such, his "hand *was* a weapon" (Brook 2012, 11), while the nanoagents that had grafted the "mechanical apparatus to human flesh" (Brook 2012, 11) also make him "stronger" (Brook 2012, 12) than an uninfected person like Annika. However, in certain circumstances Annika too can be considered to have powerful mechanical body extensions: she is highly trained in driving machines known as "trolls" and when she does so she sees "the engines as a heart and the machinery as muscle and sinew, extensions of her own" (Brook 2012, 328). Even with respect to Annika and David's muscularity, there is reciprocity of appreciation. Certainly, Annika is attracted to David's muscles (Brook 2012, 199 and 344). However, she herself has well-developed muscles and David is clearly strongly affected by them: he thinks her "arms were so incredible, strong with sleek muscles" (Brook 2012, 315) and when he sees her at work in the engine room of an airship "Shock and desire pummeled David like iron fists. [. . .] Spanner in hand, she tightened the bolt over a valve. Smooth biceps flexed beneath skin glistening with perspiration. [. . .] David's pulse pounded in his ears" (Brook 2012, 89). Annika, then, is a strong, competent protagonist whose muscularity is as attractive to her partner as his is to her; physical strength is not, in this novel, linked to masculine Otherness.

Riveted, in fact, seems to deliberately invoke, only to then undermine, common forms of gendered Othering. Gendered markers of Otherness take many forms. As already mentioned, there is a tendency for heroes' greater height to be used to emphasize their masculine Otherness. For example, in Zoë Archer's *Warrior*, the heroine is "a tall woman, but her clothing looked so delicate and feminine beside his [. . .], and something as ordinary as her sock became ethereal and tender when draped over his rough leather boot" (2010, chap. 16). In *Riveted* one might expect a similar feminization of the heroine and masculinization of the hero to result from the differences in their height given that, early in the novel, we learn that although Annika rarely feels small, she does when standing next to David (Brook 2012, 18). However, as David's aunt observes in conversation with him, both his parents were tall, his "mother in particular" (Brook 2012, 35). His height is thus framed not as a marker of masculinity but as a genetic inheritance, with emphasis placed on the height of the female parent, not the male, thus minimizing the potential for his height to be a marker of gendered Otherness.

An even more comprehensive rejection of a romance commonplace can be found in the novel's reversal of the "frequently used device" of "the eroticized difference between male and female [. . .] encoded in skin tone" (Talbot 1997, 109). Although having a father who was a native New Worlder sets him apart from "the whites" (Brook 2012, 155), *Riveted* eschews any association between darkness and masculinity: David's hair is "as black as" (Brook 2012, 14) Annika's but no darker and his complexion is probably somewhat lighter than hers given that she looks as though she is of African descent (Brook 2012, 55). Moreover, when Annika describes David to others she notes that he has "the same coloring" (Brook 2012, 133) as Källa, Annika's (non-biological) sister.

Similarly, although "In many [. . .] cultures [. . .] the battle injury or scar is the man's red badge of courage, the emblem of manhood" (Gilmore 1990, 70), Brook's novel rejects any linkage between scarring and masculinity of the kind to be found in Zoë Archer's *Warrior*. In *Warrior* scars are explicitly described as external proof of masculine martial prowess and sexual appeal:

> scars marred the perfection of his form. There, on his left shoulder, a round, puckered mark showed he'd been shot. And stretching from just under his ribs [. . .] a long, raised ridge made by—a jagged knife? [. . .] There were more scars, more tales of battles and meetings with death, on his legs, his back. [. . .] It was [. . .] a testament to his capability, his will to survive. (2010, chap. 11)

Thus although the heroine may have briefly "winced to think of the lengthy, unpleasant recovery from such a wound" (2010, chap. 11), the fact remains that she considers his "masculine beauty, not marred but made more perfect by the numerous scars that crossed his flesh" (2010, chap. 13).

In *Riveted* David's scars are also a testament to his "will to survive" but, in much greater measure, they are a testament to his mother's "capability" and not to his: he was only a child when a huge explosion tore apart their home and she died shielding him with her own body (Brook 2012, 103). Whereas scars such as those borne by the hero in *Warrior* seem to enhance his masculine sexual appeal by acting as "a testament to his capability," Annika's response to David's scars treads a middle path between vilification and eroticization. She observes them matter-of-factly and far from linking scarring to masculinity, she treats it as a commonplace fact of life: "someone with no scars was either very lucky or hadn't ever had to work very hard" (Brook 2012, 92). Moreover, the scarred people Annika describes in order to illustrate this assertion are all women. She herself gained a scar while "day-dreaming [. . .]. My mother [. . .] lost four toes to the ice one winter. Another girl I know had her nose torn away by a wild dog" (Brook 2012, 92).

Annika identifies hairiness as the primary difference between men and women: men, she thinks, are "much like women, but hairier" (Brook 2012, 8). This difference, however, is not appealing to her: she tells David she has "never been able to determine what 'handsome' means. You aren't as hairy as most men. I think that's lovely. So that must be how *I* determine it" (Brook 2012, 93). David's appeal to Annika, then, is certainly not based on extreme physical Otherness and this rejection of the eroticization of gendered Otherness sets *Riveted* apart from many romances.

CHANGING THE CONTEXT

Riveted thus both bears witness to the early twenty-first-century romance community's debates about Otherness and seeks to make its own contribution to challenging Othering. As such, *Riveted* seems to express a recognition both that "yo soy yo y mi circunstancia, y si no la salvo a ella no me salvo yo" (Ortega y Gasset 1914, 43–44) (I am myself and my context, and if I can't save it, I can't save myself). As a text which exists within the *circunstancia* of the conventions of the romance novel, it works to bring about change.

Riveted can certainly be read as an indication of support for those authors who remain Othered and excluded from mainstream success in romance publishing and who work to change the romance community's attitudes. In the years since *Riveted* was published their struggle has continued. The #We-NeedDiverseBooks campaign was launched in the spring of 2014 in response to "the lack of diversity in kidlit" (WNDB, n.d.) and later the same year K. M. Jackson created a romance-specific #WeNeedDiverseRomance to address the lack of diversity in romance caused by

> years and years of the "norm" being books by Caucasian writers and book[s] by writers of color being labeled as other and shelved separately if picked up by a mainstream publisher. And if not picked up by a publisher then self-publishing being the other option for an author of color where discoverability is even more difficult. [. . .] It would be great to also address the lack [of] POC [People of Color] staffing in publishing. [. . .] #WeNeedDiverseRomance is also shouting out to the persons with disabilities and the LGBTQ [. . .] community. We are all here, all having been marginalized and all fighting the good fight for our truths to be told. (2015)

K. M. Jackson's hashtag, then, is not simply about increasing the diversity among the characters in romance fiction: it is also about bringing to the fore works created by authors who are still Othered by the publishing industry. As she states, they have "truths to be told."

An episode in *Riveted* demonstrates why it is important to seek those truths directly from those involved. Early on in the novel a very minor incident is recounted involving García, the first engineer of the steamship *Phatéon.* He left his post unexpectedly after his "wife came to visit" (Brook 2012, 49). García's motivations, however, are unknown and so his crewmates attempt to guess them in order to fill out the story. Mary, one of Annika and García's colleagues, ascribes his departure to his wife's dislike for him "going from port to port." Annika, though,

> thought that Mary was only telling her own truth, not García's. [. . .] Mary had lain with many other men than her husband. Considering how devoted García had been to his wife, [. . .] Annika thought he'd left because he couldn't bear to leave her alone any longer.
>
> But Mary wouldn't have assumed that. People never believed of others what they couldn't imagine of themselves. (Brook 2012, 55)

Annika may not be entirely correct about the limits of other people's imaginations, but the fact remains that the only way to find out the truth would have been to ask García himself. Certainly, a careful observer such as Annika is more likely to approach the truth than one like Mary, who is blinkered by their own prejudices and experiences, but even Annika cannot know and express García's truth in the way he would himself.

Publishers are perhaps less interested in Others' truths than Annika is. The authors of a series of reports on the state of racial diversity in romance publishing, who had initially believed that once their data demonstrating the "widespread systemic racism within romance publishing" was "collected and publicly released, publishers would immediately make strides toward correcting this imbalance," were compelled to state in 2019 that there had "been zero progress" after three years (Koch and Koch 2019). It is possible that

> white readers might be more willing to embrace black stories than white publishers and editors have traditionally assumed. At the same time, it seems likely that white readers' racism has played a role in the industry's persistent exclusion of black stories. Several black authors described meeting white women at book signings who would ask to get a book signed, but emphasize that they were buying the books for a black friend, or a black colleague, certainly not for themselves. Others had seen or heard comments from white readers that they found happy stories about black women unrealistic. (Beckett 2019)

Othering shapes identities, beliefs, and desires; there are many who prefer to avoid texts which might flip them, tipping over their prejudices and preconceptions.

NOTES

1. It should be noted that *Riveted* is not unique in addressing Otherness explicitly. In an analysis of various novels by Mary Balogh, for example, Ria Cheyne has highlighted the ways in which "Characters' own ideas of disability change and develop—her contact with Lizzie leads Claudia to comment 'I have just realized that *all* girls are different from the norm. In other words, the norm does not exist except in the minds of those who like tidy statistics'" (2017, 212). Zoë Archer's *Warrior* (2010), which I contrast with *Riveted* later in this chapter, is another example.

2. I am not suggesting that this feeling is universal, but it must be fairly common given that there is a well-known proverb which "*The Macmillan Dictionary of Quotations* [. . .] and *Evan's Dictionary of Quotations* [. . .] both give [. . .] as, 'All the world is queer save thee and me, and even thee art a little queer'" (Anderson 1993, 173). Admittedly the proverb comes at the issue from a reversed perspective to Annika's since it classifies the self as "normal" and everyone else as Other. Since the proverb is an old one, the word "queer" in this context simply means "odd" and does not refer to sexual orientation.

3. There are, of course, a substantial proportion of romances which emphasize similarity and familiarity. jay Dixon, for example, has noted the existence of "the boy hero of the 1920s and 1930s, [. . .] the boy-next-door of the 1950s" (1999, 63). Although David initially appears

to be a stranger, it is later revealed that his aunt is a long-term work colleague of Annika's and he himself is Annika's (non-biological) cousin.

4. In other cultural contexts "the color black is most often associated with implications of evil, filth, depravity, and fear, the color white is most often associated with notions of purity, truth, innocence, goodness, and righteousness. These two contrasting color symbols permeate a great deal of Western culture and can be discerned in everything from classical fairy tales to popular film and literature" (Sidanius and Pratto 1999, 47). Romances would appear to be eroticizing rather than denigrating darkness (albeit generally within a rather restricted range of darkness given that so many of the "tall, dark, and handsome" heroes can nonetheless be classified as white), but it is still associated with Otherness and at least a degree of danger.

5. The "first African American line of romances from a major publishing house was launched by Kensington Press in 1994" (Markert 2016, 165).

6. Readers have not limited themselves to withholding their dollars. Harlequin published *Adam and Eva*, a romance by Sandra Kitt "with black characters in 1984, but after *Adam and Eva* [. . .] Harlequin got scads of letters complaining about the book, including one from a Philadelphia woman who said, 'Those people should have their own series'" (Grescoe 1996, 279). Harlequin Mills & Boon appears to have bowed to consumer pressure: though they intermittently retested the response of their readership by publishing the occasional novel with one or more black protagonists in a line where this was the exception rather than the norm, the vast majority of Harlequin's black protagonists have appeared under the Kimani imprint, dedicated to African American romance. Other publishers without a dedicated African American imprint have "filter[ed] an occasional African American author into their generalist romance lists. This increases the chances that a more diverse audience will read the book. This is complicated, however, by the cover illustrations. The cover is likely to feature a picture of an African American if the author is African American, and this can be off-putting to a white reader" (Markert 2016, 246). Clearly, the racism of white readers has played a considerable role in the segregation of African American romances.

7. In the years which followed the survey, the organization came to include "an LGBT special interest chapter": "On May 1, 2009 the Rainbow Romance Writers special interest chapter was officially accepted by the Romance Writers of America" (Rainbow, n.d.). In 2012 the Tulsa, Oklahoma chapter attempted to exclude LGBT submissions from a writing contest; after opposition to the move they canceled the competition (Flood 2012).

8. Jan Grue's research on the origin of the phrase found that "While it is difficult to track the precise origin of the term 'inspiration porn,' according to Google Trends it entered general usage in August 2010, although [. . .] there are not many references prior to Young's (2012) article 'We're Not Here for Your Inspiration,' published on the Australian Broadcasting corporation's website" (2016, 839).

9. In 2017 I tweeted a link to an abstract of an earlier version of this paper and Brook responded with a set of tweets which confirmed that the text of *Riveted* had indeed been shaped by the romance community's discussions around Otherness. She stated that she was "heavily influenced by [Monica] Jackson's posts, as well as @Ridley's re: disability and the way it's presented" and indeed that she had been "Influenced by so many debates around Romancelandia actually. The discussions/criticisms readers have definitely gave me new ways of looking" (Brook 2017).

REFERENCES

Anderson, Charles R. 1993. "The Exchange." *RQ* 33, no. 2: 172–74.
Archer, Zoë. 2010. *Warrior*. New York: Zebra. Kindle.
Archer, Zoë. 2012. "Why Steampunk?" *Steamed!: Writing Steampunk Fiction*, 2 April 2012. https://ageofsteam.wordpress.com/2012/04/02/why-steampunk-by-zoe-archer/ .
Archer, Zoë. n.d. "Bio." http://zoearcherbooks.com/home/bio/ .
Barlow, Linda, and Jayne Ann Krentz. 1992. "Beneath the Surface: The Hidden Codes of Romance." In *Dangerous Men and Adventurous Women: Romance Writers on the Appeal of*

the Romance, edited by Jayne Ann Krentz, 15–29. Philadelphia: University of Pennsylvania Press.

Barot, Len. 2016. "Queer Romance in Twentieth- and Twenty-First-Century America: Snapshots of a Revolution." In *Romance Fiction and American Culture: Love as the Practice of Freedom?* edited by William A. Gleason and Eric Murphy Selinger, 389–404. Farnham, Surrey: Ashgate.

Beckett, Lois. 2019. "Fifty shades of white: the long fight against racism in romance novels." *The Guardian*, 4 April 2019. https://www.theguardian.com/books/2019/apr/04/fifty-shades -of-white-romance-novels-racism-ritas-rwa.

Brook, Meljean. 2009. "Steampunk." 28 October 2009. http://meljeanbrook.com/steampunk/.

Brook, Meljean. 2012. *Riveted*. London: Penguin.

Brook, Meljean. 2017. Tweets of 17 June 2017 https://twitter.com/DrLauraVivanco/status/ 876089856077770752.

Burge, Amy. 2016. *Representing Difference in the Medieval and Modern Orientalist Romance*. London: Palgrave Macmillan.

Burley, Stephanie. 2000. "Shadows & Silhouettes: The Racial Politics of Category Romance." *Paradoxa* 5, no. 13–14: 324–43.

Carrie, S. 2012. "*Riveted* by Meljean Brook: A Guest Review by CarrieS." *Smart Bitches Trashy Books*, 3 Sept. 2012. https://smartbitchestrashybooks.com/reviews/riveted-a-guest-review-by-carries/.

Cheyne, Ria. 2017. "Disability Studies Reads the Romance: Sexuality, Prejudice, and the Happily-Ever-After in the Work of Mary Balogh." In *Culture—Theory—Disability: Encounters between Disability Studies and Cultural Studies*, edited by Anne Waldschmidt, Hanjo Berressem, and Moritz Ingwersen, 201–16. Bielefeld: Transcript. https:// www.degruyter.com/downloadpdf/books/9783839425336/9783839425336-012/978383942 5336-012.pdf.

Dixon, jay. 1999. *The Romance Fiction of Mills & Boon, 1909–1990s*. London: UCL Press.

Flood, Alison. 2012. "Ban on same-sex stories in romance competition causes outcry." *The Guardian*, 8 Feb. 2012. https://www.theguardian.com/books/2012/feb/08/ban-same-sex-ro-mance-competition.

Giggles. n.d. "Riveted." *Mrs Giggles.com*. Archived on 5 Sept. 2015. https://web.archive.org/ web/20150905095119/https://mrsgiggles.com/books//brook_riveted.html.

Gilmore, David D. 1990. *Manhood in the Making: Cultural Concepts of Masculinity*. New Haven: Yale University Press.

Grescoe, Paul. 1996. *The Merchants of Venus: Inside Harlequin and the Empire of Romance*. Vancouver: Raincoast.

Grue, Jan. 2016. "The Problem with Inspiration Porn: a Tentative Definition and a Provisional Critique." *Disability & Society* 31, no. 6: 838–49.

Jackson, K. M. 2015. "#WeNeedDiverseRomance . . . tweet on . . . tweet on . . ." 30 June 2015. http://kmjackson.com/2015/06/weneeddiverseromance-tweet-on-tweet-on/.

Jackson, Monica. 2005. "What It's Like." In "At the Back Fence Issue #209." *All About Romance*, October 15, 2005. http://allaboutromance.com/at-the-back-fence-issue-209/.

Jagoda, Patrick. 2010. "Clacking Control Societies: Steampunk, History, and the Difference Engine of Escape." *Neo-Victorian Studies* 3, no. 1: 46–71.

Jane. 2012. "Best of 2012 by Jane." *Dear Author*, 21 December 2012. https://dearauthor.com/ need-a-rec/recommended-reads/best-of-2012-by-jane/.

Karen. 2012. "RIP Monica Jackson, Author, Warrior . . . Friend." *Karen Knows Best*, 17 May 2012. http://karenknowsbest.com/2012/05/17/rip-monica-jackson-author-warrior-friend/.

Koch, Bea, and Leah Koch. 2019. "The State of Racial Diversity in Romance Publishing 2018." *The Ripped Bodice*. https://www.therippedbodicela.com/sites/therippedbodice-la.d7.indiebound.com/files/2018%20diversity%20study.pdf.

Markert, John. 2016. *Publishing Romance: The History of an Industry, 1940s to the Present*. Jefferson, NC: McFarland.

Moon, Sarah. 2012. "Review: *Riveted* by Meljean Brook." *Clear Eyes, Full Shelves*, 12 September 2012. https://www.cleareyesfullshelves.com/blog/review-riveted-by-meljean-brook .html.

Ortega y Gasset, José. 1914. *Meditaciones del Quijote*. Madrid: Publicaciones de la residencia de estudiantes.

Pagliassotti, Dru. 2013. "Love and the Machine: Technology and Human Relationships in Steampunk Romance and Erotica." In *Steaming Into a Victorian Future: A Steampunk Anthology*, edited by Julie Anne Taddeo and Cynthia J. Miller, 65–87. Lanham, MD: Scarecrow Press.

Rainbow. n.d. "History of the chapter." Archived version from 10 July 2013. https://web.archive.org/web/20130710142629/http://www.rainbowromancewriters.com/node/15 >.

Ridley. 2011. "Ridley says." *Smart Bitches, Trashy Books*, 12 Nov. 2011. http://smartbitchestrashybooks.com/2011/11/gs-vs-sta-characters-with-chronic-conditions/#comment-179337.

Ridley, 2012. "If You Like Books About Characters with Disabilities." *Dear Author*, 7 May 2012.   https://dearauthor.com/need-a-rec/if-you-like-misc/if-you-like-books-about-characters-with-disabilities/.

RWA. 2016. "Important Message Regarding 2005 'Definition of Romance' Survey." 4 April 2016. https://web.archive.org/web/20161221082122/https://www.rwa.org/p/bl/et/blogid=20&blogaid=1483.

Sidanius, Jim, and Felicia Pratto. 1999. *Social Dominance: An Intergroup Theory of Social Hierarchy and Oppression*. Cambridge: Cambridge University Press.

Talbot, Mary. 1997. "'An Explosion Deep Inside Her': Women's Desire and Popular Romance Fiction." In *Language and Desire: Encoding Sex, Romance and Intimacy*, edited by Keith Harvey and Celia Shalom, 106–22. London: Routledge.

WNDB. n.d. "Frequently Asked Questions." Accessed 20 May, 2019. http://weneeddiversebooks.org/faq/.

Young, Stella. 2012. "We're not here for your inspiration." *ABC*, 3 July 2012. http://www.abc.net.au/news/2012-07-03/young-inspiration-porn/4107006.

Chapter Nine

Representations of Otherness in Paranormal Romance

Race and Wealth in Nalini Singh and J. R. Ward

María T. Ramos-García

When talking about romance in general critics have often pointed to the pervasiveness of whiteness as the standard for beauty and love (Kamblé 2014; Hobson 2015), and the debates on this topic have reached beyond the usual publishing circles to be discussed in mainstream media (Rosman 2017; Becket 2019). Authors of color are scarce, and often relegated to publishing lines designed intentionally for a niche market, while many white authors depict worlds in which only white characters reach a Happily-Ever-After (HEA), and which conspicuously lack diversity even among secondary characters. They depict a world in which whiteness is not only the norm, but the only reality. All this has become the subject of an ongoing controversy in Romancelandia, quite visible in the current debates in the Romance Writers of America (RWA), and the recent report on diversity by *The Ripped Bodice* which are discussed elsewhere in this volume. For thirty-eight years the RWA has awarded prizes annually to outstanding romance novels in a range of categories. At the time of this writing, the winners for 2019 have just been announced and two African American authors have won. None had before.

Within this general tendency to marginalize authors and characters of color, it is important to study any deviations from the norm in order to understand not only how this racial system works, but also what its limits and contradictions are. Romance series are an ideal ground to explore representations of many forms of Otherness. The addition of one or more new viable couples in each installment brings with it a wide range of heroes and heroines within the same narrative world, providing a diverse cast of characters

127

deemed worthy of a HEA and thus reflecting the range—and the limits—of that diversity. That is, they define the limits of inclusion: what kinds of Otherness can be accepted or assimilated, and what kinds of Otherness are permanently relegated to the margins of the fictional world. Furthermore, paranormal romance, because it inserts fantastic elements into our world or a world similar to ours, is a subgenre exceptionally well positioned to reveal the underlying politics of acceptance, since it portrays a dual articulation of Otherness, both literal and metaphorical, as well as their intersections. That is, characters (human or otherwise) may be identified through physical traits and/or background as belonging to what we usually call a human race or ethnicity, as they would in any other romance. Simultaneously, the very existence of non-human or not-quite-human beings creates another kind of metaphorical Otherness. That is the case, for example, in Charlaine Harris's *Sookie Stackhouse* novels and their television adaptation *True Blood*, in which the prejudice against vampires has often been identified by critics as a metaphor for homophobia (Dhaenens 2013; Missari 2015). So, as with sexuality, quite often the metaphorical Otherness stands for race, ethnicity and/or cultural differences. The fantastic Other often works as way to tackle more explicitly difficult topics, such as race, which might be uncomfortable for readers in a realistic setting. The fantastic Other becomes a "safe" Other, in spite of the clear dangerousness of the fictional characters.[1]

This dual articulation of realistic Otherness and fantastic Otherness in serial paranormal romance, combined with a multiplicity of couples, with different combinations of supernatural (or human) species and racial coding, make it an ideal ground to explore complex interactions of conscious and unconscious attitudes toward Otherness in authors, editors, and readers. Who deserves a HEA, and with whom, and, even more importantly, who is excluded from one, reveals the limits of acceptability and desirability within the fictional world. Furthermore, it also reveals the intersections of race with other forms of Otherness, such as sexuality and socioeconomic status. However, paranormal romance is not by any means univocal in its approach to race and ethnicity. Also, the complexity of story lines that extend in some cases over more than thirty books, and the presence of the monstrous in complicated and sometimes contradictory ways, resist a simplified division into progressive and reactionary texts.

This chapter, then, will address some of these issues in two paranormal romance series by two authors who have received some critical attention, and who sit, in many ways, at opposite ends of the diversity spectrum. I am well aware I am just scratching the surface with a preliminary analysis of race and its intersections in J. R. Ward's *Black Dagger Brotherhood* series (2005–present), and Nalini Singh's *Psy-Changeling* series (2006–present).

J. R. WARD AND *THE BLACK DAGGER BROTHERHOOD*

Amanda Hobson (2015), talking about vampire romance, declares that: "One of the most glaring and intriguing aspects of these vampire romance novels is their consistent whitewashing. Just where are all the undead heartthrobs of color, and why are they seemingly absent? . . . where are the women of color as female leads?" (23). One of her main examples is Ward's *Black Dagger Brotherhood* (BDB) series, in which vampires are defined, in the glossary that precedes most volumes in the series, as follows:

> *vampire (n.)* Member of a species separate from that of Homo sapiens. Vampires must drink the blood of the opposite sex to survive. Human blood will keep them alive, though the strength does not last long. Following their transitions, which occur in their mid-twenties, they are unable to go out into sunlight and must feed from the vein regularly. Vampires cannot "convert" humans through a bite or transfer of blood, though they are in rare cases able to breed with the other species. Vampires can dematerialize at will, though they must be able to calm themselves and concentrate to do so and may not carry anything heavy with them. They are able to strip the memories of humans, provided such memories are short-term. Some vampires are able to read minds. Life expectancy is upward of a thousand years, or in some cases even longer. (Ward 2015a, xii–xiii)

Although some members of the species belong to the working class, for the most part these vampires are obscenely rich, and Ward rejoices in the continuous display of conspicuous consumerism and luxury product placement. According to Hobson, of all the series she examined this one contained:

> the more problematic exploration of race and ethnicity as these vampires are portrayed as gun-wielding, hard-fighting, steel-edged thugs complete with hard-core rap and a type of slang based on Black vernacular. Yet they are indeed white, and therefore, the representation of Blackness, here, is interpreted through white vampires, and a white female author. The Brotherhood, for all intents and purposes, performs in Blackface, putting on the stereotypical and mediated image of Black masculinity for the purpose of prurient entertainment. (35)

While the characters do, indeed, use slang, it does not follow the morpho-syntactic features of African American Vernacular; other than the fact that they listen to rap music (as many white people, including the author, do) there is no reason to conclude they are performing black masculinity or blackface. Mary Bly also observes their affected hyper-masculinity but associates their dress and attitude not only with hip-hop culture, but also with Hell's Angels bikers and their image of "righteous bad guys," although the Hell's Angels are largely white and have been accused of being white supremacists (64).[2] That is, she sees their dress, language, and music choices as those of "bad boys good at heart," and "announcing opposition to the legal system" (64) without indicating race identification per se. According to Bly "The American nature of the brothers runs in their blood with their vampire genes. Their sartorial characteristics and normative behavior are intrinsically American, and thereby, reassuring" (70). But their identification is unequivocally as white Americans. All the older vampires came from the "Old Country," clearly identified as northern European via frequent flashbacks to their past lives in some of the novels. The detailed physical descriptions indicate a variety of eye and hair colors, and white skin. Although Ward has claimed repeatedly that her vampires are not human, and hence not part of the human racial system (Michelleti quoted in Hobson, 36) there is a clear racial coding, which becomes more evident when other paranormal groups enter the scene, as will be seen later.

In this world in which vampires are a different species, humans are for the most part in the background, unaware of the vampires and other species who live among them. In the first book in the series (*Dark Lover* 2005) Wrath, the king of the vampires, despises humans, who treated him badly when he was a weak orphan centuries ago. That hatred, contextualized in this way, is understandable, and is undermined when he falls in love and eventually mates Beth, who is half vampire and half human. In the second novel of the series, *Lover Eternal* (2006), the pattern is repeated, with Mary, one hundred percent human, mating the vampire Rhage, her life extended to be as long as Rhage's by the Scribe Virgin, goddess creator of the vampires and often *Deus ex machina* in the series. Vishous's mate, Jane, in *Lover Unbound* (2007), the fifth book in the series, is also human, although she dies and is then returned as a ghost. The only two human males who mate vampire women (Butch and Manny Manello) turn out to be the offspring of vampire males with human women. All of them are described as white. As is the case in other romance series, "marrying-up" is a lot easier for women than it is for men. Butch eventually undergoes the transformation into vampire. Manello chooses not to, although his longevity has been guaranteed by mating the semi-goddess daughter of the Scribe Virgin. Still, his physique and personality are strongly associated with the vampires he chooses to live with:

> Manny was well built for a non-vampire, with an athlete's body that he continued to keep up after mating V's sister, Payne. But the strongest thing about him? His confidence. Trained in the human world, the former Chair of the Department of Surgery at St. Francis Hospital downtown radiated the kind of my-way-or-the-highway attitude that fit right in with the Brothers. (Ward, 2015a: 221–22)

It should be noted his attitude is not perceived as a personality flaw, but as a right earned due to his physical and professional attributes and achievements.

Class is, in Ward's world, the product of genetics and personal achievements, although the latter are implicitly attached to the former.

After Manello's pairing with Payne in the ninth installment in the series, *Lover Unleashed* (2011), humans have appeared only as background, sexual objects, annoyances, or potential recruits for the undead *lesser* society, with only one exception, again, a woman (Sola) paired with a vampire (although the couple doesn't reach their HEA until *The Thief* (2018), so no human entered the fictional world as an eligible partner for almost one decade). Most disturbingly, as the series advances, the dismissal of normal humans turns into contempt and even hatred, as characters start to call humans "rats without tails."[3] The expression becomes common with *Lover Reborn* (2012), although it is initially only used by characters who, at that point in the series, are defined as antagonists and lacking a moral compass. However, in *The Shadows* (2015a) the expression is used twice by two main characters, and the same occurs in *The Beast* (2016), where the vampire Rhage opines:

> Shit knew those rats without tails never went anywhere without two things: a half dozen of their evolutionarily inferior, nocturnally codependent, fuck-twit buddies, and their goddamn cell phones . . . the fact that humans couldn't stick to their core competencies of ruining the environment and telling each other what to think and say was only one of the reasons he hated them. (3)

Later on, Vishous complains that "[h]e'd beyond had it with humans. He had real work to do, but noooo, he was once again wiping the asses of these rats without tails so that the rest of them didn't get upset that vampires walked among them" (2016, 13). The mentions of the racial slur continue in *The Chosen* (2017), in which humans start to be described as an invasion:

> As a two-hundred-plus-year-old Shadow, Trez had long viewed those rats without tails as an inferior, inconvenient clutter on the planet, rather like ants in one's kitchen or mice in the basement. Except you weren't allowed to exterminate the humans. Too messy. Better to tolerate them than risk a species exposure by murdering them just to free up parking spaces, supermarket lines, and your Facebook feed. (42)

While in *Dark Lover* the king's prejudice against humans had been tempered when he fell in love with the half-human Beth, the contempt of the warriors for humans becomes a leitmotif in more recent books, in a manner reminiscent of white supremacist discourse.[4] In a 2016 interview for *Louisville Magazine*, Jenni Laidman asked the author:

> Q: Throughout the books, there's a theme of the humans being "rats without tails." But, they're getting together with humans, and the Queen was human. Why are they still being disrespectful of the humans?

A: You know, a lot of people have asked that question. And I just don't have a good answer.

The slur "rats without tails" has disappeared in her most recently published novels in the series, *The Thief* (2018) and *The Savior* (2019), and two fully human heroines have again been included through mating in the BDB world and granted eternal life. Ward is very aware of her target market and may well have realized she could be alienating part of her readership. Given that, as Bly deftly demonstrates, her initial books were dealing with the post-9/11 crisis, it is hard not to see the increasingly offensive treatment of humans within the series, which coincides with diatribes about Millennials, jokes about hybrid cars, and some mentions of right-wing media in the period right before and after the election of Donald Trump to the presidency of the United States, as a political positioning regarding who does or does not belong in the country. This interpretation is reinforced when we explore the treatment of other beings within the series.

In addition to vampires, Ward also introduces three other fantastic groups that she describes as subspecies: the *symphaths*, the *shadows*, and the *doggen*. The *symphaths* are the only Others described as monstrous. They have barbed penises and each of their hands has six elongated fingers with an extra knuckle. The glossary in the series describes them as a "[s]ubspecies within the vampire race characterized by the ability and desire to manipulate emotions in others (for the purposes of an energy exchange), among other traits. Historically, *symphaths* have been discriminated against and, during certain eras, hunted by vampires. They are near extinction" (Ward 2015a, xii). They feed off the emotions of others in a parasitic manner, so they could be considered the real vampires in the series.[5] Only two half-breed vampire/*symphaths* (conceived through rape), Rhevenge and Xhex, become protagonists in the series, and both do so by assimilating into vampire society, something they achieve, at least in part, by repressing their *symphath* instincts through the use of drugs or self-inflicted pain. The *symphaths* are forced by the vampires to live in a colony, isolated from the rest of society, be it human or vampire. Rhevenge eventually becomes the king of the *symphaths*, imposing vampire values on *symphath* society in the best colonizing tradition. The *symphaths* do not appear much in the series, and they are always presented as extremely dangerous and unpredictable, but they are asked to go to war with the vampires when the vampires are threatened, like an allied (but subordinate) country.

Although the vampire species is clearly white, there are, as Hobson points out, two identifiably black characters in the *BDB* series: the twins, iAm and Trez. They are members of another related supernatural species, the *shadows* or *s'Hisbe*, with a different culture characterized by a vague Orientalism and different powers, who are part of the vampires' world. She explains that

Ward embeds iAm and Trez in criminal activities, such as drug dealing: "The Shadows, the visually Black men in the series, live in the shadows of the vampire society as criminals and as outsiders because of their racial identity further making Ward's diminishment of race suspect" (37–38). This interpretation is problematic, since iAm and Trez became drug dealers as employees of Rhevenge (the half-vampire ally of the Brotherhood) and some of their best customers are precisely the protagonists of the series, and other vampire characters are also drug dealers. In *The Shadows* (2015a), the book that came out right after the publication of Hobson's chapter, Trez and iAm have moved to live with the Brotherhood, and the king of the vampires is willing to start a war with the *shadow* queen to protect them. Their position, then, is not that of marginalized characters, but well integrated—albeit genetically different—ones. In an interesting twist, Ward describes them as looking black, but not "being" black. When in *The King* (2014) Trez is trying to get back into the club he owns:

> he somehow made it to the front of the line and—"What the fuck—he doesn't belong here! Why're you letting him in!" As Trez realized he was the subject up for discussion, he stopped and looked over his shoulder. . . . Probably played a lot of World of Warcraft or whatever it was—and that made him forget that if you were going to be a bigoted big-mouth, you'd better be able to back shit up . . . "I own this place," Trez said in a low voice. "So the question is, why the fuck should I let you in." He glanced at Ivan. "He's not welcome here. Ever." (49)

Then he explains:

> As a Shadow, he was used to being stared at—regular vampires didn't know what to do with his kind, and frankly, he didn't really care for them, either. In fact, he'd been brought up to believe that the two shouldn't mix—. . . Oh, and as for the human world? Everyone assumed he was black and attached their own racial associations, good and bad, to that—but there was the irony. He was neither "African" nor "American," so none of that shit applied to him in spite of the fact that his skin happened to be dark. That was humans for you, though—self-absorbed to the point where they just had to see themselves in all situations. Meanwhile, there were whole other species walking among them, and they were none the wiser. Although . . . that being said . . . if some misguided dumb-ass tried to pull the racial shit with him at his own front door? Then the idiot could fuck off. (49–50)

In *The Shadows* their identity as looking like, but not "being" African American is reiterated when iAm reflects on his experience as the new owner of an Italian restaurant:

> Everyone from the waiters to the chefs to the busboys had assumed he was an African-American, and the deep pride and tradition of Italian ownership, cook-

ing, and culture would have worked against anyone who didn't have Sicilian blood in his veins. As a Shadow, he understood the deal better than they knew. His people didn't want anything to do with vampires or symphaths—and certainly never those rats-without-tails humans . . . Over a year into his ownership, though, everything was all good. He had proved himself to everyone from the customers to the staff to the suppliers . . . He was treated with respect that bordered on worship. Wonder what they'd think of him if they knew he wasn't from Africa, he did not identify as American—and more to the point, he wasn't even human. (42)

The *shadows* are "not black" in the same way the vampires are "not white," but clearly their appearances mean that the vampires are identified by humans as white Americans and the *shadows* as African American, although interestingly the latter's place of origin is never revealed. To complicate matters, they are the only group in the series that does not have an entry in the glossary. Hobson considers the fact that other characters refer to them as "The Moors" to be an indication that the depiction of their culture is intended to create an association between the *shadows* and Muslim cultures (37). There are other indications in *The Shadows* that confirm her interpretation. The first female *shadow* who appears in the book, a princess pretending to be a servant, is dressed in what can best be described as a burka: "her body and head draped in the pale blue of her station, her face covered with a mesh mask that showed him [Trez] absolutely nothing of her eyes or features" (207). Later on, when she is revealed as the princess, she confronts the executioner, forcing him to look at her, and "it was the first time in her life a male had ever seen her face" (215). The clothing of male servants is called *farshi*, which is a type of dress worn by upper class Muslim women in the Indian subcontinent. If we eliminate the "h" that Ward adds to many words, Farsi (or Persian) is the language spoken in today's Iran. The *shadow* palace is full of decorative tiles and the characters kneel "on woven silk mats" (557). So, we find a deliberately vague Muslim flavor with no specific geographic location. Although their culture is supposedly a matriarchy led by a queen with her female offspring as heirs, it is a society in which sexual repression makes the traditional (male-dominated) vampire society appear modern by comparison. They also show extreme cruelty (the new female baby born to the queen is summarily executed when the court astrologists decide she is not the rightful heir to the throne), and servants are treated as slaves, something that has been forbidden in vampire society, albeit only relatively recently. In this context, it is precisely the rejection by Trez and iAm of *shadow* society that makes them acceptable to the "mainstream" vampire society. In this novel, iAm finds his HEA with the princess of his own race—thereby providing the vampires with an ally in what before had been a closed-off society. Meanwhile, Trez, who is in love with a (white) female vampire, sees her die, her body progressively turning into stone. This subplot is the only example of an un-HEA in the series so far, to the disappointment of many of Ward's readers. In subsequent novels there are indications that she has reincarnated and Trez will eventually be reunited with her, but this potential delayed resolution does not detract from the fact that the first interracial couple in human terms (black and white) ended in death.[6] At the same time, the once self-contained *shadow* society has been breached. Since his self-exiled brother, iAm, is now the mate of the new queen (after the execution of her mother), this small society is now strongly influenced by someone in the debt of the vampires.

The third additional species, the *doggen*, suggests a more blatant case of prejudice, not based on skin color, but on social class, since they seem to be white skinned like the vampires (although there are barely any physical descriptions of *doggen* in the books at all). They are described as "[m]ember[s] of the servant class within the vampire world. *Doggen* have old, conservative traditions about service to their superiors, following a formal code of dress and behavior. They are able to go out during the day, but they age relatively quickly. Life expectancy is approximately five hundred years" (Ward 2015a, x). Only one *doggen*, Fritz, has enough relevance to be an individualized character, and his role in the series is that of a dutiful butler who is not just happy assisting his masters, but is deferential and subservient in the extreme. Examples of this attitude abound in all the books, but are probably more prevalent in *Lover Unleashed*, with examples such as: "The ordering didn't take longer than a minute, and Fritz was thrilled by the request. Usually after Last Meal, the butler and his staff retired for a brief rest before the daily cleaning started, *but they would much rather have been working*" (281, emphasis mine). The name's resemblance to a dog's is not just a coincidence, and occasionally Fritz is described as a puppy, or even overtly compared to a dog, as when "[t]he old *doggen* smiled so widely, the wrinkles in his face made him look like a Shar-Pei" (Ward 2011, 390). The *doggen* would have a similar function to that of the house-elves in the *Harry Potter* books, were it not for the absence of a Dobby and a Hermione to problematize their role. Needless to say, no *doggen* love story has even been hinted at in the series so far. Their position as a species whose role is to serve another (inherently superior) species is so naturalized within the series that although Fritz appears in almost every single book, his role is always to provide food or transportation, or occasionally comic relief, but there is never any information given about any interests he might have outside of his servant role. When asked in a recent interview about a possible love story for Fritz, Ward, who usually promises a book on every other character, replied: "No, that just wouldn't be interesting" (Ward on Facebook, 2019). If romance tells us who deserves to be loved, clearly those in the service industry are excluded. In this manner, a division of labor is assigned a separate species, creating a physiological justification for a class distinction.

Ward creates paranormal beings from different species to represent different races in a manner that exaggerates their differences and shows a clear
preference for the white (vampire) race, accepting only exceptional members
of other groups into the fold. Not only that, other fictional "races" are clearly
described as inferior due to both their cultures and physiologies. Eventually,
and through violent coups, both the *symphaths* and the *shadows* become led
by allies of the vampire king, in the best colonial tradition. She also creates a
different species for the servants (the *doggen*), who relish their subservient
roles, described as "natural." At the same time, the actual humans are described as inferior and despised. While the BDB books center, for the most
part, on whiteness, the Othering of characters is not done strictly across color
lines. However, genetics do take an oversized role in this world, which
naturalizes servitude and racial inferiority. In spite of the role that Butle-
resque performativity plays in gender identity in Bly's analysis, she points
out how essential genetics is in the world of the BDB. Its importance is even
greater when it comes to race. On the other hand, Ward clearly supports
marriage equality, being one of the first authors to devote one of the books in
her mainstream romance series (*Lover at Last* 2013), to the HEA (complete
with a wedding) of a gay couple, and including another male/male HEA in a
subsequent novel (*Blood Fury* 2018), illustrating how different categories of
diversity can intersect in complex and contradictory ways.[7]

NALINI SINGH AND THE *PSY-CHANGELING/TRINITY* SERIES

Of Indian origin, born in Fiji, Singh's family moved to New Zealand when
she was still a child. Her background makes her an unlikely candidate for the
success she enjoys in the U.S. mainstream romance market. One of her
series, *Psy-changeling,* is a perfect example of a color-blind society in human
terms. The kinds of racial tensions and prejudices that in our world are often
caused by race or skin color are translated in her fictional world into conflicts
among three races (using the author's terminology): the changelings, the Psy,
and the humans that are distinguished by their specific supernatural abilities
(or lack thereof) and do not coincide with the common race distinctions,
based on coloring and physical features, that exist in the real world. The
changelings are animal shifters, physically strong and with a reputation for
displaying emotions and being comfortable with their "animal side." Traditionally they have been perceived as less intelligent due to the importance
they give to emotion and the senses, although in the series it is evident they
are not lacking in brainpower. The changelings are organized in packs led by
an alpha. The packs usually only have members who change into the same
animal species, although they are willing to accept human partners or other
changelings that mate into the pack. When one parent is a changeling, the

changeling genes are usually inherited by any offspring, and when both parents are changeling but belong to different species their offspring will inherit the animal of the most dominant parent. Packs are organized internally in hierarchies based on dominance, although the system is presented as benign, so less dominant members of the group are also valued and cherished. In some ways, the packs are presented as idyllic. Changeling packs usually live away from urban areas, with plenty of land for their animals to roam. However, many packs are comfortable with progress and are engaged with the world at large. They also own corporations that control multiple business ventures and their residences are protected with the latest technology.

The Psy are somehow the opposite of the changelings: they are urban and cerebral. They possess psychical powers of different kinds and to different levels. Some are telepathic, some telekinetic, some can predict the future, among other possibilities. The strength of those powers depends on the individual. The strongest telepaths may be able to kill someone without touching them or control the actions of several people at the same time. A telekinetic of high power is able to teleport, carrying objects or other people with them, anywhere in the world. Due to the high frequency of violence-inducing mental illnesses in their ranks, about one hundred years before the beginning of the series they decided to condition their children to eliminate emotions. By and large, the Psy seem to control the world's economy and power structures. All Psy need psychic feedback to live, which is provided through the "Net," a mental construct that links all the Psy in the entire world. However, their control is slipping, because the "silence," as they have named their emotion suppression system, is failing and is creating a significant number of psychopaths within their ranks. Later on in the series it is revealed that a group of Psy who rejected silence and disappeared, covertly mixing with humans and changelings, has developed new abilities. Still, the majority of the population are "normal" humans, who have a minor role in the series in comparison with the other two groups.

The three groups exist globally and interbreeding within each group has led to mixing of physical characteristics such as skin-color, especially among the Psy, who conceive artificially and choose parenting partners from across the world with the purpose of enhancing the psychic abilities of their offspring. In a dystopian alternative history/near future, the races have remained separate for a century, and there is a powerful taboo against intermarriage between the races, but mostly among the Psy, that is shattered within the narrative. Prejudices and stereotypes are rampant, and the main theme of the series is the reconciliation between the three races. Amanda Hobson acknowledges the racial diversity in human terms among the characters in Singh's novels but she criticizes the fact that "[n]o character, thus far, has been described as Black or as African or African-American in decent [*sic*] though many of the characters have a racially mixed background" (26). This criticism reflects a U.S.-centric view of race, based on a simple contrast between black and white. Singh doesn't often provide real-world racial categories, preferring to describe the richness and diversity of skin tones, and eye and hair color in her characters, in accordance with the scientific belief that there are no separate races among humans. Still, some of her characters can be described as black or African American based on their physical description. The curly, unruly hair and dark skin of the female protagonist of *Hostage to Pleasure* (2008), Ashaya Alaine, is frequently mentioned:

Her pale blue gray eyes were unusual for her dark skin tone. (27)

"electric coils" (44)

"a woman with pale blue gray eyes, curly dark brown, almost black hair, and mocha skin" (64)

"[. . .] her hair tumbled around her in crackling waves. It was just past shoulder length, but so curly, so wildly beautiful that the animal in him was entranced by it." (134)

"'My skin?' [. . .] 'It's brown.' 'It's melted chocolate and coffee with cream'" (219)

In the same novel, a minor character (albeit not a North American) is also described as black and highly attractive: "His ebony skin, stretched smooth over the oval of his skull, seemed to soak in the light, rather than reflect it, but it was the aristocratic lines of his face that held the eye. According to the human media, Henry Scott was considered both handsome and distinguished" (47). In fact, more direct descriptions of origin are scarce and even when present there is more emphasis placed on visual characteristics than on geographic or national labels, as in the following description of a character— Aiden—who appears in this book for the first time and whose name is not revealed until later in the series: "this guy's ancestors had come straight from some part of the Chinese subcontinent. He was all sharp bones, olive skin, and slanted eyes lashed with ridiculously long lashes. His hair was cut short but it was oil-slick black, straight as a ruler" (279). Although the racial composition of the main cast of characters is varied according to real-world criteria, Singh's earlier contemporary novels, written prior to this series, portrayed a much whiter world. Jayashree Kamblé has observed this evolution in Singh's work, that took place while writing *The Psy-Changeling* and *Guild Hunter* (2009–present) series. It seems quite likely that the author felt more freedom to choose the ethnicity of her characters once she had acquired a solid reputation in the international market.

Paranormal romance is a relatively new subgenre that became established in the 1990s, but its presence was relatively minimal until after the 9/11 attacks, when its popularity increased substantially. Another romance subgenre that rose significantly during the same period and has received more critical attention is the sheikh novel. In his Otherness, the sheikh hero has a lot of commonalities with the paranormal one, at least with the initial paradigm of most paranormal series, since a significant majority of the series begin with a human woman meeting a supernatural man. Although, as we have seen in this chapter, the formula gets a lot more complicated as series develop, some of the analytic tools utilized in the study of sheikh romances can be also applied to paranormal ones. In *An Imperialist Love Story* (2015) Amira Jarmakani states that the union between the sheikh and the heroine "is meant to be symbolic of the exceptionalist technology of liberal multiculturalism, where ethnic and cultural differences are commodified and capitalized into spicy details that give the exceptional-universalist power its flavor" (19). By the same token, Singh's world emphasizes that the characters are widely dispersed geographically and celebrates the diversity of the hues of their skin and the languages they speak, but it is, nonetheless, a world centered on the United States (most of the action takes place in San Francisco and the surrounding area), where most of the leaders of the world order reside. It is also a world in which cultural differences have, for the most part, disappeared. The harmony the series aspires to comes at the expense of any substantive regional differentiation.

Kamblé emphasizes the distinctive role of the extended family in these texts, specifically in the changeling packs, which "introduces into romance fiction a social structure that challenges the entrenched one (of the exclusionary romantic couple and their nuclear family); this alteration bears traces of the traditional family-centric romance narratives in South Asian and South Asian immigrant cultures that Singh is likely acquainted with" (154). In the best analysis to date of Singh's work, Kamblé concludes that:

> Singh's inclusion of interracial couples counters the narrative of white reproduction that lies within the romance genre, a part of its episteme as a twentieth century form. Moreover, her conceptual innovation of making the family a part of the romance suggests the culturally hybrid nature of her novels, one that is made possible by the paranormal romance's carnivalesque format. It is such developments, such spaces of "local" culture that might be able to create a more refined version of the popular romance, which could contribute to a heightened awareness of the inequity that lies in racial difference. (156)

This liberal multiculturalism is somewhat negated, however, by the globalism of the dystopian society represented, in which regional cultural differences have been virtually obliterated (the extended families mentioned in the narrative are created by the changelings, and are not a regional development).

Following the analysis proposed at the beginning of this chapter, comparing the intersections of fantastic and realistic Otherness, Singh creates a post-racial world, in which color doesn't exist, or, better said, doesn't matter, while at the same time criticizing the metaphorical racism that created conflict among the different fictional racial groups, and undermining the supposedly objective reasons for their segregation. Furthermore, the strong differences amongst the three races are presented as artificial and minimized, supporting the universalist perspective that cultural differences are not that important and deep down we are all the same.

Jarmakani also emphasizes how the values of humanist liberalism (which include multiculturalism) become intertwined in post-9/11 sheikh novels with neoliberal economic values. This latter aspect of her criticism resonates strongly in Singh's case. The series depicts the development of a global revolution—through interracial parings, but also conspiracies, violence, and strife—to break barriers, that is, to eliminate the fictional racial segregation. But the impulse that brings about this change, under the cover of the love story, is economic. In the first book in the series (*Slave to Sensation*, 2006) the protagonist couple are introduced, of all places, at a business meeting and, highly unusually for Psy and changelings, are required to work together on a project, the reason being that the DarkRiver changelings have become an economic power, at a level previously reserved to the cerebral Psy:

> DarkRiver's business interests were extensive enough to rival their own [the Psy family of the female protagonist]. The world was changing under the noses of the Psy, the human and changeling races no longer content to be second best. It was a measure of their arrogance that most of her people continued to ignore the slow shift in power. (7–8)

It should be noted that while the business world is a common setting for contemporary romance, it is significantly more rare in the paranormal sub-genre, where the wealth displayed is usually explained through compound interest or is gained for the most part off-scene. However, business and commerce figure prominently in this series, and one of the main arguments for collaboration between the races is economic, in support of free trade in a globalized market. The forces opposing integration are not only seen as murdering and cruel, but also as economically exploitative, which the series argues is due to their opposition to free market capitalism, as is directly stated in *Allegiance of Honor* (2016):

> There were no doubt business owners—Psy, human, and changeling—pissed off because Trinity [the movement to unify the different groups] had facilitated an explosion of cross-racial business networks. Great for clever operators who were good at what they did. Not so good for those who'd been coasting

by with substandard work because competition wasn't as accessible to their clients. (19)

The reader is supposed to take a statement like this one at face value, since the motivations seen in the enemies of the new organization range from protecting personal business interests to individual psychopathy and a desire for power. There are also others who act out of fear of the unknown and distrust for the Other, especially when that Other can kill with just a thought. However, somehow, the complexity of factors becomes subsumed into an economic appeal for free trade. Participation in the humanist, multicultural project becomes dependent upon the acceptance of the economic rules of the West. Once we establish the connection between liberal universalism and neoliberal capitalism, Singh's utopian vision no longer appears so benign.

CONCLUSION

The two series examined here are long and ongoing, with thousands of pages accumulated over far more than a decade, and more work needs to be done to tease out all the implications for Otherness—and more specifically racial Otherness—in them. There is also an unavoidable evolution in the authors and their worlds over the years, an evolution that is ongoing, since the series have not reached their conclusions. Ward has moved away from the typical romance structure, and since 2014 some books in the BDB series do not contain the HEA of a new couple. Then in 2015 she added the spinoff *Black Dagger Legacy*, which still includes the characters of the main series, although it centers on a new generation of fighters, but guarantees the romance experience in each novel. As for Singh, with *Silver Silence* (2017), the sixteenth full novel in her series, she has declared that she is beginning what she calls "the second season" of the series, called now Psy-Changeling Trinity, in honor of the Trinity Accord between the three groups (human, Psy, and changeling). Additionally, these series are not necessarily representative of the paranormal romance field; in fact, it could be argued both are outliers. I would tentatively conclude that although the predominant whiteness that affects all romance is also present in this subgenre, the dual articulation of real and fantastic Otherness produces more nuanced and complex (and often more explicit) approaches to race, making it a perfect site for further exploration of this issue. Ward and Singh also make clear, in very different ways, how inextricably connected race, money, and, in the case of Ward, social class, are in these fictions, and how politics and the economy are very real issues in these worlds of fantasy.

NOTES

1. This contradiction has been pointed out by famous African American romance writer Beverly Jenkins, regarding white readers who refuse to read romance with black heroes or heroines because they claim they cannot relate: "You can relate to shapeshifters, you can relate to vampires, you can relate to werewolves, but you can't relate to a story written by and about black Americans?" (quoted in Becket 2019)

2. Ralph "Sonny" Barger, one of the most notorious Hell's Angels, in an interview with BBC's online Chris Summers in 2000, stated that "The club, as a whole, is not racist but we probably have enough racist members that no black guy is going to get in it."

3. Although a few readers in reviews make some observations regarding this terminology applied to humans, some even enjoy it, as is the case with Lotusland Lady's review of *Blood Fury* (2018) on Amazon: "I particularly enjoyed the scorn with which the merging of a human wedding and a vampire mating is portrayed. Humans, [sic] those rats without tails, rarely come out well in these books. Why is that so appealing to the human reader? Not sure, but it is clearly part of the fun."

4. After the 2016 election, as has been the case in other popular culture media, the political references have also become more open, with comments extending to cultural changes and young generations, as is the case with iAm in *The Chosen* (2017):

> In large measure, his clientele were millennials, that generation born between 1980 and 2000. Defined by the Internet, the iPhone, and a lack of economic opportunity, at least according to the human media, they were a demographic of lost moralists, committed to saving each other, preserving the rights of everyone, and championing a false utopia of mandated liberal thinking that made McCarthyism look nuanced. (41)

Later on, even the vampire king is mocked when he is compared to young humans: "'I don't know when Wrath turned into a fucking Millennial.' Tohr started pacing around. 'But maybe he should get off the throne and start sharing Snapchats about how everyone needs to forgive and get along. Throw a fucking bunny face on himself and do a guided meditation on unity. This is insane.'" (293)
There are other ideological positionings: also in *The Chosen*, it is casually mentioned that Vishous watches Fox News and CNN, while in *The Shadows* Paradise, who becomes the protagonist of *Blood Kiss* (2015b), the first book in the *Black Dagger Legacy* spinoff, reads the tabloids *Daily News* and *The New York Post*, instead of *The New York Times*. Rupert Murdoch's political media is given quite a presence in a series in which characters supposedly do not care about human affairs, but only for the period 2015–2017. Later on, the references disappear. The role of current politics in the series, and more widely, its larger presence in American popular culture since 2015, is an area that deserves further critical attention.

5. It should be noted that the *symphaths* are also described as androgynous, in a sharp contrast with the hypermasculinity displayed by all the heroes in the series, another venue for future exploration into the complex gender politics of the series.

6. At the time of this writing, the resolution of Trez's story with the reincarnation of his white vampire mate is announced to take place in a novella (not a regular installment of the series), *Where Winter Finds You*, to be published November 26, 2019.

7. *Blood Fury* is technically not a book of the *Black Dagger Brotherhood* series, but of its spinoff *Black Dagger Legacy*. Since both series share the same fictional world and take place simultaneously, I am including both in this analysis.

REFERENCES

Becket, Lois. 2019. "Fifty Shades of White: The Long Fight Against Racism in Romance Novels." *The Guardian*, April 4, 2019. https://www.theguardian.com/books/2019/apr/04/fif

ty-shades-of-white-romance-novels-racism-ritas-rwa. Accessed August 3, 2019.

Bly, Mary. 2012. "On Popular Romance, J. R. Ward, and the Limits of Genre Study." In *New Approaches to Popular Romance Fiction: Critical Essays*, edited by Sarah S. G. Frantz and Eric Selinger, 60–72. Jefferson, NC: McFarland.

Dhaenens, Frederik. 2013. "The Fantastic Queer: Reading Gay Representations in *Torchwood* and *True Blood* as Articulations of Queer Resistance." *Critical Studies in Media Communication* 30, no. 2: 102–16.

Hobson, Amanda. 2015. "Brothers under Covers: Race and the Paranormal Romance Novel." In *Race in the Vampire Narrative*, edited by U. Melissa Anyiwo, 23–43. Rotterdam: Sense Publishers.

Jarmakani, Amira. 2015. *An Imperialist Love Story. Desert Romances and the War on Terror*. New York: New York University Press.

Kamblé, Jayashree. 2014. *Making Meaning in Popular Romance Fiction: An Epistemology*. New York: Palgrave Macmillan.

Koch, Leah and Bea Koch (n.d.) "The State of Racial Diversity in Romance Publishing Report (2016, 2017, 2018)." In *The Ripped Bodice*. https://www.therippedbodicela.com/state-racial-diversity-romance-publishing-report. Accessed August 3, 2019.

Laidman, Jenni. 2016. "The Anti-Romantic: J.R. Ward's Commercialized Creativity." *Louisville Magazine*. October 4, 2016. https://www.louisville.com/content/anti-romantic. Accessed July 28, 2019.

Lotusland Lady. 2018. "Black Dagger Lite, missing the testosterone, but still a good read." Customer review of *Blood Fury* on Amazon. https://www.amazon.com/Blood-Fury-Black-Dagger-Legacy-ebook/product-reviews/B06ZZ9Q9L5. Accessed July 28, 2019.

Missari, Stacey. 2015. "Queer Resistance in an Imperfect Allegory: The Politics of Sexuality in *True Blood*." In *Race, Gender, and Sexuality in Post-Apocalyptic TV and Film*, edited by G. Gurr. New York: Palgrave Macmillan.

Rosman, Katherine. 2017. "In Love with Romance Novels, but Not Their Lack of Diversity." *The New York Times*, October 10, 2017. https://www.nytimes.com/2017/10/10/style/romance-novels-diversity.html?login=smartlock&auth=login-smartlock. Accessed August 3, 2019.

Singh, Nalini. 2006. *Slave to Sensation*. New York: Berkley.

Singh, Nalini. 2008. *Hostage to Pleasure*. New York: Berkley.

Singh, Nalini. 2016. *Allegiance of Honor*. New York: Berkley.

Singh, Nalini. 2017. *Silver Silence*. New York: Berkley.

Ward, J. R. 2005. *Dark Lover. A Novel of the Black Dagger Brotherhood*. New York: New American Library.

Ward, J. R. 2006. *Lover Eternal. A Novel of the Black Dagger Brotherhood*. New York: New American Library.

Ward, J. R. 2007. *Lover Unbound. A Novel of the Black Dagger Brotherhood*. New York: New American Library.

Ward, J. R. 2011. *Lover Unleashed*. A Novel of the Black Dagger Brotherhood. New York: New American Library.

Ward, J. R. 2012. *Lover Reborn. A Novel of the Black Dagger Brotherhood*. New York: New American Library.

Ward, J. R. 2013. *Lover at Last. A Novel of the Black Dagger Brotherhood*. New York: New American Library.

Ward, J. R. 2014. *The King. A Novel of the Black Dagger Brotherhood*. New York: New American Library.

Ward, J. R. 2015a. *The Shadows. A Novel of the Black Dagger Brotherhood*. New York: New American Library.

Ward, J. R. 2015b. *Blood Kiss. Black Dagger Legacy*. New York: New American Library.

Ward, J. R. 2016. *The Beast. A Novel of the Black Dagger Brotherhood*. New York: New American Library.

Ward, J. R. 2017. *The Chosen. A Novel of the Black Dagger Brotherhood*. New York: Ballantine Books.

Ward, J. R. 2018. *Blood Fury. Black Dagger Legacy*. New York: Ballantine Books.

Ward, J. R. 2018. *The Thief. A Novel of the Black Dagger Brotherhood.* New York: Ballantine Books.

Ward, J. R. 2019. *The Savior. A Novel of the Black Dagger Brotherhood.* New York: Ballantine Books.

Chapter Ten

"There's Something Charming about a Man with an Accent, Isn't There?"

The Representation of Otherness in Three Novels by Lisa Kleypas

Inmaculada Pérez-Casal

Multiculturalism and the (under)representation of racial or ethnic, cultural, and linguistic difference within mass-market romance fiction are keenly debated topics in Romancelandia these days.[1] In 2018, the Ripped Bodice bookstore in the United States released *The State of Racial Diversity in Romance Publishing Report*, in the hope that "providing clear data would contribute to the work that authors of color had been doing for decades to prove that there is widespread systemic racism within romance publishing" (Koch and Koch 2019, 1). As owners of the first bookstore devoted entirely to romance fiction, Leah and Bea Koch's study shows that "for every 100 books published by the leading romance publishers in 2018, only 7.7 were written by people of color. That compares to 6.2 % in 2017 and 7.8 % in 2016" (Koch and Koch 2019, 4). These figures clearly cast a (racist) shadow over an industry that flaunts its power to give visibility to, even normalize, particular social situations such as an active female sexuality or multiculturalism (e.g., Krentz 1992; Kahn 2015; Rodale 2015).

Paradoxically, the romance novel shows an unflinching attraction for non-Anglocentric elements. Otherness gives the romance fantasy a distinct flavor, emphasizing the genre's escapist function by literally taking the reader to faraway lands to experience non-Western customs. Often, these romantic landscapes are combined with exotic and picturesque (male) characters who, almost invariably, are shaped by Western cultural stereotypes. This interest in the Other, however, is hardly surprising. As Joane Nagel (2003) has pointed out, sexuality and ethnicity are deeply interrelated:

> Ethnic boundaries are also sexual boundaries. Ethnicity and sexuality join together to form a barrier to hold some people in and keep others out, to define who is pure and who is impure, to shape our view of ourselves and others, to fashion feelings of sexual desire and notions of sexual desirability, to provide us with seemingly "natural" sexual preferences for some partners and "intuitive" aversions to others, to leave us with a taste for some ethnic sexual encounters and a distaste for others. (1)

Since romance novels focus primarily on intimate relationships, the (ethnic) features of the Other are integral to the notions of "desirability" that Nagel mentions, and largely condition who marries whom in these texts. In this respect, the genre can both challenge and reinforce racial/ethnic boundaries, by depicting interracial/interethnic unions or by building ethnosexual frontiers.

The popular Regency and Victorian romances emerge as two of the most conservative subgenres. Arguably, ethnic and cultural diversity are rendered more invisible here than anywhere else in the genre. Paramount examples in these subgenres such as Stephanie Laurens's *Cynster* series or Julia Quinn's *Bridgertons* focus almost exclusively on the lives and loves of upper-class, (white) British characters. Kristin Ramsdell (2012) has attributed the success of historical romance to "our not-so-latent yearning to escape, if only for a moment, to a time when life was simpler, better defined (especially regarding roles and rules), infinitely more exciting, and much more romantic" (191). In accordance with this escapist function, the approach of these narratives to history seems generally selective. Mainstream Regency and Victorian romance novels have created very specific chronotopes, in which dukes, earls, and viscounts populate London soirées or enjoy life in their ancient manor houses.

Some of Lisa Kleypas's historical romances follow this pattern, but others do not. As Jayashree Kamblé (2014) has observed, her books often reflect class struggles in which low-born heroes reach the top of society by deploying an entrepreneurial, capitalist mentality (47). In addition, it must be noted that some of these heroes also present traces of cultural, ethnic, and/or linguistic Otherness that are essential for the construction of their identity. The fact that Kleypas depicts this type of hero from time to time suggests that she has a recurring interest in representing and discussing the experience of being Othered. However, as Kamblé has also contended, romance novels "can be seen to contain a narrative that normativizes [. . .] whiteness" (2014, 131), even when the characters are manifestly portrayed as racially or ethnically different.

The present chapter seeks to contribute to the ongoing debate about the romance novel's ethnic politics at the textual level. For this, it examines Kleypas's representation of ethnic, cultural, and linguistic difference in three case studies: Derek Craven (*Dreaming of You*, 1994), Cam Rohan (*Mine Till Midnight*, 2007), and Rhys Winterborne (*Marrying Winterborne*, 2016). These pages study the ways in which these three male protagonists perceive their own difference either as a drawback or as a positive element. In addition, this analysis shows the various responses that this successful and reputed author gives to being Othered by looking at the novels' happy ending and the consequences it entails for the heroes' Otherness; that is, whether the heroes' difference is assimilated as Kamblé suggests, or celebrated at the end of these stories.

DEREK CRAVEN AND THE EFFACEMENT OF DIFFERENCE

Derek Craven is one of Kleypas's landmark protagonists, and one of the most popular characters in the genre's recent history. He appeared for the first time in *Then Came You* (1993), where he was presented as an outsider, repudiated by the powerful aristocracy depicted in the novel. Derek's marginalized status is related to his lack of respectable origins: an orphan boy, he grew up in the poor London streets until he managed to make a fortune through dubious means. By the time *Then Came You* begins, Derek is already established as one of London's wealthiest men, but he remains an outsider to the "good" society in Regency England.

Dreaming of You (1994) narrates Derek's struggle to hide his Cockney origins. Despite the fact that at times he seems proud of his personal achievements, symptomatic of the genre's complicity with capitalist values (Kamblé 2014, 47–48), the plot makes it clear that Derek seeks social integration. A "flawed" society constitutes, according to Pamela Regis's taxonomy, one of the eight defining elements of romance novels. This society "always oppresses" the protagonists in some way, and it may play a part in keeping the lovers apart (Regis 2003, 31–32). In order to achieve their happy ending Derek and his heroine, Sara, must overcome class distinctions; that is, they must eliminate difference first. Over the course of the novel, the hero tries desperately to conceal his personal history and the characteristics that mark him as an Other: he dresses like a nobleman, behaves like a nobleman, and tries to speak like a nobleman as well. For the most part he succeeds, except with regards to his accent. Both *Then Came You* and *Dreaming of You* attempt to reproduce Derek's Cockney accent and its distinctive features, mainly represented in the text by the H-dropping phenomenon. This feature serves a clear purpose, as it helps to distinguish the hero and other low-born men from the aristocratic characters. When Derek encounters the heroine for the first time, she immediately perceives this difference: "'Elp me up,' he said roughly, surprising her with his accent. She wouldn't have expected a man wearing such fine clothes to speak with a cockney [*sic*] twang" (Kleypas 1994, 6).

Progressively, the traces of Derek's Otherness begin to fade. Halfway through the novel, before the hero and heroine marry, Derek has already started to speak like a gentleman. At this point, the textual representation of Cockney English is restricted to other working-class characters. The prostitutes and most notably Ivo Jenner, a man whose personal trajectory resembles Derek's, continue to *talk* and behave like Others. This situation is most visible near the end of the story, in an altercation between Derek and Jenner. The text goes to great lengths to emulate the Cockney pronunciation that Jenner is supposed to have: "Aye. I admit to that, but I 'ad nofing to do with this. I came 'ere to do Crawen a frigging *favor*, damn 'is eyes!" (Kleypas 1994, 351; italics in original). Early in the novels, readers are told that Derek's accent surfaces whenever he is "considerably excited or angry" (Kleypas 1994, 57), yet it is noticeably absent in this argument with Jenner, and in his final love declaration, arguably the highest emotional peak in the book:

> "When they said you were dead. . ." He paused while a tremor took hold of him and forced himself to go on. "I thought I was being punished for my past. I knew I wasn't meant to have you, but I couldn't stop myself. In my whole life you were what I wanted most. All along I've been afraid you'd be taken from me." (Kleypas 1994, 362)

The epilogue confirms that Derek has finally made his way into the upper class, and the heroine tells us that he is now "universally praised for his 'reformation'" and known as a "public benefactor" (Kleypas 1994, 368). He attends various social events with his wife, and participates actively in reformist policies, rubbing shoulders with the same people who had previously rejected him. These remarks evince Derek's status as a fully integrated individual, but his acceptance obviously comes at the cost of his difference. Derek's most distinguishing trait, his accent, is neutralized in order to prosper in aristocratic English society.

IDIOSYNCRASY AND PRIDE: CAM ROHAN

Approximately a decade after *Dreaming of You*, Kleypas devised the character of Cam Rohan. Kleypas's romance novels are frequently grouped into series, joined together by recurring characters. Cam appears for the first time as a secondary character in *Devil in Winter* (2006), the third volume in the *Wallflowers* series. *Mine Till Midnight* (2007), in which Cam is the hero, inaugurates a different series popularly known as the *Hathaways*. Cam's prolonged presence within Kleypas's fiction—he is a recurrent character in the four remaining *Hathaway* novels—reveals a more complex portrayal of his Otherness across the different texts.

Cam is succinctly introduced as "Mr. Rohan," "the Gypsy," or "half-Gypsy," since he is also Irish on his father's side (Kleypas 2006, chap. 7). His physical description corroborates his difference, describing his coloring in detail: "The swarthy hue of his skin and the inky blackness of his hair betrayed his heritage, not to mention his first name, which was common for a Romany" (Kleypas 2006, chap. 7). Cam also emphasizes his origins by wearing jewelry and arranging his hair in a more Roma style. His uniqueness and physical attractiveness are thus enhanced, verging almost into stereotype when he is compared to an outlaw (Kleypas 2006, chaps. 7 and 20). Perhaps more importantly, though, Cam's Otherness is continuously reiterated through his deployment of Romani culture. He often tells stories and gives glimpses of his native traditions, which he considers wiser than English ones. Despite his marked difference, Cam is much appreciated by the other characters. He works at Jenner's, a gentlemen's gambling club, occupying a position of responsibility as *factotum*: managing clients, other employees, orders, etc. In both *Devil in Winter* and *Mine Till Midnight,* this hero demonstrates that the prejudices held against the Romani people as inferior, "lazy, rootless wanderers" are outright racist or, at the very least, ill-founded (Kleypas 2007, chap. 18).

Mine Till Midnight offers a mild commentary about hybridization and its impact on the hero's identity. As Cam confesses to the heroine Amelia Hathaway, a gentlewoman he met by chance outside Jenner's: "I'm a half-breed—*poshram*, they call it—born of a Gypsy mother and an Irish *gadjo* father. And since the family's lineage goes through the father, I'm not even considered Roma" (Kleypas 2007, chap. 5; italics in the original). Cam feels isolated from both the Romani and white communities because of his mixed-race background. He longs to return to the Romani lifestyle of his early childhood, when he lived with his mother's clan or *vitsa* until he was mysteriously abandoned in London and found employment at Jenner's. Cam is aware that he is internalizing *gadjo* or English culture and is manifestly afraid of losing his ethnic and cultural roots: "He had forgotten things; words, stories, the songs that had lulled him to sleep as a child. [. . .] And that made him fear he was no longer Roma" (Kleypas 2007, chap. 7). In the first half of the novel he plans to join a group of traveling Romanies. Yet Cam's Irish half, "renowned for its fierce love of land" (Kleypas 2007, chap. 12), together with his attraction to an English gentlewoman, clash with Cam's desire to adopt a Roma way of life and to preserve his Otherness. Consequently, the book's conflict focuses on the hero's negotiation of his ethnic origins, his longing for freedom away from the strictures of British aristocracy/Englishness, and his love for an English woman in a predominantly racist (and classist) Victorian society.

Cam and Amelia's courtship ends with the heroine's love declaration, and the hero's tacit agreement that he has found his "tribe" within Amelia's family (Kleypas 2007, chap. 22). This statement indicates that, on this occasion, Otherness finds a happy ending. Nevertheless, both the omniscient narrator and Cam put great emphasis on the Hathaways' unconventional behavior, highlighting the fact that they are *not* like other English people. They generally disobey the rules that govern the aristocracy, the first of which is ethnic purity. In this respect, Cam's union with Amelia, sister to a viscount, and the fact that he largely continues to act according to the customs of the Roma (e.g., clothing) in subsequent novels, undermines the ethnic boundaries upheld by his contemporary society.

It must be noted, however, that later novels reveal that Cam's marriage to Amelia is conducted primarily in "the way of the *gadje*" (Kleypas 2008, chap. 19). Clearly, the rigid gender norms that govern the Roma community, where a woman is "treated as a subordinate" (Kleypas 2008, chap. 19), are hard to reconcile with the ideal equal partnership demanded by (Western) romance readers. Additionally, Cam and Amelia's love can triumph because the walls surrounding the Hathaways' family estate create a sanctuary where difference is accommodated and naturalized. Subsequent books mention that Cam and his children dress like Romanies when they are at home, for instance, and Cam also acts as the Patriarch, mediating between the different family members and providing advice and comfort when necessary. Outside the walls of the manor, however, Cam is never completely reconciled with the all-white aristocratic society, and his marginal status is repeatedly asserted through the derogatory comments of secondary aristocratic characters. Racism lurks in the final pages of *Mine Till Midnight*, when Cam implies that their children will be considered Roma and will face ostracism (Kleypas 2007, chap. 22). Therefore, the symbolic "remake" of society that Regis (2003, 31) considers a necessary element of the romance novel is not complete in this case.

Kleypas's deployment of language as an integral part of Cam's Otherness also deserves some commentary. The heroine in *Devil in Winter* notes that Cam possesses "an unusual accent, cultured, but *tainted* with hints of cockney [*sic*] and a sort of foreign rhythm, all blended in a unique mixture" (Kleypas 2006, chap. 7; emphasis added), but his dialogue is invariably presented in perfect English, with some Romani words appearing occasionally. The previous description appears to be sufficient to remind readers of the hero's Otherness, and the reference to his "tainted" accent enough to separate him from the upper-class, English characters. Remarkably, however, other lower-class characters such as Joss Bullard, one of Cam's co-workers at Jenner's and the villain in that story, have their (Cockney) speech reproduced in the text. This is particularly noticeable when both characters interact, as happens in this fragment:

"Are you mad?" Cam demanded in a flare of rage. "What's the matter with
you? We're talking about Jenner's daughter. You shouldn't have done it even
if you'd been given a bloody fortune!"

"She's never done nofing for Jenner," Bullard interrupted harshly, "or
nofing for the club. But she comes 'ere at the very last to watch 'im kick off,
an' then she takes everything. Bugger the 'igh-kick bitch an' 'er sodding
'usband!" (Kleypas 2006, chap. 12)

Although both men have spent a considerable amount of time in London's
working-class streets, in both cases from a young age, Bullard's Cockney
pronunciation is the only one that is represented in the text. The novels make
a clear distinction between Cam and the upper-class English characters as far
as culture and physical appearance are concerned, but they largely code them
as equal when it comes to the representation of oral speech. The reasons why
Cam is so obviously separated from fellow lower-class men such as Joss
Bullard are unclear, but in this case, it appears that the textual representation
of the hero's linguistic Otherness could reduce his desirability if there was
both an ethnic and class difference in his persona.

Similarly, the very few Romani words that appear in the novels, particularly in *Mine Till Midnight*, largely present Cam's exoticness in a stereotypical way. Frequent endearments such as *"monisha"* serve to create a sense of
intimacy between Cam and Amelia. The second language mainly has a romantic and erotic function, as can be seen in the following passage: "Cam
lowered her to the blankets, in the pool of dancing firelight. And he whis-
pered in the old language, telling her that he wanted to chase her as the sun
chased the moon across the sky, he wanted to fill her until they were *corthu*,
one being, joined" (Kleypas 2007, chap. 15; italics in the original). In this
respect, Cam is very similar to other bilingual romance heroes discussed in
this volume, whose limited use of their native language perpetuates their
exotic image while simultaneously permitting them to be assimilated culturally and ethnically.

There is another character in the *Hathaway* series, Kev Merripen, whose
attitude towards his ethnic and cultural background is the exact opposite of
Cam's. Despite their similarities (they are both Romanies, raised by *gadjos*,
and eventually are revealed to be brothers), where Cam flaunts his difference,
Merripen largely conceals it. As Amelia observes, Merripen is secretive and
reticent to explain his culture to others (Kleypas 2007, chap. 5). Jayashree
Kamblé has already conducted a thorough analysis of this character in relation to whiteness. This character exhibits a marked Protestant ethos, represented mainly by sexual restraint, and a capitalist mentality that extols entre-
preneurship and technical innovation, among other things. Both Protestant
and capitalist values are regarded by this critic as defining elements of white
male masculinity, which leads her to interpret Merripen's final ascendancy to
the peerage in *Seduce Me at Sunrise* (2008) as a co-optation of (white)

Western identity (Kamblé 2014, 142–44). Admittedly, Merripen assumes the title of Lord Cavan from his grandfather, willingly takes on the (white) role of landowner and seemingly forsakes his Otherness in favor of whiteness with the approval of other (white) characters in the series. Despite the fact that he is also revealed to be the son of a nobleman, Cam opts for maintaining his difference.

Kleypas has not elaborated on this dichotomy between Cam and Merripen. Therefore, we can only speculate about the reasons why one of the characters embraces whiteness, whereas the other preserves for the most part his ethnic and cultural pride. All things considered, though, by giving Cam and Amelia a happy ending that allows the hero to maintain his Otherness, even if this happens only in the domestic space, Kleypas appears to be defending multiculturalism as well as cross-cultural relationships.

THE AMBIVALENCE OF RHYS WINTERBORNE

Welshman Rhys Winterborne is one of Kleypas's latest creations. As a member of a peripheral, traditionally oppressed community within the United Kingdom, this hero possesses a distinctive culture and language that clash with the normative English society in which the courtship takes place. Even though it may be surprising to a contemporary readership, the Welsh condition of the protagonist, in tandem with his inferior social class, are regarded in the novel as different, marginalized and Othered by other characters. This is owed to the fact that historically, the late Victorian period in which the plot develops was characterized by the subjugation of non-English peoples (e.g., Welsh, Irish, Indian).

Like Derek and Cam, Rhys makes his first appearance as a secondary character. In *Cold-Hearted Rake* (2015) he is presented as a wealthy, shrewd businessman, a self-made man who tries desperately to fit into a rigid class system which alienates him both for his working-class background and his Welsh origins. The first chapters of *Marrying Winterborne* revolve around the hero's decision to marry into the English nobility. For Rhys, marriage to a gentlewoman is a prize for his business success and, simultaneously, it gives him the opportunity to assert his power over the English, embodied here by the heroine/wife, Lady Helen Ravenel. The hero believes that inter-ethnic relationships disrupt the social order and can help bring down the English ruling class. Significantly, the combination of English and Welsh blood would produce a superior race in his eyes: "Think of our children, *cariad*. Sturdy Welsh stock with a Ravenel strain. They'll conquer the world" (Kleypas 2016, chap. 4; italics in the original). This final claim seemingly legitimizes hybridity, albeit in a way which endorses ethnic stereotypes.

Needless to say, Rhys's attraction to Helen eventually turns into love, thus changing his original intentions. He soon perceives the social stigma attached to his origins as a disadvantage for the woman he loves, and he warns Helen about the dominant social prejudices which define the Welsh as "morally backward, lazy . . . even unclean" (Kleypas 2016, chap. 14). At the same time, however, Rhys internalizes some of them. His great height, muscular build, and more revealingly, his rampant sexuality, are all attributed to his Otherness:

> On the rare occasion when he'd enjoyed the favors of an upper-class lady, she had wanted to be taken roughly, as if he were a simple brute who was incapable of gentleness. Rhys had appreciated being spared any pretense of intimacy. He was no Byron, no poetry-spouting connoisseur of seduction. *He was a Welshman with stamina.* (Kleypas 2016, chap. 4; emphasis added)

This passage equates Rhys and the Welsh with sexual power and prowess, a theme that is repeated several times throughout the book, and one which the hero clearly approves of. Similar remarks appear, if less frequently, in relation to Cam in *Mine Till Midnight*. Indeed, an overflowing sexuality is often an intrinsic quality of romance heroes. As Kleypas herself has declared on various occasions, the alpha hero possesses a series of attributes, including his ability to please the heroine sexually, which are indispensable for the romance fantasy (Wendell and Tan 2009, 72–73). This association, however, becomes problematic whenever the hero is constructed as racially or ethnically different, since colonial discourse has historically deployed the notion of an uncontrollable sexuality to define and subjugate the Other.

Besides creating one of the novel's major conflicts, Rhys's Otherness helps to develop attachment and intimacy between the couple, as Helen's attempts to learn Welsh and Welsh mythology demonstrate. This is a significant departure from the other books that have been analyzed so far, in which the heroines remained largely unaffected by their heroes' linguistic difference. Amelia, for instance, does little to accommodate Cam's background or to learn more about the rich Romani culture. While she welcomes the knowledge that Cam transmits about Roma traditions, she never partakes of Cam's culture in the way Helen does in *Marrying Winterborne*. Rhys finds Helen's interest flattering, not least because his own attitude towards his native culture is quite ambivalent.

Once more, language is a key element in the construction of the hero's identity. Welsh words are present amidst Rhys's dialogue in English. Even the noises he makes, like the onomatopoeic "Wfft" which appears repeatedly throughout the book and refers to "a Welsh sound of disgruntlement" (Kleypas 2016, chap. 16), are a constant reminder of the hero's characterization as a Welshman, emphasizing his different origins. Simultaneously, language adds to the romantic fantasy. Some of the Welsh words that appear frequently in the text are endearments to Helen (e.g., "*cariad*") or, alternatively, they boost the erotic atmosphere in sexual scenes:

> "When the man thrusts inside the woman," he said, breathing with increasing difficulty, "the word is *dyrnu*. To thresh." He began to kiss his way down her body, savoring her warm skin with its faint dusting of talcum. After blowing lightly against the protective curls of her sex, he murmured, "This is a *ffwrch*. A furrow to be plowed." He leaned close enough for her to feel the tip of his tongue as he drew it along the innocently closed seam. Her thighs trembled on either side of him. "And the word for this"—he paused to search deeper, finding the shy bud still hidden beneath its hood—"is *chrib*, a bit of honeycomb." (Kleypas 2016, chap. 18; italics in the original)

Occasionally, the novel transcends this erotic use of language and makes some interesting political remarks. Kleypas addresses language difference explicitly, and presents her characters discussing the official policies that discourage linguistic pluralism in favor of a single national language, (i.e., English). Rhys, for instance, recalls being advised by his mother not to speak Welsh because "it was bad for business" (Kleypas 2016, chap. 14). The story also presents a social backlash against non-English identities, personified in the figure of Lord Vance. This character's enmity with Rhys is a consequence of the anti-Welsh policies that Vance pushes for as a member of the British Parliament. In addition, he is said to have written some pamphlets to blacken the reputation of Welsh people in London. The fact that Rhys and Vance are sworn enemies makes readers sympathetic to the hero and the Welsh, as victims of oppression by the dominant (English) culture. Thus, *Marrying Winterborne* appears to vindicate difference as something positive by linking it to the hero. Helen's and Rhys's wedding in the town of Caernarvon in Wales may be read as an indicator of the novel's desire to escape the racist prejudices associated with London. The couple's adoption of Helen's young half sister, whom they rename Carys, "loved one" in Welsh, may also be interpreted as a challenge to English authority and supremacy. Finally, the glossary of Welsh terms included at the end of *Marrying Winterborne* further proves the importance of language to the novel. Significantly, that is not the case with *Mine Till Midnight* or *Seduce Me at Sunrise*, where no such thing appears.

Yet the final marriage union does not entirely overcome the barrier posed by the hero's different ethnicity. On the one hand, the evil represented by Lord Vance is only temporarily neutralized. Rhys exhorts him to abandon England, but there is no reassurance that this will happen, or certainty about how long Vance's exile would last. On the other hand, while the marriage between Helen and Rhys could be interpreted as a symbolic reconciliation between the English and the Welsh, the novel makes it clear that the hostility that Helen will be facing for marrying downwards and into another ethnic group will continue beyond the happy ending. The (English) society that oppresses the protagonists still prevails, and unlike in *Mine Till Midnight*, there is no haven available for them. Rhys and Helen reside in London, the heart of the centralizing and homogenizing English politics of the late Victorian period in which the novel is set.

CONCLUSION

Popular romance fiction is currently facing a set of challenges in relation to cultural, linguistic, and racial/ethnic diversity. Protests against the publishers' biased practices, together with a growing awareness of multiculturalism, have prompted a process of critical self-reflection in the romance novel community that might even affect subgenres that have traditionally focused on white Anglo-Saxon characters, as is the case with Victorian and Regency historical romances.

This chapter has focused on three of Lisa Kleypas's hero figures and analyzed the ways in which this historical romance author has written about Otherness and the experience of being Othered. In the first case study, Kleypas portrays a hero who achieves social integration by sacrificing his difference. In the other two examples, however, this author attempts to present Otherness in a more favorable light, with characters who celebrate their difference despite the threat of alienation under the English elite that governs the novels' setting. With this, I am by no means arguing that Cam Rohan or Rhys Winterborne are perfect representatives of Otherness. Language, for instance, remains a controversial issue. Helen Winterborne's comment in relation to her beloved Rhys: "There's something charming about a man with an accent, isn't there?" (Kleypas 2018, 62) evinces that in the texts analyzed here, language acts as an indicator of Otherness that the heroes use primarily to fuel the romantic fantasy.

There is no doubt that there is still work to do in relation to racial/ethnic clichés and the accurate representation of diversity in mainstream romance fiction. Kleypas's 2018 release *Hello Stranger*, for instance, was much criticized for its degrading and racist portrayal of an Indian woman as a sexual guru, who teaches the hero how to please women. As Elyse (2018), from the influential blog *Smart Bitches, Trashy Books* observed, this stereotyping:

> perpetuates that [sic] idea that women of color are nameless, identity-less beings that White men get to have sex with because they're just so sexual in nature. Ethan then takes his sexual knowledge from this woman of color and brings it to his White one-true-love. This woman's culture and knowledge exist only in service to the White hero.

This scene has already been revised and the offensive content removed entirely from the book. But if anything, it shows that for the romance novel to be truly revolutionary and inclusive, it is imperative that the different parts of Romancelandia continue to monitor the various representations of Otherness in these texts.

NOTE

1. Catherine Roach (2016, 197) defines Romancelandia as "the physical community of authors, readers, and publishing professionals who engage with the genre and to their lively online discussions on reviewer websites, blogs, and Twitter." Arguably, scholarly criticism of popular romance novels is also a part of this community, since the boundaries between academia and fandom have become increasingly blurred in recent years.

REFERENCES

Elyse. 2018. "Book Review: Hello Stranger by Lisa Kleypas." *Smart Bitches, Trashy Books*, accessed March 5, 2018, http://smartbitchestrashybooks.com/reviews/hello-stranger-lisa -kleypas/.

Kahn, Laurie. 2015. *Love Between the Covers*. DVD. Directed by Laurie Kahn. USA, Australia: Blueberry Hill Productions.

Kamblé, Jayashree. 2014. *Making Meaning in Popular Romance Fiction: An Epistemology*. New York: Palgrave Macmillan.

Kleypas, Lisa. 1993. *Then Came You*. New York: Avon Books. Kindle.

Kleypas, Lisa. 1994. *Dreaming of You*. New York: Avon Books.

Kleypas, Lisa. 2006. *Devil in Winter*. New York: Avon Books. Kindle.

Kleypas, Lisa. 2007. *Mine Till Midnight*. New York: St. Martin's Press. Kindle.

Kleypas, Lisa. 2008. *Seduce Me at Sunrise*. New York: St. Martin's Press. Kindle.

Kleypas, Lisa. 2015. *Cold-Hearted Rake*. New York: Avon Books. Kindle.

Kleypas, Lisa. 2016. *Marrying Winterborne*. New York: Avon Books. Kindle.

Kleypas, Lisa. 2018. *Hello Stranger*. New York: Avon Books.

Koch, Bea and Leah Koch. 2019. "The State of Racial Diversity in Romance Publishing Report." The Ripped Bodice, accessed May 7, 2019, https://www.therippedbodicela.com/ state-racial-diversity-romance-publishing-report.

Krentz, Jayne Ann, ed. 1992. *Dangerous Men and Adventurous Women: Romance Writers on the Appeal of the Romance*. Philadelphia: University of Pennsylvania Press.

Nagel, Joane. 2003. *Race, Ethnicity, and Sexuality: Intimate Intersections, Forbidden Frontiers*. New York: Oxford University Press.

Ramsdell, Kristin. 2012. *Romance Fiction: A Guide to the Genre*. Santa Barbara, CA: Libraries Unlimited.

Regis, Pamela, 2003. *A Natural History of the Romance Novel*. Philadelphia: University of Pennsylvania Press.

Roach, Catherine M. 2016. *Happily Ever After: The Romance Story in Popular Culture*. Bloomington: Indiana University Press.

Rodale, Maya. 2015. *Dangerous Books for Girls: The Bad Reputation of Romance Novels Explained*. Self-Published: Amazon.

Wendell, Sarah and Candy Tan. 2009. *Beyond Heaving Bosoms: The Smart Bitches' Guide to Romance Novels*. New York: Fireside.

Index

About the Contributors

Aline Maria Pinguinha França Bazenga is assistant professor at the University of Madeira (Funchal, Portugal) and a researcher of the Centre of Linguistics of the University of Lisbon (CLUL, Lisbon, Portugal). Member of the *Research Team on Dialectology and Diachrony* (https://clul.ulisboa.pt/pessoa/aline-bazenga), since 2011 she is the linguistics coordinator of the Encyclopedic Dictionary of Madeira Project (CLEPUL/APCA), and the AR-POFAMA Project (Spoken Portuguese in Madeira Island Archives) at CIERL-UMa. She is also a member of the International Working Group on Non-Dominant Varieties of Pluricentric Languages (http://www.pluricentriclanguages.org/about-us/ndv-working-group). Her research interests include Sociolinguistics, Language Contact, and the study of the variety of Portuguese spoken on the island of Madeira.

María Isabel González-Cruz is a full professor in English Studies at the University of Las Palmas de Gran Canaria, Spain, where she teaches Pragmatics. She has published widely on the Anglo-Canarian socio-cultural and linguistic contact and its bibliographical production. In addition to several books, she has written a number of chapters and articles on issues related to sociolinguistics, pragmatics, ELT, and lexicon, particularly on Anglicisms and Hispanicisms, in international journals such as *English Today*, *Lexis, Pragmatics*, *Intercultural Pragmatics,* and *Sociocultural Pragmatics.* Co-editor of the *Revista de Lenguas para Fines Específicos* between 2009 and 2015, she has led the Research Team *Sociocultural and Sociolinguistic Studies* since 2004. She also coordinated the interdisciplinary research project FFI2014-53962-P, *Discourses, Gender and Identity in a Corpus of Popular Romance Fiction Novels Set in the Canaries and Other Atlantic Islands,* funded by the Spanish government between 2015 and 2018.

Johanna Hoorenman is lecturer in American literature at Utrecht University, the Netherlands. Her research interests are in American poetry, posthumanism, and American popular romance fiction. She is currently working on a comprehensive study of Native American–themed popular romance novels, informed by Native American studies and Cultural Memory studies.

Maureen Mulligan is a senior lecturer at the Universidad de Las Palmas de Gran Canaria, Spain, where she teaches courses on British Theatre and British Cultural History. She studied at New Hall, Cambridge University, and at Goldsmiths, London University. Her research field is women's literature, and especially women's travel writing, focusing on British travelers during the period of the British Empire and the post-colonial period. Recent publications include articles in journals such as *Studies in Travel Writing*, *Studia Anglica Posnaniensa*, *Journal of Tourism and Cultural Change*, and *Journeys*, and chapters in edited collections by the University of Hong Kong, Routledge, and John Benjamins.

Inmaculada Pérez-Casal specialised in English Studies at the Universidade de Santiago de Compostela (Spain) after graduating in English Language and Literature in 2013. In 2014, she completed an MA dissertation on the contemporary American romance genre, and she is currently writing her PhD thesis on the same topic, applying genre and gender studies to study the development of the romance novel in English. Her research interests include feminism and gender studies, literature by women, as well as popular literature and cultural studies.

María del Mar Pérez-Gil is an associate professor of English at the University of Las Palmas de Gran Canaria, Spain. Her research interests include gender, ethnicity, cultural and national identity, and the discourse of the exotic. She has published in several journals, including *Studies in the Novel*, *Critique: Studies in Contemporary Fiction*, *The Journal of Popular Culture*, and *The Journal of Men's Studies*.

María T. Ramos-García is a professor of Spanish at South Dakota State University, but in the last few years her attention has shifted to paranormal romance and urban fantasy in English. She regularly presents at IASPR and PCA on these literary genres, and teaches the course "Love, Monsters, and Global Conflict: Paranormal Romance and Urban Fantasy in the 21st Century." She is the author of the chapter on paranormal romance and urban fantasy in the upcoming *Ashgate Guide to the Study of Popular Romance*.

Ramón E. Soto-Crespo is associate professor of English at the University of Illinois at Urbana-Champaign. His essays have appeared in *Atlantic Studies, American Literary History, Modern Language Notes, Modern Fiction Studies, Contemporary Literature,* and *Textual Practice.* He is the author of *Mainland Passage: The Cultural Anomaly of Puerto Rico* (2009), which won honorable mention at the 2009 Modern Language Association Prize in United States Latino and Chicano Literary and Cultural Studies. His book *White Trash Menace and Hemispheric Fiction* is forthcoming in January 2020.

María Jesús Vera-Cazorla is associate professor in the Department of Modern Languages, Translation and Interpreting at the University of Las Palmas de Gran Canaria. Her main lines of research are the methodology of teaching foreign languages and the history of language teaching. Member of the research group "Sociolinguistic and Sociocultural Studies," she has collaborated in several national research projects, including "Discourse, Gender and Identity in a Corpus of Popular Romance Fiction Novels Set in the Canaries and Other Atlantic Islands." Recent publications include articles in journals such as *Historia Caribe* and *History of Education & Children's Literature* and chapters edited by Tirant Lo Blanch.

Dr. Laura Vivanco is an independent scholar whose PhD thesis from the University of St. Andrews was published in 2004 as *Death in Fifteenth-Century Castile: Ideologies of the Elites.* After changing field from Hispano-medievalism to popular romance studies she has written many articles on a variety of issues relating to romance novels as well as two books: *For Love and Money: The Literary Art of the Harlequin Mills & Boon Romance* (2011) and *Pursuing Happiness: Reading American Romance as Political Fiction* (2016).